SADDLE SEAT EQUITATION

REVISED EDITION

SADDLE SEAT EQUITATION

REVISED EDITION

HELEN K. CRABTREE

DOUBLEDAY
NEW YORK LONDON TORONTO SYDNEY AUCKLAND

To my parents, who shared my dream, to my husband, who made it come true, and to the Equitation Horse—the noblest animal I know.

PUBLISHED BY DOUBLEDAY

a division of Bantam Doubleday Dell Publishing Group, Inc.
666 Fifth Avenue, New York, New York 10103

DOUBLEDAY and the portrayal of an anchor with a dolphin
are trademarks of Doubleday, a division of Bantam Doubleday
Dell Publishing Group, Inc.

Some of the material in this book has appeared in different form
in *Saddle and Bridle* magazine, and permission for adapted use
is gratefully acknowledged.

Library of Congress Cataloging-in-Publication Data
Crabtree, Helen K.
　Saddle seat equitation.
　1. Saddle seat equitation. 2. American saddle horse.
I. Title.
SF296.S23C7 1982 798.2′4 81-43770
　　　　　　　　　　　　　　　　　　AACR2
ISBN: 0-385-17217-6

8　10　12　13　11　9　7

Contents

Introduction

This book on Saddle Seat Equitation concerns itself with the teaching of both horse and rider—from the very first lesson up to the AHSA Medal Finals. Because he is most beautifully suitable for the job, we use the American Saddlebred as the perfect mount for the job. However, other breeds are useful and workable for the seat taught in this book. The show ring can be the ultimate goal, but this basic saddle seat—the psychology of the horse, training procedures for both horse and rider—in fact, everything within these pages can be applied even to the most modest forms of riding and training. There are few "backyard" horses who could not become better sources of pleasure and learning for the novice horseman if his owner only knew how to go about the problem of self-education. This problem is dealt with here for the rider himself, and for those who will teach.

Not only does the saddle seat present a beautiful picture, but it is one of the most adaptable styles of riding known to man. In this book, the "instructor" is anyone who helps a rider and who exercises or trains a horse. The tremendous increase of interest in riding has forced many friends or parents into the role of instructor. The demand for good instruction far exceeds the supply of qualified teachers in most areas. If you have a good public stable nearby, you are indeed fortunate. If you are like the majority of riders who want to learn to ride well and have no access to professional guidance, then we hope that this book will help your aspirations come true.

The secret of doing anything well is practice, especially when we are dealing with animals. The horse is a lovable animal and, treated with common sense and compassion, is willing and able to learn. But he learns only by repetition—a repetition that should represent only the things we wish to teach the horse. You must recognize from the beginning that both horse and rider develop those skills that they repeat most often. If you ride a horse for thirty minutes, doing all the wrong things for twenty minutes, then slaving over the good points for ten minutes, in spite of your earnest intentions you have literally trained the horse to develop the wrong habits, not the right ones. For the student rider, we will reap the same results. While riding, like any sport, is controlled by the mind, the body develops muscular habits, and this development comes only through practice. The rider who only "knows" how to ride is that wooden figure on a horse who appears to be taking constant inventory of his anatomy. The thorough rider is one who has put in so many hours of practice in correct form that the body itself will take over on "automatic pilot" to free the mind to the fascinating world of complete control over the actions of the horse. This is true horsemanship—the acquired ability to produce the maximum performance of the horse through the perfect form and control of the rider.

Perfection breeds perfection, and the rider must attain his own apex of hands and seat before he can expect to attain complete control over his mount. This problem of self-perfection is very difficult to solve unless you have instruction from the ground. Almost any spectator at a horse show, given enough time, could judge an equitation class. Recognizing what is right is the easy part of any evaluation. What is difficult is the ability to correct mistakes. Anyone can tell a rider that his feet are too far forward, but the complete instructor must be able to tell him not only that his feet are too far forward, but how to get the feet back into position.

Since we do start with the first day for the beginning student, you will find that the instruction at this level is, of necessity, simplified for immediate understanding. As the rider progresses, the same subjects will occur again and again in increasing depth. As I have discovered in teaching riders who come to our stable from all parts of the United States, the instructor must never presume that the rider has complete cognizance or mastery of the fundamental principles of equitation. When you hear a very successful trainer refer to a "one-two-three-four trot," then you know that experience is not always enough. This trainer may be good, but how much better he would be if he understood the mechanics of the gaits. Many riders are showing in advanced equitation classes, and some are winning, who have never established a correct basic foot position. How much better they would ride and what reserves of horse performance they would discover if they would learn the underlying principles of basic horsemanship!

So many good horses are mediocre performers because the rider will "ride down" to what he considers is the inferior ability of the horse. This is what equitation is all about—the goal is the absolute maximum of horse performance. The extent of the rider's achievement is certainly limited by the capacity of the horse, but most riders never do find out just how much the horse can do.

When a trot is called for in the show ring, the mere fact that the rider puts his horse into the gait is not enough. It is how well the horse does that gait, step by step. Even the lowliest of pleasure horses has his own peak of perfection, and the most interesting and rewarding thing a rider can do is to advance his own training and that of his horse until that peak is reached. This is actually what the show ring is all about for the equitation rider. The first sentence of the introduction to the American Horse Shows Association movie, *Saddle Seat Equitation,* is "Equitation is a means, not an end within itself." The show ring is a tangible test of what the rider has accomplished. More than that, it gives him a chance to have his accomplishments evaluated by an expert. Every class is an opportunity for learning, and the show should always be kept in this perspective.

Equitation classes are for the young, but the practice of good equitation is for every person who rides a horse. You may ride just the saddle, or you may ride the whole horse, body and mind. For the latter group, those who hope to get the most out of this wonderful sport of riding, this book is written. It is not only instructional but, in its own way, chronicles equitation from 1958 through 1980. Nowhere else is there any sort of recorded history of this most important facet of the horse industry.

Since the original SADDLE SEAT EQUITATION was published in 1970 we seem to have entered a "Golden Age" of equitation. Classes of fifteen to twenty riders under eleven years of age are not uncommon. And these youngsters are riding and obtaining superior performances from mounts that would have been years ahead of their riders a decade ago. The riding skills exhibited in the older age groups and in the preliminary qualifying classes of the "Good Hands," AHSA Medal, and the UPHA Challenge classes are magnificent, vying for quality of horse and rider with the open three-gaited classes and in many instances exceeding them.

The United Professional Horsemen's Association Challenge Cup classes with stated emphasis on the showing of the horse have greatly influenced the advanced horsemanship that makes equitation an exciting spectator sport as well as attaining the high degree of horse training that I have always felt was true equitation.

Ten years pass quickly and while certain styles are transformed and show routines differ to meet the changing times, in essence, the basics of riding do not change. For this reason, in revising and updating this book, I have altered very little of the first part of SADDLE SEAT EQUITATION. References to trainers, riders, and teachers who are no longer active have been retained. My reasons are many and, I believe, justified. Many instructors and riders have made significant contributions to this sport. They should not be forgotten merely because they are no longer "household words." Without their dedication and hard, unselfish work, equitation as we know it today would not have been possible.

In the mid-'6os only a very few were teaching the all-encompassing "horse training" version of equitation that is the expected norm today.

I recall taking nine riders to the Illinois State Fair Horse Show one year and seeing all nine retained in the ring to work for the championship while all of the other riders were excused. Certainly that is one of my proud memories, but it can never happen again, nor should it. Now there are many talented, experienced instructor-trainers throughout the country who have come up through the ranks—ten and under all the way to amateur status and finally into the very profession itself, so today good advanced training is available to any youngster or anyone who wants it.

There has been criticism to the effect that the quality of horses now showing in equitation places these events out of the reach of some owners. In some cases this may be true, but it has always been true. What is so rewarding, however, is that the present better-informed teachers and students have learned to improve the performance of their horses so much that those which were formerly the dull, placid "equine vehicles" are much, much better horses whose use and value have vastly increased because of their equitation training and improved presentation. Happily, Saddlebred Pleasure Equitation is now firmly established, thus rounding out the options so that all riders have an equal opportunity to participate.

I am delighted to add to this new edition chapters dealing with Arabian, Morgan, Saddlebred Pleasure, and Walking Horse Equitation. The emergence of equitation as an important facet of these three breeds has been phenomenal in just the past ten years. I am pleased to know that SADDLE SEAT EQUITATION has been the handbook for many of the riders and instructors. It is thrilling to be able to devote many pages to the specifics of the different breeds whose proponents have recognized that equitation is the fountainhead of training. It is a deep satisfaction to see the young riders given their rightful chance to compete and excel.

In this book we advance to the more sophisticated levels of riding—the in-depth understanding of not just what the horse has done and how best to deal with it but, most importantly, what the horse is going to do and how we may anticipate his actions. Only through a thorough understanding of the original—yes, the primeval—instincts of a horse can a trainer-rider make intelligent decisions in the guidance and control of that horse. It is not enough to have advanced to the point where we can deal with mistakes. The thorough rider must, through constant intelligent and consistent control and directives, gain the horse's trust to the point where the rider may confidently expect favorable responses. Just because we, as riders, know that we are right does not assure us of the horse's compliance and immediate response to our commands, correct though they may be. No, we must earn a horse's trust. Until that rewarding moment when the rider's understanding and the horse's trust have blended the rider will be TAKING A RIDE, not MAKING A RIDE.

The prospects are limitless. What a challenge for the instructor when he realizes that only he or she, as teacher, can place a ceiling on the rider's attainments! As Plutarch taught, a child's mind is not a vessel to be filled but a fire to be kindled.

We may create a feeble flame or a glorious blaze, but until we dare to try, who knows?

HELEN K. CRABTREE 1982

1

Selection of the Instruction Horse

If you do not already own your own horse, then you must find a horse to use for teaching. The selection of a horse for instruction is of the utmost importance and, whenever possible, it is a time when competent professional help should be solicited. Perhaps you are not located near an academy or training stable, but you should make every effort to seek out a trainer or instructor who will give a lot of thought to the horse to which your child will entrust his future pleasure and safety. Older horses that have seen their best days in the show ring are, without a doubt, the best selection. Very young horses that are gentle and dependable enough for a beginner generally prove to be too slow and lazy after any use at all. The oldsters should be workably sound, but a few blemishes—a bad tail, dead splints, or some other toll of the years that depreciates the horse's show value—should not stand in the way.

If you are looking for manners, experience, willingness, soundness, beauty, youth, action, and so forth, then you are looking for something well-nigh impossible to find and equally difficult to pay for! In necessarily sacrificing some qualities, let it be age, beauty, and action —the frosting on the cake—but never in your most optimistic mood should you choose a "looker" over a "doer." There will be plenty of time for a flashy show horse after the child has learned to ride completely. Truly never was a saying more honest than "Handsome is as handsome does." It will be worth every dollar invested and every hour spent to place the selection of this first horse with a qualified agent. Tell him how much you can spend and give him the complete history of your child's experience, if any, and an unbiased evaluation of his aptitude.

The fit of the horse to the rider is of the utmost importance. A small rider can ride even a tall horse if the barrel of the horse is reasonably small. One must be careful, however, not to select a horse with rough or long gaits. The beginning horse is ideally proportioned as follows.

HEIGHT: 15 hands to 15.2. (A hand is 4 inches, measurement to be taken from the highest point of the withers to the ground.)

GENERAL CONFORMATION: Moderate weight and substance. Avoid horses with very flat backs and overly fat or widely sprung ribs. Riders cannot drop their legs down the sides of such horses.

GAIT: The trot is the most important gait to analyze in the beginner's horse. It should be very even (identical stride on either diagonal is a must) and of a moderately short stride. For this reason, the smaller horses, who naturally tend to shorter strides, are best suited to this job. The short trot must be smooth and graceful, not "peggy," as a short, jolting trot generally precedes a short, jolting canter.

HEAD AND NECK: If a horse carries his head and neck fairly high, it will be easy to teach a rider rein control, since the rider's hands and the horse's mouth are close together. A long-necked, low-headed horse is very difficult for the rider to control, because he is forced to use a long rein. When such a horse raises his head abruptly, the rider finds himself with a lap full of reins and no control. This is one time when a rather short-necked horse is preferred.

If the horse has the aforementioned qualities, we can assume that he will have an easy-riding canter. If, however, he is stiff-legged on his canter and there is nothing that shoeing or training can do to remedy the fault, then you had better continue your search. I cannot overemphasize that the horse must be unusually patient and even-tempered. He will have to put up with a lot before the student has learned to ride. Test the horse thoroughly for his manners and disposition. Ask to see the horse ridden repeatedly at all three gaits, and begin your scrutiny of the animal in the stall.

While a seller may avoid volunteering information prejudicial to the sale of his horse, very few sellers will deliberately misrepresent a horse. If the buyer will state his honest needs and explain that the horse must be suitable for beginning instruction, this will surely rule out horses of evil temperament from the start. Many trainers and dealers are honestly unaware of the qualities necessary for this particular type of horse, so it is advisable to ask the following questions: Is the horse quiet in the stall? Will he kick or bite? Can he be trimmed with the electric clippers? Does he haul well? Will he haul in a single stall? Will he haul in a trailer by himself? Is he reasonable to load in the van or trailer? Will he stand tied? Some horses are halter pullers —they will pull back and break away, so it is an important consideration, particularly in the beginning horse, which will undoubtedly be handled and shown at one-day shows where no box stabling is available.

After observing the horse in the stall, watch him being saddled. Occasionally you may find a horse that is girth bound—one that will rear and fall backwards as the girth is clinched up. Looping a lasso around the flanks, with the end of the rope drawn forward through the horse's front legs, up through the ring of the halter, and then tied to a stout mooring, will generally break a horse of this annoying habit, but it is a cure that is best administered by a professional handler, and anything even remotely associated with rearing should be immediately ruled out for the young rider.

After you have watched the horse in the stall and have seen him saddled, ask the seller to ride him for you. The horse should stand quietly while being mounted and should remain standing until signaled to move out. Watch the horse's first steps very keenly, as most lameness will show up before the horse warms up. Request turns to both right and left. Proceed to the ring and have the horse shown at all three gaits both ways of the ring and parked in the center.

Now it is time for you to try the horse. After mounting in the center of the ring, ride the horse immediately to the out-gate and stop there. A well-trained horse should stand at the gate with very little restiveness and should willingly turn away from the gate. Any tendency to balk, rear, or back when asked to turn away from the gate or the stable should warn you away from the horse. Almost any horse will hesitate at this command, but any signs of any form of balking are *big trouble*. This lesson horse should help a rider, not argue with him. Another good temperament test is to ride the horse up to the stable entrance and ask him to turn away and walk back to the ring. Stopping the horse out of all three gaits while facing towards the gate are also good tests.

Ride both diagonals. Most sound horses will feel the same on both diagonals. However, many horses will have been ridden only on one and will tend to skip a step in order to move the rider back to the accustomed diagonal. If this is the case, this tendency can be overcome with repeated riding of the less favored diagonal, and while we would rather have a horse that is already trained to both, it is not too difficult a problem to correct. If the horse trots in such a manner that it is practically impossible to post a specific diagonal consistently, then in all probability the horse is lame. If the difficulty becomes more pronounced as the horse is trotted in a circle, then you should heed the obvious warning, terminate the ride, and ask to see something else.

If the horse has passed all tests satisfactorily up to this point, dismount and, after the horse has had the tack removed, pick up each foot and inspect the wall of the hoof. It should be smooth, free from horizontal ridges or a dished profile, which indicates previous foundering. Look for any vertical cracks in the hoof. Those cracks at the hairline or any that have obviously grown down from this band are quarter cracks, and in the majority of cases will cause lameness. While some cracks are caused by blows, they generally indicate a weak hoof and unfortunately recur. It is wise to inquire if the horse has ever had quarter cracks. Some horses are never bothered by them and, since they are very common, this is one time that you could use some good professional advice. If you know that the horse has shown consistently and soundly with quarter cracks, then you may take the calculated risk. But, suffice it to say, we would all rather buy a horse without them. Friction tape bound snugly around the hoof each time the horse is exercised will generally keep the crack from splitting, and your blacksmith can shoe the horse to help keep him sound. Be sure to remove the tape after each ride, as the constriction can cause contracted heels. The shoes should be of medium weight, under twenty ounces, and open at the heel. A closed or bar shoe generally indicates a history of lameness and is another calculated risk. Here, again, it is wise to know your seller.

As you were watching the horse being ridden, you should have watched him from front and back. If a horse is hitting his knee or ankle with the opposite foot you will generally be able to see this. However, it is a good practice to scrutinize the legs, knees and ankles very carefully. Run your hands down the bones. If there are abrasions at the inside of the knees or ankles, the horse is probably interfering. This is a very serious fault, as the circling and maneuvering called for in equitation work will cause the evenest of horses to brush occasionally; thus a horse that is built to interfere will be in constant trouble. Mushy or enlarged tendons at the back of the front legs indicate more trouble. The tendons should be hard, tight, and well defined. Road puffs (small knots at the sides of the ankles) generally appear on horses that have had considerable use. They seldom cause trouble and, with proper shoeing and a relatively short foot, you should have no problems here at all. Hard knots on the inside of the cannon (shin) bone may be "splints." If they are old splints, not feverish or tender to the touch, they will probably never cause trouble. A splint is a bony outgrowth that "cements" a separation of the vestigial splint bone from the cannon bone and, unless it is extremely large and near the knee, seldom causes lameness. Have the vet check a splint if you are in doubt.

If the horse has satisfied you thus far, ask to see the bridle. If his mouth has felt suitable and the horse has a nice, even head carriage, then it is smart to bit and bridle the horse just as he was rigged when he suited you. Whenever it is possible, try to buy the bridle with the horse—he will have enough to do to accustom himself to new riders without adjusting to a different bridle. And if it is a set-tail horse, buy the tail set, too, as it will be properly fitted.

For insurance purposes, it will be necessary to have a licensed veterinarian examine the horse. This is advisable under any circumstance, as the layman is certainly not as qualified to judge for soundness—and particularly so for eyes, as proper lights and knowledge are required. Any seller refusing the privilege of vetting a horse obviously has something to hide. The cost of having the horse examined is assumed by the purchaser.

2
Tack

After the lesson horse has been bought, the tack must be selected. The saddle must fit both rider and horse, while the bridle is mainly concerned with horse only. Saddle fit is easy to understand, but the matching of bridle to horse requires a lot of thought and understanding. For even the experienced trainer, this can present a problem —especially with horses whose disposition or conformation causes difficulties. However, since the lesson horse should be free from temperamental faults and his build is likely to be average, generalizations should cover the problems of tack.

The bridle should be kept clean and supple at all times. This should go without saying, and yet we often fail to do this because the animal is being used only at home at first, and the obvious necessity for public perfection is missing. But cleanliness in tack is important at all times, since dirty leather can be extremely uncomfortable to a horse's head and may actually cause sores.

The selection of the proper curb bit is probably the most important choice in fitting the double bridle. While the rise of the cheeks (length from the mouth to the cheek-strap attachment) varies somewhat, unless you specify a special measurement here, this is standard. The variables that most concern the average teacher are width of the mouth (it should be wide enough to allow free movement of the cheeks of the bit without rubbing the horse's jaws) and length of cheeks. The longer the cheek, the more severe the bit, since the curb operates on the lever principle. An average curb would measure from 4¼″ to 4¾″ mouth with cheeks 7″ to 8″ long. Longer cheeks would prove too severe for the beginner's inexpert hands and would tend to pull the horse's head too low.

The port, or curved part, of the curb bit probably represents more originality in training devices than any other facet of tack. Ostensibly, it provides added space for the horse's tongue. Extremes of height and construction can make the port a very uncomfortable instrument, and such extremes should never be employed for novice riders. A medium port is always best on the lesson horse. Wrapping the mouth bar on each side of the port with a soft, adhesive-type rubber tape is frequently a wise thing to do, as it will diminish the annoying effects of spasmodic rein handling by the beginner. Examine the horse's mouth and chin every time you use him, and if there is ever any evidence of chafing, wrap the curb chain with two thicknesses of the rubber.

Snaffle bits generally fall into two categories—smooth and rough. The smooth snaffle should be used, being certain that it is not too wide. It should never pinch the corners of the mouth, but since it is a jointed bit, if it is too long it will point acutely at the joint, which will force it forward and downward under the mouth of the curb. Obviously, whenever the curb is employed, the point of the snaffle will dig into the tongue. The rings at the ends of the bit should be fairly small to lessen the chance of involvement with the curb chain.

Twisted-wire snaffles or those of twisted metal are more severe and also imply some sort of correction. Horses who pull or tend to carry

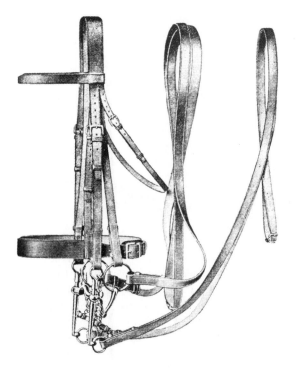

Weymouth bridle. A good, sturdy-type bridle for instruction. The reins shown are ⅝″ curb and ⅞″ snaffle. These reins would be too large for the small rider; we suggest the Standard Show reins—⅜″ curb and ½″ snaffle. *Courtesy Sickles, Inc., St. Louis*

their heads too low will be helped with these rough snaffles—but, again, the lesson horse should not present these problems to the beginning rider.

After each ride, the bridle should be wiped off, if not cleaned with tack soap. The bits most certainly should be cleaned with a sponge, then dried. Dousing the bits in the water bucket every time the bridle is used may be better than not cleaning them at all, but it will rot the leather and is an expensive time saver.

The caveson should be snug. You may find that tightening this noseband will keep a horse from chewing excessively at the bits, but extremely tight cavesons generally goad a horse into head tossing. Comfort is the keynote of the bridle. A badly fitting bridle will cause control problems.

Next to the investment you will make in the lesson horse, the most important purchase will be the saddle. First of all, it must fit the horse. For this reason, you would be far ahead to solicit the help of an

If the instructor wishes to dress up his school bridle, he may buy the fancy brow band and caveson set, or add the colorful brow band and the plain "King's Genius" style caveson. *Courtesy Miller's Saddlery*

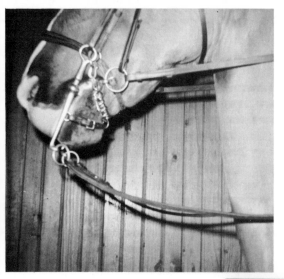

Here we see the caveson too low. Aside from the fact that the position is ugly and tends to make the horse appear coarse-headed, the flagrant fault is that any action of the snaffle bit will pinch the horse's mouth against the caveson. This is a very common, careless fault. The curb bit shown here has a sliding mouthpiece that moves upward as the rein is pulled. Many trainers like this type bit, as it encourages tongue movement and a moist, responsive mouth.

Some common bridling faults: Throat latch too light; caveson fastened over snaffle and curb cheeks; curb chain hooked behind snaffle bit; cheek-strap keepers out of place.

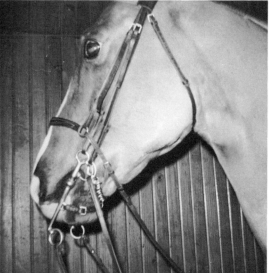

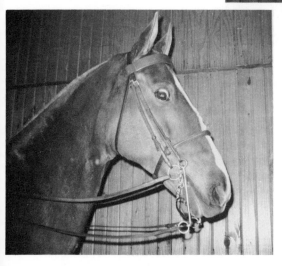

Regular double bridle showing plain curb bit and snaffle. The caveson is not interfering with the action of the bits. Here the snaffle headstall has been shortened to keep the bit high in the horse's mouth, also allowing adequate room for the curb chain in position behind the curb and in front of the snaffle. *Photos by author*

HOW TO MEASURE A SADDLE

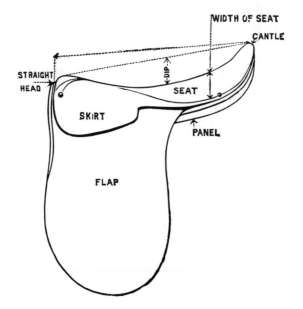

Length of tree is from head to cantle.

Width of seat is from belly to belly.

Dip: Place ruler on head and cantle and measure vertically from center of seat.

HOW TO ORDER SADDLES

Give size of saddle wanted or height and weight of rider.

Width and length of girth.

Width of stirrup leathers.

Width of stirrups.

If not specified, average sizes of girth, leathers and stirrups will be furnished.

experienced trainer or tack supplier. And buy a good English saddle. Whenever you can, buy a good, used saddle, since new saddles are stiff and slick. A pony saddle will not fit a horse, because it will not be broad enough in the pommel. The general line of the seat should be horizontal. Because the pony saddles are narrow, they will tilt upward in front, thus forcing the rider back and away from his feet. Too many people think that because a saddle's length is right for a rider it will suit the job. It must fit the horse, thus permitting the rider's

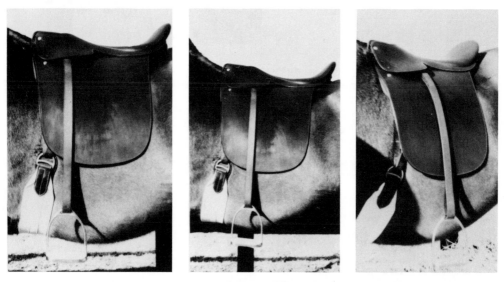

STIRRUP POSITION 1   STIRRUP POSITION 2   STIRRUP POSITION 3

THE CRABTREE STAKE AND EQUITATION SADDLE

After a lifetime of frustration in trying to fit assorted shapes of riders into stereotyped saddles that all shared a common fault—stirrup leathers hung too far forward—I finally found a tack dealer, Bobby Beech of the National Bridle Shop in Lewisburg, Tennessee, who shares my feeling that a saddle must fit the rider and the horse, not vice versa. The Whitman Saddlery Company has turned out our innovation to perfection.

The above pictures clearly show how the stirrups may be adjusted for all types of riders and horses. Not shown is this same saddle with a lower, modified cantle.

How many hours of struggling I would have saved myself and my riders if I had had this saddle in the past. *Photos by author, courtesy of the National Bridle Shop and Whitman Saddlery Co.*

When a saddle is too long, the rider will have difficulty in keeping forward in balance over the stirrups. There will be a tendency to grip in strongly at the knees, causing great torso tension. Additionally, the riding coat will catch under the rider's seat rather than flow back from the hips at the trot. On short-backed horses, the extra-long saddle will be shoved forward into the horse's shoulders by the thrust of his hind-quarter action.

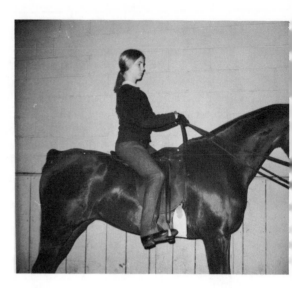

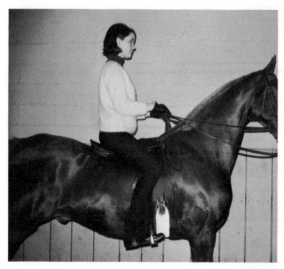

In the saddle that is too short, the rider is forced out of basic position. In order to sit properly, the knees will be jack-knifed too far forward of the leather.

Proper length of saddle: The distance from buttocks to knee places the knee in position on the stirrup leather while seating the hips in the depth of the cantle. The forward mounting of the girth on the cut-back saddle equalizes the rider pressure at the cantle, and the drawing back of the lower leg during posting further distributes rider weight throughout the seat of the saddle. *Photos by author*

proper alignment on his back. It is possible that the horse may have high withers or a prominent backbone that will be chafed by the pommel or channel of the saddle. To buy a saddle to fit such problems is almost impossible. Should you be confronted by this dilemma, use a thick, clean saddle pad or a pommel pad. Home-fashioned "saddle blankets" are not only unsightly but they frequently wrinkle and cause saddle sores.

Since riders' sizes vary greatly, there is no definite rule to help in the selection of the saddle. However, assuming that the rider is average size, the following measurements will serve as a reference:

6 to 8 years   14″ Saddle
8 to 10 years   16″ to 17″ Saddle
11 to 14 years   18″ to 19″ Saddle
15 to 18 years   20″ to 21″ Saddle

If you are selecting a new saddle, ask the dealer to permit you to try it on the horse. Be sure to place a clean towel on the horse, as a dirtied saddle will not be returnable.

If you select a new saddle, ask the dealer to stain it for you. This not only gives an attractive finish but will preserve the leather. Most dealers are happy to perform this service, and they can certainly do a better job than you can.

A 14″ child's saddle that properly fits down on the horse's back and withers, creating a horizontal "floor" in the seat of the saddle, which permits the child to sit where his build places him.

When the saddle does not fit the horse, the floor will be slanted, not horizontal. The bad results are twofold: The rider will be constantly trying to climb up the slanted seat to get his body over his stirrups, and the concentration of rider weight on the cantle will cause a sore back on the horse.

Photos by author

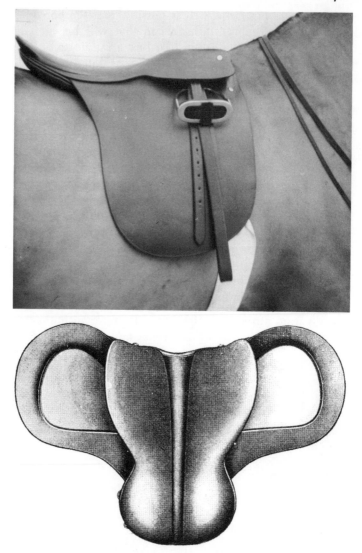

The greatest economy in tack is to buy the best and then take care of it. The beautiful cut-back show saddle will serve every purpose from beginning instruction to the show ring or bridle path. When you select your saddle, order your tack-cleaning supplies at the same time. Your dealer will equip you properly and show you how to care best for your purchases. We show the underside of the saddle to remind you that this part of the saddle should be cleaned every time it is used. You will be protecting your tack and your horse. *Top photo by author, bottom photo courtesy of Sickles, Inc., St. Louis*

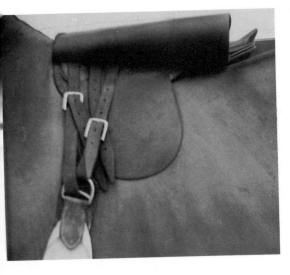

The girth should buckle in the first and third billets, with the front buckle higher. This will make a depression for the knee, whereas parallel buckles will form a lump beneath the knee. Tuck the first and second billet ends under the third strap.

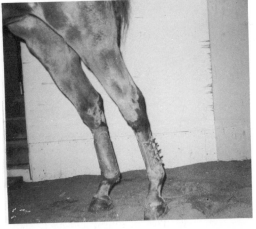

Horse cross-tied in stall. The sheepskin covering on nose and crown of halter protects the horse from chafing, especially on long trips. The tail boards in the stall keep the horse from rubbing against the walls to remove the tail set. With the horse thus tied, he may be groomed from both sides in safety.

Shin boots should be used during schooling of any individual work that involves circling. Without the boots, an inexperienced horse may "interfere," striking the ankles and shins. After the horse has learned the patterns, he seldom requires this protection.
Photos by author

The best girth is of the Y construction—and is called a Humane Girth. Make sure that it is of the proper length, so that, when pulled into the suggested position on the billets, there are still several holes to go. Your new leather will stretch somewhat. Buckle to the front and rear billets, making sure that the ends of the billets are tucked under to keep them from catching the reins. Surely you are aware that some horses will swell up as they are girthed, so do check the tightness of the girth twice.

Stirrup irons should be fitted with rubber pads. The stirrup width will vary with foot size. Never fit the boot tightly in the stirrup. Equally dangerous is the very large stirrup that might permit the rider's entire foot to slide through. Without pads, riders will feel insecure and will tend to "clench" the stirrup bar, an action that is almost certain to result in feet slipping in or out of the stirrup.

3

A Simple Explanation of Aids and Diagonals

Aids are the means by which the rider controls the actions of his horse. At the very beginning of instruction, the aids will probably not be referred to as such when addressing the student. It is apparent that the beginner should be taught in the simple, everyday terminology for the first few lessons. Our first concern is establishing the rider's control over the horse, so we use phrases that are immediately understood. At the outset, it makes more sense to say, "Push his rear around with your right leg," than it does to tell him to use the right leg aid. This is not a problem in semantics at all. For those who have had instruction enough that some elements of form and control are already automatic, then surely they are ready to react to the more formal and concise phraseology of the aids. The beginner is not ready.

The selection of terminology must be made by the instructor on the basis of the level of understanding of each individual pupil. I feel that a detailed explanation of aids in the opening lesson is just too much to digest at first. In due time, the teacher can give the more detailed explanation of the aids. By then, the rider has already been employing them, and the understanding is much greater, since the learner is acquainting himself only with the phraseology. He has already physically used the aids. For this reason, such simple explanation of aids at this time is more for help in understanding the teaching instructions that follow than as a lesson for the student.

The natural aids are the hands, legs, voice, and body weight. The primary action of the hands is to guide and halt the horse. To turn to the right, the right rein is drawn back. This is the direct rein. The other, or left, rein is called the bearing rein, and the amount of simultaneous pull on this rein controls the extent to which the horse turns on the direct rein. A slight crossing over of the left hand to make the left rein push on the horse's neck can assist in the turn while also limiting it. Were it not for the limiting action of the bearing rein, the acuteness and the speed of the turn could not be controlled. Obviously, a turn to the left simply reverses the identity and actions of the hands. The leg aids are simpler in application than the hands, but because it is possible to get "from here to there" without them, we often fail to teach them sufficiently. In turning to the right, the right leg presses simultaneously with the pull of the right hand. The opposite is true at the left turn. A push-in, direct at the girth, will cause the horse to bend his body at this point, resulting in a turn that is in balance and a movement that employs the total horse. I call this an inside leg aid for speedy identification. The leg aid behind the girth strongly influences the position of the rear of the horse as well as being an indication of stride as in the push-off in the canter. Leg aids used simultaneously tend to move the horse forward.

The voice is generally limited to two sounds, a cluck and "Whoa." The word to stop, "Whoa," should be delivered in a commanding tone —tell him, don't ask him—but the word "Whoa," when used as a soft, long-drawn utterance, has a calming effect as well as directing the horse's attention to the rider. The cluck can be used either as an indication for speed, forward movement, or as a quick bid for the horse's attention. To be effective, it should be used deliberately.

The fourth natural aid is the body weight. As a hiker will subconsciously move under the shifting weight of his knapsack, so will a horse react to the rider's position on his back. In its crudest form, body weight adjusts to the direction of the horse and is not an aid at all but a reaction to the direction of the horse. This your beginner will probably do at first. When the weight shift slightly precedes the actions of the horse, only then is it truly an aid. Remember the exact term—aid. This is the line of communication between rider and horse, not horse and rider.

There are two common artificial aids—the whip and spurs. Spurs are absolutely unwise for beginners, as they only implement the leg aids and require infinitely more tact and discretion than any beginner could have. The whip is generally used as an emphasis quickly following, or used in conjunction with, the other aids. It can be used for correction, but certainly never in the case of the beginning rider. It should be explained in this manner to the new student and described as a routine part of the horse's training in order to avoid the natural feeling that the whip represents punishment and that the rider either fears an uncontrolled reaction from the horse or he is reluctant to "hurt" the horse. If the rider is assured that neither is the case, then he will learn the use of this aid as easily as he learns to use the reins.

A trot is a two-beat gait. The right front and left hind feet strike the ground simultaneously, followed by the left front and right hind. If the rider is posting with the motion of the right front and left hind, he is said to be posting the right diagonal. If he is moving with the other pair, then he is posting the left diagonal. For identification from the saddle, the shoulder that is moving up and down with your posting action is the diagonal you are riding.

4

Preparing the Lesson Horse

Presuming that you now have the proper horse, but that the task of working the horse and teaching the child falls to you, then all thought about and preparation of the horse should be in relation to how the horse will be ridden by the child and not by an adult. To amplify this statement, let me cite the problems in the order of their occurrence from the initial lesson:

The horse must stand quietly for any length of time. When you mount, you should sit there for several minutes, manipulating the reins, making stirrup adjustments and many other motions that are sure to occur the first time the child gets up. Surprisingly, some horses have never been taught to stand after mounting, and many an old show horse has shoved into high gear the minute the right foot hit the stirrup.

One should teach the horse word commands. Always say "Whoa" when halting the horse. It will help the young rider to stop the horse without unnecessary rein pulling, which frequently develops head throwing in the horse who has not yet become accustomed to the clumsiness of the beginning rider.

A small enclosure or ring is another necessity. An area sixty to a hundred feet square or any approximation of this will serve the purpose. The horse should be trained in this area so that he will learn to adjust his gaits to the confines of the small space. Ordinarily the horse will shorten his stride somewhat, which is exactly what we want him to do to accommodate the beginner. A long, lofty-striding horse is almost impossible for the novice youngster to adjust to. I recall hearing an instructor tell a rider repeatedly to hold her legs quiet at the canter on a horse who must have sailed ten feet at every stride. Obviously, such a horse was less than ideal for the job. Shoeing the horse with an even-weight or a toe-weight shoe with a short foot will aid in shortening the stride and will help keep the horse sound for the many hours of riding ahead.

While leg aids are very necessary to the correct and complete control of a horse (the most common aid being the use of leg pressure behind the saddle skirt to turn the horse's hind quarters), the adult should try to use his aids in much the same way that the shorter-legged child will use them. Obviously a low heel aid is wrong, because the child cannot reach that low area. A high calf pressure will reach the same area that a child will reach with his heel. For this very reason I find that toeing a horse on the elbow to signal a canter is wrong. A child simply cannot reach a horse's elbow with his toe, so this necessitates teaching the horse to canter from hand signals, leg aids back of the saddle, and the placement of the horse's body. I further feel that toeing a horse into the canter requires expert skill and timing and that by the time the rider has developed this proficiency he is then capable of securing his gaits by more subtle means. So, in preparing the horse for cantering, one should make the horse canter frequently, stopping him mainly with the voice and starting him with a light hand. A short whip may be used to signal the start if it is synchronized with the lifting of the horse's head to the rail. At all times the gait originates from a walk.

To encourage a horse to shorten his stride and maintain perfect balance it is a good practice to establish the canter on the rail and then pull toward the center and describe a smaller circle. A canter originates in the hind quarters of the horse, and the greater part of his weight should be carried at the rear. This results in a collected gait, in which the hind legs are well under the body and the motion is high in front, as compared with the uncollected canter, in which the horse appears to be going downhill and the high motion is at the back. To keep this collection, make sure that the horse is taught to canter with the head well up until he learns this balance for himself. You may be sure that the beginner will not be able to elevate the horse's head at first. If you are fortunate enough to get the ideal horse, he will already canter in this desired fashion; but since horses are creatures of habit, it will then follow that you must continue to train him in his good habits, or you will lose what you were so lucky to start with.

Let me impress upon you the necessity for working the horse for the moment at hand. If a rider is in the elementary stages, then the training should consist of the identical workouts that the horse will be called upon to do with the child.

One of the most common and aggravating habits that a horse can develop in a few rides by a beginner is a tendency to cut corners and to pull away from the rail. If the rider will learn to shorten the rail rein first and to keep it somewhat shorter, then "cheating" by the horse may be forestalled. However, if the horse does begin this fault, it is a good idea to have someone stand in the center of the ring while you train and, at the first step away from the rail, use a long whip hard on his front legs. It should not take too many lessons to correct this particular transgression. However, be sure that the correction comes from the ground man and not the rider, because the horse would be quick to detect a change of riders; but since the teacher will be standing in the middle of the ring during instruction, the horse will naturally assume that he is being corrected even before he makes the mistake. Do not attempt this correction while the student is up, as the horse will cut quickly for the rail and could jump from under the beginning student.

It has been my further experience that, in the case of a horse with a tendency to pull, it is better to rig the curb chain severely while training the horse and ease it back when the beginner gets on. A good horse for the job will not be a puller, but some horses can get a little careless about their mouths after a few rides with the negligible control of the beginner. If you try twisting the chain or changing to a more severe bit to be used by the beginner, then you may be in trouble, as all severe bitting devices should be used with the utmost tact and discretion to accomplish a purpose. Any methods used by the trainer should make the horse more attentive to the weak rein work of the beginner.

The new student should be neatly attired in comfortably fitting jodhpurs or blue jeans. If jeans are used, they should be secured under the instep with elastic or snap-on straps. Loose-fitting pants legs twist and slide on the saddle and generally cause skin burns. Never permit the rider to wear loafers or other loose-fitting shoes. Regulation jodhpur boots are best, and laced oxfords are adequate. If the boots are new, suggest that the rider wear them a day or two before the first lesson. New boots are quite stiff in the sole, and since complete freedom of the ankle joint and instep are necessary right from the beginning, any constraint of the boots will cause a great deal of difficulty. A comfortable shirt with a long tail will do. The shirt should be tucked in so that you will be able to see the exact posture of the torso. Bulky sweaters or jackets can hide a multitude of sins. The instructor must be able to see the back and shoulder positions clearly at all times.

5

First Lesson

The basic factor in teaching anyone to ride is the immediate establishment of control over the horse. Merely sitting atop the animal is a strange, new experience, and the rider's only reassurance that the horse will behave and co-operate is for him to learn how to handle and adjust the reins even before he moves the first step. Not only does it satisfy this need for security and safety, but it starts him right out learning something definite, which adds a sense of accomplishment.

I like to use a mounting block for the average beginner on his first day of instruction. Most riders are interested in getting on immediately and "riding," so the quickest way up seems to be the best. For very small riders, a "leg up" is good. Have the rider stand at the side of the horse facing the saddle and grasping the sides of the saddle skirt with both hands. Now the rider bends the left leg at the knee and an attendant grasps the knee with his left hand and the ankle with the right and lifts the rider straight up into position on the saddle. Explain to the student that he should arch his back and stiffen the elbows to make the desired mount. Many children will limber up and lie across the saddle if not told this in advance.

In following lessons the riders should hold the reins in the left hand as they mount. For taller riders, the conventional mounting should be taught by the second or third lesson, when some rapport has been established between rider and horse. To mount, grasp the center of the snaffle rein with the right hand and take this rein in the left hand at the horse's neck just in front of the saddle. Pull the rein up tight. Then grasp the curb rein with the right hand and place it loosely in the left. The rider will thus be holding the horse snugly on the snaffle and loosely on the curb. This hold will control the horse and prevent any dangerous jabbing of the horse's mouth in the event that the rider's hand should slip at any time during the mounting. Now face the rear of the horse and grasp the far side of the stirrup and turn it at right angles to the horse and place the left foot well into the stirrup. Take a hop step closer to the horse and take hold of the cantle of the saddle with the right hand followed immediately by a spring off the right foot upwards and clearing the hind quarters with the right leg to settle down into the saddle. Obviously, the right hand slides forward as the body clears into the saddle.

As soon as the rider has mounted the horse and placed both feet in the stirrups with the balls of the feet at the back edge of the irons, his hands should be placed on the reins in the proper grip. Any rider who is over six years of age should be able to handle ⅜″ double reins. The reins should be grasped two in each hand, with the little finger around the snaffle rein while the next finger holds the curb. The ends (bight) of the reins follow the palm and come out of the hand to be held between the thumb and the middle joint of the first finger.

It takes very little time to show the rider the next step, which is how to shorten the reins. So many riders become frightened on their first ride because they keep getting longer and longer on the reins, with less and less control. To shorten the reins, maintain the original hold and grasp the left reins just below the left thumb with the right fingers and then slide the left hand forward on the reins. Repeat the procedure for the other hand. To lengthen, relax the grip and slide both hands back at the same time.

At the standstill, have the rider practice shortening and lengthening the reins several times. This attainment of rein dexterity cannot be stressed too much. I know that it is the most important single step in the first lesson because over the many years of using this method we have never had one fear case develop because of lack of control. It is imperative that the rider learn rein handling first, so that he may concentrate on his body and leg position. For this first lesson starts the rider out right and he will make a daily progress, or he will start out wrong and as soon as it is time to begin posting he will be in trouble and will have to go back to the fundamental lesson, unlearn the bad habits, and start all over. A rider is very anxious to absorb every word at first, because everything is new and he is dependent on his teacher for his safety. It is that elementary. But as soon as the rider has gained some amount of control and self-confidence, then he begins to do what comes naturally. If you are lucky and everything he does is right, then all is well; but this phenomenon seldom exists, and we generally find that the rider clutches around the horse with his legs rather than using the combination of body weight and stirrups to gain thigh contact with the horse.

Proper foot and leg position are one and the same. Feet assume the ideal position with the toe about 15° out from parallel with the horse, and the heel slightly lower than the stirrup bar. This foot position is not attained by turning the toes in nor by rotating the ankle joint out, but by placing the foot evenly on the stirrup. Then, holding the entire leg steady from the hip down, swing the heel down and out, which will turn the entire leg at the hip joint until the knee and thigh are in close, comfortable contact with the saddle. Never try to grip with the knees. Instead, swing the lower leg into position, and a natural, unforced knee and thigh contact will result. The rider should be able to sit erect, glance down at his leg and see the entire leg and foot. If the side of the foot is hidden, then the calf is clutched in too much. The opposite extreme of swinging the lower leg out too far will also result in the same stiffness that gripping causes and will tend to make a rider sway-backed.

If the hands and legs are in the proper position, then the torso will generally follow along in good form. Merely keeping the rib cage high will take care of posture faults. Bad torso faults generally result from faulty balance, which is caused by improper foot and leg positions. So, you see, the literal foundation of the foot in the stirrup is the key position in all of riding. Horsemen have a favorite saying, "No foot, no horse," which I would like to paraphrase to read, "No foot, no rider."

I have found that the easiest way to make foot position clear to a rider is to draw the empty stirrup away from the horizontal the approximate distance it will be when the foot is in the stirrup. Point out that the stirrup bar is no longer horizontal, but that it is slightly slanted upward at the outside. Then tell the rider to place his foot

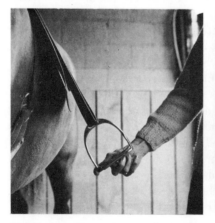 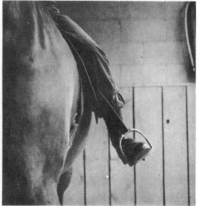

Hold the stirrup away from the horse's side at the approximate distance it will be when the foot is in the stirrup. Emphasize the slant of the stirrup bar.

The foot is on the slanted bar, with the resultant good knee and thigh contact.

Photos by author

evenly on this slanted surface and you will get the desired foot and ankle position. Explain that only by keeping the foot surface slanted will the knees push into the saddle to give the rider a firm and close knee and upper leg. If riders have difficulty in placing the foot correctly, I generally get results with, "Just relax the ankle a little bit and try to show me the bottom of your foot."

A general rule for stirrup length is that the hanging stirrup should touch the rider on the point of the ankle joint. Riders with round, stocky legs may need the stirrups raised one hole, while very thin-legged students may need to lengthen the leather one hole.

Size of the saddle is most important. The length is dictated by the rider's height and length of leg. Ideally, with proper stirrup length, the buttocks will be well back in the depth of the seat (just fitting into the upward curve of the cantle) and the knee joints will be exactly covering the stirrup leathers. Knees pointed far ahead of the leathers indicate a saddle that is too short, while knees back of the leathers result from a saddle that is too long. Shortening the stirrups until the knees reach the leathers will not remedy this fault at all. The heels should be located almost directly below the hip joint, and shortening the stirrups will only move the knees and hips farther out of alignment.

For small children it is extremely dangerous to have the stirrup too large. The entire foot could force through, and in case of a fall, the rider could be dragged. Stirrups that measure no more than one inch

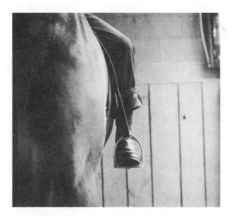

This picture clearly shows what happens when the stirrup swings into the side of the horse and the stirrup bar is not slanted. Not only is any knee grip gone, but the entire leg from the hip joint on down is rotated out, and there is practically no firm support in the upper leg. The greatest fault that arises from this stirrup position is the tendency for the teacher to ask the rider to grip with the knees. This will only add stiffness to all other faults. The obvious correction is to slant the foot on the stirrup bar; then all leg faults will correct themselves. *Photo by author*

wider than the sole of the boot are safe. Very wide stirrups are not only dangerous, but they are difficult for the child to keep at right angles to the horse's sides. Rubber stirrup pads should be used.

Now with hands in control, at waist height and at a rather short and comfortable length of the reins, have the rider start the horse at a walk. Of course, the horse is gentle and steady-mouthed and you are working in a small enclosure. The first half hour should be used in practicing starting, stopping, reversing, and any form of guiding exercise that the age and ability of the rider indicate. Recently I had a little four-year-old girl who learned a lot of control by making her horse walk to the end of the training aisle and touch his nose to the wall. She would not have understood my warnings not to let the horse cut corners, but she did understand the positive game of touching the wall. It was the first thing she reported to her mother, that she had "made" the horse do something. And that was the first lesson. It is never too soon to teach even the youngest rider that riding is what you can make the horse do, not merely how pretty you can look on his back.

Setting up a guiding course is simple and presents another positive goal for a rider. I often drop pieces of paper at twenty-foot intervals and have the rider guide the horse in and out of the markers. Several years ago I was amazed to discover how very little the average equitation rider really knew about elementary guiding. He could follow the rail around a ring because the horse was trained to do so, but when called upon for the easiest figures off of the rail, he was at a loss. There has been some justified criticism of equitation riders on this account. In this regard, there is much to be said for pleasure riding and hunting. Such lack is the fault of the instructor, however, and not of the show seat and is easily corrected when detected. That is the great factor in favor of individual workouts off of the rail—both in instruction and in the show ring.

The final phase of this first lesson is a review of all skills learned and an introduction to proper dismounting. To dismount, have the rider grasp all reins in the left hand. Place this left hand firmly on the pommel of the saddle. Now stand up on both stirrups. Remove the right foot from the stirrup, completely standing on the left stirrup, and balancing on both hands at the front of the saddle. Draw the right leg over the horse's back as the right hand slides to the back of the saddle. Make sure that the rider keeps the left leg rigid and transfers his complete weight to the hands before removing the left foot from the stirrup. Then slide slowly to the ground with the head held high. Most beginners will try to reach for the ground with the right foot before they have pulled the left foot free and can easily get hung in the stirrup and frightened, so particular attention should be paid to the fact that the rider must be completely supported on his hands (with rigid elbows) before he begins the descent.

If a rider can mount and dismount quickly with complete control over the horse and himself, with particular care to stay off the curb rein, then that is sufficient for the first few lessons. It is our belief that first things come first and that each lesson should embrace only one or two new skills well learned, with a constant check and review on past learning. I have found that thirty-minute lessons are best. Riders and horses should work hard for the entire lesson, a near impossibility for the longer lessons. Brevity inspires the teacher also.

6

Second Lesson

Learning to post is one of the greatest single skills any rider faces. It can be fun, and it can be frustrating. How easily a rider learns to post depends a great deal on natural rhythm and co-ordination, but it is no real indication of future promise in a rider. One of my quickest riders to post had a very limited future, while another, who is now at the top in her age group, bobbed around for two or three lessons before she and the horse got together. Sometimes it takes a lot of persistence. Several years ago I was riding instructor at MacMurray College, and one of the most enthusiastic freshman students was having a bad time learning to post. Everyone in class was posting but Kathryn, and finally, in desperation, I mounted her on a very methodical, rough-trotting horse. After taking quite a beating, Kathryn finally began getting with the horse, and by the end of the lesson had started posting. Wishing to point out the rewards of persistence, I halted the class and commented on Kathryn's achievement.

"Oh, yes," she beamed, "I finally got it in the end!"

At the start of the second lesson, the rider having learned seat, hands, and rein handling in the first lesson, it is advisable to retrace that first learning in a few minutes of practice.

Now, place a bandage around the horse's neck at such a length that it will pull up to about three inches above the pommel of the saddle. A narrow leather strap may be used, but I prefer the ordinary type of knit leg bandage always found in every stable. It is easy to tie at any desired length, it does not cut into the horse's neck like a strap, neither will it cut into the rider's fingers. By referring to the bandage as a "necktie," and because it is not leather, there is never any confusing of it with the reins.

At a standstill explain the mechanics of a trot. It is a two-beat, diagonal gait that causes a rhythmic bounding of the saddle which in turn signals the rider to rise up and down in the motion known as posting. It is very necessary to stress now and remember always that *posting is a movement caused by the horse, not an exercise to avoid*

Position of fingers holding "necktie." *Photo by author*

the motion of the horse. Next, have the rider extend the forefinger of each hand to grasp the necktie. The function of this aid must under no circumstances ever be misunderstood. It is not to hang to, or keep from falling off, and it is never to be used to pull up out of the saddle. Rather, it is a subtle aid to the rider, both mental and physical, the same sort of help one gets from the reassuring feel of a bannister on a steep stairs. Actually, the greatest benefit is to the horse. It keeps the awkward beginner from jerking the horse's mouth and consequently permits him to maintain a steady, continuous gait.

For the beginner's horse, use a smooth snaffle and an easy curb bit rigged with a rubber-wrapped chain. Merely loosening the curb chain allows too much play in the curb and can easily pinch the corners of the horse's mouth. Many instructors favor the single snaffle rein for the beginner, but I feel that avoiding the curb responsibility implies permission for the beginning rider to pull on the horse's mouth. If this sanctioning of heavy hands is not deliberately intended, it certainly is recognized as a real possibility. I have found that using the necktie will forestall any tendency for the rider to pull himself up by the reins (and discover that he can actually succeed in this bad habit). By the time he has learned balance, so that accidental jabbing of the horse's mouth no longer occurs, the rider is immediately capable of learning how to combine or separate the uses of both reins. It is a mistake to "teach down" to beginning riders, and if the necktie is used until bal-

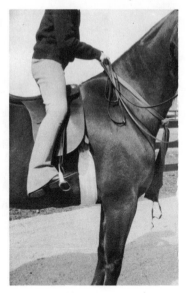

Fig. A   Fig. B

Fig. A Fault: "Necktie" too long.

Here we see the necktie in use at the standstill. It is obvious that the rider is out of balance. With this long rein-hold the hands are drawn too close to the body and we find the rider pulling herself up and forward with the tie. The forward thrust of the head and forward slant of the stirrup leather attest to the unbalanced effort of the rider to rise on the stirrups. The tie must never—under any circumstances—be used to pull the rider up.

Fig. B Correct length and use of "Necktie."

With the tie at the proper, shorter length, the rider has established an independent balance on the horse. The knee is forward on the stirrup leather, the foot is directly under the weight of the body, and the hands are kept properly forward by the tie. With this good balance, the tie assumes its proper function—merely to steady the beginner's hands so that the horse's mouth will be protected, thus assuring a steady, consistent rate of speed at the trot. *Photos by author*

ance is independent, then the sophisticated rein handling of double reins is possible at all age levels.

Remaining at a standstill, with the rider's fingers hooked over the necktie, count "up-down" in the rhythm that the horse will trot, and have the rider try the posting. This may be followed by having the rider try this same exercise with the horse at a walk. We use this step only with naturally timid riders, to whom everything must be taken in very gradual steps. Most riders are now ready to try their wings at the trot, and the balance of lesson time may be consumed in alternating the trotting practice with the rein handling and guiding learned the first day. I cannot stress too much that a rider must be kept learning to maintain interest, and one skill well learned each time is progress. These first lessons should be in a small ring or enclosure. If there are no such facilities, then it is advisable to ride alongside to help keep the horse at a steady, even gait and well in control, so that the beginner can concentrate on his posting.

In this very beginning of posting, the rider is mostly concerned with his efforts to stay on top of the horse. This is why we may have the stirrups up a little from normal. With exceedingly timid riders it is permissible on the first posting lesson to place the feet extra far through the stirrup; not up to the heel, but with the ball of the foot at the front of the stirrup bar. Remember, one should be sure that the stirrups are small enough for the rider. Large-width stirrups will hang parallel to the horse's sides, and the stirrup leather will not make the half turn to permit the stirrup to hang at right angles to the horse's sides, thus twisting the stirrup away from the foot.

Beginners will be exceedingly awkward on the first few tries, but generally time will take care of the co-ordination of motion between horse and rider. Counting along with the rhythm of the horse is a great help and such admonitions as "slower" or "faster" should be called in that rhythm. It is good to impress upon the rider that the posting motion is very slight. In fact, it seems to clarify the movement to explain that, in posting, the motion is not actually complete but rather that the rider starts up and then descends. This explanation will prevent the usual practice of the rank beginner who rises, hangs momentarily in the air, and then falls back into the saddle. I have had considerable success with very small children in likening posting to sitting at the dinner table. Then the person starts to rise from the chair, changes his mind, and sits again.

In some cases, especially where the rider has either had some slight experience riding ponies with a western saddle and sitting the trot, or where a rider has been on a horse a time or two and has had a scare —in these cases, you may find that the rider will refuse to rise from the saddle at all but will hunch down in the saddle and cling there like a leech. If this is so, it is advantageous to have someone demonstrate posting to the rider. In fact, this is wise with all beginners. If this visual aid does not get results, then the instructor should mount a good, gentle horse, secure a lead shank to the caveson or snaffle ring of the lesson horse, and ride alongside the student. Take a slow trot and grasp the rider's belt in your right hand and literally boost the rider up-down in the proper rhythm. This generally brings immediate results, as there is assurance in the closeness of the instructor; and the rider will find that what you have been saying is really true, that it is easier and more comfortable to post than to sit the trot.

As this lesson proceeds and you discuss the rider's progress repeatedly, be sure to impress him with the fact that the saddle boosts the rider aloft and that his main problem is controlling the time and manner of descent into the saddle.

When the rider begins to post, it will probably be for only a few successive steps. Be sure to tell him when he is correct. Many riders actually believe that they are posting if they bounce in rhythm. Also, be very careful that the necktie is the proper length. If it is too long, the rider will clutch at the tie, shoulders shrugged and elbows tense and overdrawn, and in this position he is almost certain to attempt to pull himself up by his hands. Shorten the tie until the hands are somewhat ahead of the pommel. Make sure that the tie is long enough to keep the hands above the withers, not down to the saddle.

Some riders will hunch the back and drop their hands. Arching the back will raise the chest and elevate the hands to the proper height. If the tie is too short, it will not only pull the hands down, but it will cause the rider to reach too far forward and destroy his balance. This imbalance and fear of toppling forward will keep the rider tense in every part of his body, and he will never learn to distribute his weight on the stirrups and throughout the upper legs and seat until the hands are moved back.

At this stage of development, certain faults begin to show up and should be corrected before they become muscular habits. While learning, the rider must concentrate very, very hard to perfect good form, for this is the style that he will have forever, and if it is well learned he can soon go on to the fascinating business of getting the desired performance from his horse. Right now, the main accomplishment is merely to do the mechanics of the walk and trot when called. He is at that "one-two-slide" stage of dancing class, posting being a deliberate "up-down" exercise which the muscles will soon learn to take over instinctively. Again, let me stress that the rider be instructed to rise with the movement of the saddle.

Lunging and pumping come from posting that is ahead of the horse's motion and come entirely from the efforts of the rider, not the combined movement of horse and rider. Generally, it is caused by feet thrust too far forward, which calls for a strenuous bounding by the rider to get the body above the feet. By pointing the knee forward and drawing the lower leg back (until the rider can see only his toes below the point of the knee) the rider can line his posting weight over the base of support, the stirrup. This is not only a beginning fault, but one commonly encountered in the show ring. It can often be the result of a very ambitious rider who tends to overdo many things. By waiting in the saddle and making a conscious effort to slow the posting tempo, many riders can correct this lunging, high post. Just remember, the time the rider spends out of the seat of the saddle is dictated by the rhythm of the trot, but the distance the rider rises depends upon the speed of the rider's own movement. He may post slowly for a short rise, or post fast and get to the moon and back. But do keep in mind that the feet must be under the body to permit the slow tempo, otherwise he will tense and fall back hard in the saddle.

The exact opposite fault to the lunging, high post is what we call "popping" from the saddle. Whereas in the lunge the rider has too much weight on the stirrups and not enough in the saddle, in "popping" too much impetus comes from the saddle, where the rider is heavy and late in rhythm. Also, in this case there is insufficient weight in the stirrups, which generally results in considerable leg movement. Instead of a posting movement which is predominantly up-down, as it should be, the "popping" post is predominantly forward and back, as if the rider were hinged forward at the knee. To correct this fault is generally much more difficult, as it ordinarily shows up in the more advanced riders and has been a habit of longer duration. Frequently, changing to a short-treed saddle and dropping the stirrups a hole or two will force the rider over his feet. For if a rider attempts to pull his feet back under his body (rather than push the body forward over the feet), he will often tense up in the shin muscles, point the toes, and add more faults to his problem. Once the rider has corrected his fault in the shorter saddle, by practicing leaving the saddle a fraction sooner and by consciously trying to force the weight more evenly down the entire leg and foot, he may return to the longer saddle that fits him. Quite often it will help to shoe the horse with a decided toe-weight shoe to lengthen his stride, as this habit generally starts with a short-gaited horse.

7

Third Lesson

By the time of the third lesson, the beginner should have a fairly good idea of posting. Of course it goes without saying that all riders differ in their learning. I would like to suggest, however, that in the very young riders, eight years or under, instruction should be given twice a week. You will find that the small fry will forget quite a bit of the instruction in weekly lessons, and especially for the first eight or ten times there is much to be gained by having the lessons at closer intervals.

This third lesson generally introduces the rider to the beginnings of form in riding and adds "how to do" to the "what to do" of the first two sessions. It must be made very clear that the knees should be well forward on the saddle—on, or slightly in front of, the stirrup leathers. Heels must be forced down to slightly below the stirrup level. Most children will pull the heel up as the knee moves forward, so we must be very careful here to see that the leg is properly aligned and always remains so from now on. Correction of the foot and leg position should start at the very beginning of the lesson and continue until the rider has established a good basic position. Some riders can get this within the lesson time. Whenever this occurs, we are ready to have the rider learn to post independently of the necktie.

It is a workable plan to have the rider free his right hand and ride with this hand at waist height while the other still grasps the necktie. After a few minutes, have the rider release the necktie completely and ride free. It will help to remind the rider that the reins are attached to the bits in the horse's mouth and that he must be very careful to keep a steady, constant hold on the reins. I tell the riders to pretend that they have a glass of water balanced on each hand and that they are not to spill a drop. It is too soon to launch into an explanation of "hands," collection, give and take, and many other facets of handling. Most instructors, particularly the novice teachers, are too anxious to make corrections. I can recall my own intensity with new riders—the seeing of a thousand faults and attempting to correct them all. I

Heel rising with the torso at the trot. This is generally a careless fault and can be corrected by concentrating on keeping the heel down. A simple fault but a frequent one.

would even hold the rider's foot in position and run around the ring with the horse at a brisk trot. Of course, I see the futility now and realize, as all should, that no faults are completely individual and that time and patient instruction will correct some faults to the degree that other, related faults will automatically disappear. Since foot position is the literal basis of seat and hands, we should concentrate on this area and let the hand position alone as much as possible now. You will find that most riders will ride with an extended arm, which is not too great a temporary fault if you do not let it persist too long so that it becomes a habit. If the rider has gotten a good foot position, the fourth lesson can introduce the best hand position for the individual.

I always preface the trot command with questions to young beginners. They are: "What is the first thing you do when I call for the trot?"—Shorten the reins; "Where are your knees?"—Forward; "Where are your heels?"—Down: "Where is your head?"—Up; "Where is the horse's head?"—Up; "How do we get it up?"—By shortening the reins and raising my hands. In this way the rider learns from the very first to take inventory of himself and of the horse. It is never too soon to learn that preparation for any gait is greatly responsible for the successful execution of the gait.

Now that the rider has some general idea of his basic position and how it is used to get a good position from the horse, we can analyze the placement of the arms and hands. Since the rider learned to post by grasping the necktie, he will probably be riding with an extended arm and rigid elbow. If riders are old enough to understand, we should ask them to make a 90° angle at the elbow. In the smaller riders, place their arms in the correct position, and show them by your own example what to do. Generally, if you tell them to raise the horse's head with their hands, not their arms, they will understand. It also helps to say, "Hands up, elbows down." We raise a horse's head with our hands, not our arms. For this particular lesson, the one in which the rider makes the transition from necktie to free hands on the reins, it is a good idea to have the curb chain quite loose or use a padded curb chain to protect the horse's mouth from the inexpert rein work of the beginner. Above all, do not bit the horse severely under any circumstance.

Your greatest problem now will be to get the rider's hands up to waist height. I used to tell riders to hold their hands as high as their belts, but I have found that admonishing them to raise the horse's head gets their hands up better and is not too soon to begin getting the riders interested in not only what the horse does but how he does it.

One fault to watch for in a novice rider is a tendency to slump and let the spine bow as he sits down in the saddle during posting. There are times when it is necessary to tell the rider, "Arch your back." However, it is highly probable that the rider will stiffen the entire upper body, even to the extent that the knees may stiffen and lock. I have had the best results in getting good posture with one phrase, "Pull your ribs up out of your belt." This movement results in the following improvements: The head will be high. The chest will be high. Shoulders will be squared, but relaxed and not hunched. The back will be slightly arched but supple, not stiff. And the forward and upward thrust of the chest will align the upper body somewhat forward over a three-point base of support, the pelvis and the two seat bones.

Posting is fun, but it is also very tiring to the new rider. It is wise to mix it up a bit. Return to a careful analysis of the rider's position at a walk. Teach him to guide the horse in a circle, being sure that both reins are taut. Insist that the circle be absolutely round and that the horse return to the exact spot from which he left the rail. At this early stage, emphasize proper rein tension during guiding. Most beginners will haul around on the direct rein while loosening the bearing rein completely. Obviously the horse will twist his neck, and not only the rider but the horse will be out of balance. Both reins must be fairly snug, with more pull on the direct rein. Never let the rider stick his hand out to the side to guide. Make sure that the pull is straight back, and teach the pupil to make simple turns with wrist movement only.

The proper way to reverse should be taught at this time. Bring the horse to a complete halt on the rail. As the rider holds the horse at this spot he should draw his outside (next to the rail) leg slightly back and push the horse into a pivot. At the same time, he turns the horse toward the rail, making certain that he keeps the horse's neck straight. It is important that the reverse be done from a standstill. Otherwise the beginnings of both the reverse and the canter would be identical. A horse should never have to guess what a signal means.

8

Hands

Hands are the link between the immediate command of the rider and the resulting response of the horse. To oversimplify, the hands represent the steering wheel and the brakes of the horse. There is no term in riding that is more abused or misunderstood than the term "light hands," and it causes more trouble than any other misconception that a rider could have. Many people believe that good hands are the ones that have very little contact with the horse's mouth. Nothing could be further from the truth. To illustrate, hold two strings and have someone "drive" you as we used to do when playing horse. The only possible way that you can follow the guiding of the driver is to have a firm and steady pull on the lines. To try to anticipate the spasmodic on and off jerking of the lines is very distracting and uncertain. Certainly a horse must react the same way when the reins are attached to bits that can be very severe. It must be understood, however, that this constant contact with the horse's mouth must be made through an "elastic" wrist and hand rather than a "brittle" gripping of the reins. Just as a tow chain must be taut at all times, so must the slack be taken up in the reins to keep from hitting the horse's mouth. Just how much pull should be exerted on the reins depends completely upon the horse, the problem at hand, and the degree of proficiency of the rider. For the very young rider, have the student grasp the reins in the usual manner, and then you take the reins at the bits and pull on them until the rider can feel such a pull as the horse should feel from the rider. Now, presuming that you have a well-trained horse, it is wise to explain that, in most simple guiding such as turns to the right and left and stopping, the rider starts the turn with the reins with a subtle pull, and the horse completes the turn, because he has been trained to turn when the rein is pulled. Most new riders laboriously pull the horse around the entire turn as though they were driving a tractor. They should learn immediately that a turn or stop is the horse's response to the signal of the reins. We find that serpentine work down a riding aisle at the walk and trot is of great value. It teaches a rider to make a smooth transition from one rein to the other and makes him become agile with his hands. Many new riders, particularly the very small ones, will be hesitant about any arm movement, and it is important that they get some sort of practice in rein manipulation right from the start. It is a great mistake to underestimate the capabilities of young beginners. I have an eight-year-old right now who has ridden less than twenty times who is learning to raise a horse's head and collect him. In years gone by, I thought that such work was too advanced for a youngster and merely taught the child to hold the hands up and to shorten the reins when I noticed that they were too long. Now I have found that even six-year-old children can grasp the fact that they should hold the horse's head in place, not just hold the hands at the "proper" position.

We have a favorite saying that hands are 99% brains and 1% muscle. It is indeed true that good hands are thinking hands. I have a student now who is a grown young man, who hopes to learn to show his own gaited horse. He had mastered a good, workable seat but was having considerable difficulty in the use of his hands. His hands were not tense because his balance was wrong (as may often be the case), but they were stiff and unyielding because he was trying to hold them in a set position at a certain height and with a certain rein length. When he began to be able to move his hands after practicing serpentine turns at the walk and trot, he was then instructed to imagine that his hands were the horse's mouth—to "think" with his hands and to forget "how" his hands were using the reins. He can now set a horse's head where it should be and is well on the way to having an excellent pair of hands.

There are certain "hand" problems that one has with the very small riders under eight years of age that I should like to discuss briefly. First of all, reins should be small enough. Half-inch snaffle and ⅜″ curb should be used and should be kept clean and supple. Constant practice at shortening reins should occur. We instruct beginners in a long aisleway, and it is splendid for teaching rein work. The riders are taught to shorten reins and lift the horse's head at every turn. Be sure to have these tiny riders learn to elevate the horse's head as soon as possible. If you do not, either the horse will be completely loose on a very long rein where the child will have no control at all, or the child will ride with the arms completely outstretched. This outstretched position is a very difficult habit to break and is also a precarious posture, since the slightest pull of the horse's head can topple the child forward, out of balance. There must be a certain amount of bend in the elbow to take up any head movement in the horse, and yet, if the

Seven-year-old Amy Davis was one of the most rewarding students I ever taught. She had an incredible capacity for concentration, and I believe that this picture taken at the 1980 Lexington Junior League Horse Show is noteworthy for many reasons. The pony is a superb product of her rider's determination and ability. It was no easy task to set up this rather heavy-headed pony and get the collection and balance that were the pony's maximum performance. When we refer to the use of the hands reflected in performance, this is what we mean. Just look at the eyes of Amy and the pony and you will know what total mental communication between rider and mount means. And what perfect hands! *Photo by Donaldson*

rider has a bent arm on a long rein, there is absolutely no control that far from the horse's mouth.

In some cases, where the rider is very small, it is a good idea to put an overcheck on the horse to keep him from pulling the tiny rider off balance. A word of caution, however: Be sure that the overcheck is not severe and do not try to pull the horse's head up higher than his usual, natural carriage. If you pull him up too much, you will merely swap head throwing for head pulling. If the child can learn a happy medium here—to elevate the horse's head somewhat and to have a slight bend at the elbow—then you will find that this is a safe, workable position that will adjust to perfect form as the rider matures in size and experience.

Since we are in the very early stages of learning, it is sometimes hard to know just how much information about aids should be given. I have found that reducing things to the lowest common denominator works in horsemanship as well as in mathematics. The illustration used previously about the rider's being told to "show me the bottom of your foot" appears to work as well as making a lengthy analysis of the entire foot and ankle position. As far as hands are concerned, after you have explained the mechanics of guiding and such rein work as we have already covered, it is time to make a brief explanation of the two reins and their distinctive action in the horse's mouth. The snaffle bit and the curb should be shown to the rider before he mounts. Demonstrate the direct pull of the snaffle and the leverage action of the curb with the resultant arching and lowering of the horse's neck. After the rider has mounted, and before he moves from the standstill, have him practice shortening the snaffle only. This selective shortening is done exactly as the original rein adjustment, but the rider grasps only the desired two reins, not all four. Then practice shortening only the curb. Point out the horse's reaction to the pull of the individual reins. The actual position of the hands can be a difficult thing for some riders to understand. You will get good results from the following demonstration, having the rider do the same thing along with you.

Stand on the ground with your arms hanging at your sides. Then elevate your hands as if to clasp them together at waist height. This will very closely approximate a good, workable hand and wrist position. Thumbs should not point straight up, as this makes the backs of the hands vertical and limits the action of the wrists. Neither should the hands be held parallel to the ground, with the backs of the hands completely horizontal. This position also limits the wrists, and even worse, gives a cramped, shrugged tension to the shoulders and upper arms. If you will hold a whip in your right hand so that it will lie across your left forearm, slanted about midway between your wrist and elbow, then match the angle of the left hand to the right-hand position, you will have a good basic position. The wrists must always be somewhat arched and higher than the knuckles. However, the teacher must be very careful with instructions to arch the wrists, as very often the rider will exaggerate this movement and will look like a dog begging for a bone. When you know just how high each particular horse carries his head in a collected fashion and have taught the rider to take up the slack in the reins as he elevates so that he has a firm, elastic contact with the horse's mouth, then the rider will have established the proper height of his hands and correct length of reins. It is impossible to say that reins should be held at a specific height and length, because every rider is built differently and every horse has an individual head carriage. The position must come from the best control at that very moment. It is not too early, however, to tell the rider, "Bring the horse to you; don't you go to the horse." In other words, do not let the horse pull the rider's hands out of position. The rider must get the front end of the horse right and then check himself for his own best position. You will find that good riding calls for frequent rein adjustments, and the teacher should coach this point frequently. Your rider will learn very early in the game to watch the horse's head position, and you will notice that frequent rein manipulations also tend to keep the rider relaxed in the entire upper body.

One of the most difficult and important functions of the hands is the proper use of the whip. In the first place, riders must learn to use the whip as an aid to preventing mistakes rather than solely as a punishment. I believe that my hardest job with my more experienced riders is to get them to use the whip when it is needed. A well-placed word or cluck is certainly important and will help to keep the horse up on the bit and attentive to the rider. What makes these word signals effective is the training the horse has received which associates the sound with physical action. In other words, the voice means that the horse should respond, or he will get a tap of the heel or whip. Now, if we are constantly clucking like a lonesome cricket, the effect is soon lost and the horse will pay no attention whatsoever, or he will develop the ugly habit of laying back his ears to listen to the meaningless clatter. Do use your voice, but one cluck—then use the whip smartly to reinforce the authority of the voice. The main concern here, however, is that in using the whip we do not jerk on the reins. It takes practice and lots of thought to become adept in the use of the whip.

To be of value, the whip must make the horse come alive and responsive. If we jerk the horse at the same time, he can only con-

This rider has unusually short arms and has overcompensated by riding completely on the curb rein to assure control over his pony. Taking up the slack in the snaffle would improve the picture without changing the control. Relaxing the wrists would lower the knuckles. *Photo by Morris*

clude that when he springs to attention from the whip, he is being jerked because he did wake up. So, you see, hands must be clever, even-pressured and thoughtful in the use of the whip. If you persist in roughing a horse's mouth when you use the whip, then you are doing absolutely nothing for your horse except to make him sour and resentful. A horse's mentality is limited—he learns completely by association, not by mental telepathy, so be sure that your hands do not tell a lie.

In order to set and collect the horse, more rotation of wrists and use of fingers is needed. Here the young rider is attempting to "push" the horse's head into position. The pushing hands tend to tilt the torso forward, with the resultant loss of weight in the saddle, which causes the knee to pull back. Truly, faults are seldom single. *Photo by John R. Horst*

9

Canter

The best approach to the canter is in the thorough preparation and training of the horse. Presuming this has been done, you are now ready to prepare the rider. Since most children have had little or no opportunity to see show riding, their only conception of a canter is what they see in the cowboy movies or on TV. Therefore, you must immediately correct the impression that the canter is a headlong gallop. Tell him that it is actually a very easy gait to ride. With most riders, I find that it is a good practice to refer to the canter in preceding lessons as the gait that will be their reward for having learned the more "difficult" trot. To permit a child to canter too soon often makes the rider lazy on his trot work—which indeed is work for many sessions after the posting is accomplished.

You will find that, on the third or fourth ride after learning posting, the child's interest may lag a little and that his learning progress may stay at a plateau for several sessions. That is when the instructor is smart to add interesting deviations to the routine that must be followed. Here is a good time to have the rider practice withdrawing the feet (one at a time) from the stirrups and replacing them while the horse is walking. You will find that, many times, stiff and tense feet and ankles result from the rider's fear of losing the stirrup. By practicing this replacing of the feet, that tenseness will disappear and the exercises will aid in the suppling of the ankles. Furthermore, whenever the stirrup is lost, the rider will be able to replace his foot without fear of falling.

Presuming that the rider has advanced satisfactorily with posting and that both he and the horse are ready for the canter, the first step suggested is to teach the rider to sit a jog trot. Remember, for the past several sessions he has done nothing but practice rising from the saddle in the posting motion, and now he must learn to sit the saddle completely. The jog is a slow, mincing trot that is achieved by forcing the horse forward from a walk and restraining him at a slow speed. Here is your first real opportunity to demonstrate to the child the very important practice of "collection"—the use of the legs to force the horse's hind quarters forward and the use of the hands to hold the fore quarters back so that the horse keeps in form and balance. The use of the legs in the management and control of a saddle horse is so important that it will be dealt with separately and often, for to ride a horse with the hands and reins only is only half riding.

Have the child ride this jog until he is able to sit with complete relaxation, learning to maintain an erect posture with all torso muscles pliant. To stand in the center of the ring and shout, "Relax! Relax!" will accomplish nothing. A good illustration and one that appeals to a child is to suggest that he pretend to be a rag doll and be very limber. Of course this is only an attitude of relaxation, but you will find that children have a real sense of humor, and when you can express ideas in childhood terms that catch a youngster's fancy, then your progress will be more rapid.

If the horse is very quiet and inclined to be somewhat sluggish, a whip will be needed. Hold it in the right hand with the lash end alongside the horse's right shoulder, and apply the whip with a rotating motion of the wrist. Later on, he may choose to hold the whip across the withers, but to learn to use a whip erect without jerking the horse's mouth is very difficult for the beginner. Now explain the mechanics of the canter:

It is a three-beat gait that starts with a hind foot, followed by the simultaneous stride of the other hind foot and its diagonal front foot, and completes on the remaining front foot. The motion is rolling, and should be moderately slow. Left to his own devices in the field, a horse will seldom do a collected canter as we know it. The natural gaits—walk, trot, and gallop—are progressions of speed, and so it is only by training that we get the canter, which is actually an artificial outgrowth of a natural gait, the gallop. The previous training of the horse cannot be stressed too much here, and the horse must be able to take a collected canter or it will startle the beginner and develop a fear that should never exist.

After explaining the mechanics of the canter, then show the rider what his signals should be to get the horse into the gait. There are three distinct steps that must be observed in getting a canter, and these will apply in every instance from the first lesson to the final ride in the show ring. I cannot emphasize too strongly the necessity for this procedure.

First, the reins must be shortened and the horse collected with strong leg aids used to wake the horse up and get him mentally and physically oriented to begin the first stride with the hind quarters well under him. Next, the horse should be placed at an angle towards the rail. This is done by a slight pulling of the rail rein and a pushing of the horse's haunch with the rail leg. After, and only after, the horse is in this angled position should the rider lean slightly forward towards the leading shoulder and cluck to the horse (using the whip and increasing the heel aid if the horse needs a strong signal). These steps in the proper order are positively necessary. A canter can be slow and collected only if the horse starts with the hocks well forward. He will get his hocks under him only with the good use of hands and legs, and he will get the correct canter lead only if he is placed in the proper position to start. It is too soon and too much to ask the rider to learn his canter leads on this particular lesson, but you must insist on this proper sequence because it is the only way to ensure a correct lead. Every rider in the show ring, from the novice equitation rider to the most expert professional, uses this order of aids, regardless of class or breed of horse. The professional may be so subtle that the preliminary steps are almost impossible to detect, but you may be assured that they are there. Even the Walking horse which seems to glide into the canter with no visible signal has been "set up" for the gait.

After having gone over these steps very clearly for the rider (and, if possible, having demonstrated them on another well-trained horse), have the rider start. If the rider is timid or you are not completely satisfied that the horse will keep slow, then start the canter just past the gate and go only a short distance at first, extending the length of the ride as the rider gains proficiency and control. If, on the other hand, the horse is too sluggish, then it is wise to start the canter as they approach the gate. Generally the only early faults that will occur in this session are the nervous inclination of the rider to tense up on the reins and stop the canter, a bounding from the saddle, or too much exaggeration of relaxation, which results in lounging back in the saddle and loss of weight in the stirrups. Practice, encouragement, and patience will generally correct the first fault; bounding from the saddle comes from too much weight on the stirrups, coupled with a tensing of the seat muscles and a stiffening of the spine. Going back to jogging practice may help here, as will your own explanation to the rider of his fault. Shortening the reins and correcting the torso posture will correct the third fault.

After the rider has learned to sit the canter easily and to perfect his form and keep the horse collected, the canter leads should be explained:

Although the horse starts the canter with his hind leg, a canter is identified by the front foot that consistently strikes the ground in a forward position. This is known as the leading foot and the canter may be either the "right lead" or the "left lead." As in the child's skip step, the leading foot strikes the ground ahead of the other front foot, and in executing any circle, this leading foot must be towards the center of the circle. If it is not, then the leading foot will cross in front of the other foot and cause extreme awkwardness or tripping.

Since we are confronted with turns in a riding or show ring, we must set up the proper lead, which is always towards the center of the ring. This is why we turn the horse's body towards the fence to prepare for the proper lead. In this manner, we position the horse at such an angle that he is forced to lead out with the proper foot to avoid tripping himself. To aid this stride further, we use the outside leg aid (pressing the horse's side with our rail leg). This tends to position the horse on the angle, but even more important, it causes the horse to draw forward that outside hind leg, which is the proper stride to begin the correct lead. Thus we have two influences over the horse—the leg aid, which controls the first hind stride, and the body angle, which causes the proper front stride. Identification of the lead from the saddle is very easy, as the leading shoulder appears consistently forward-striding and is obvious to see. A word of caution here, however: Since the English language is so confusing and the term "right" may mean either right and wrong or right and left, it is best always to refer to leads as correct or incorrect. The lead towards the center of the ring is always correct, and the lead towards the rail is always incorrect.

10

Analysis of Foot Position

As time passes and the riders progress with their lessons, it becomes increasingly apparent that the learning process is a nebulous thing that cannot be charted and planned for in a rigid system. Every rider differs in interest and talent, and each rider differs from lesson to lesson. Add to this factor the ever-changing horse, and you will soon learn that the problems take constant planning and altering of plans.

With most riders, there will be a steady progress up to and through learning to canter. Very often, after this point the rider will subconsciously think that he has "learned to ride," that he can control the horse at the three gaits, and "What more is there to riding?" Here is that first plateau, where the rider seems to stall on one level and fails to show the previous gradual improvement. Now the teacher is hard put to instill that same enthusiasm in the rider which breeds such pleasant progress. It has been my experience that the best approach is one of complete honesty with the rider. Tell him that the next few lessons may be somewhat boring for both of you, but that they are necessary for the development of complete muscular habits that will free the mind later on for the more exhilarating things to come. Children appreciate frankness, and they will keep interested as long as they are learning. When they know that periods of dreary repetition are a temporary necessity and not an indication that they are complete dumbbells, then they will be willing to work hard, and here is a wonderful time for a youngster to learn that hard work can be fun. You, as the teacher, will be performing a service not only to yourself and the rider, but to the parents of that rider.

I completely believe that the position and the use of the foot in the stirrup is the most important single element in riding a horse. There is much to be said for hands, but we must recognize that the feet are the literal and figurative basis of riding, and every position of the entire body and the resultant balance and control originate here.

Perhaps it would be well to begin this analysis of the foot with a negative statement. Almost without exception, any new rider, when asked to repeat what "rules for riding" he has heard, will immediately say, "Grip with the knees." And the reply is, "Do not grip with your knees." Let me explain immediately. Knee grip or contact is certainly a primary necessity, but to command a rider to grip with the knees results in the rider's pulling the knees directly into the saddle with the inner thigh muscles. This is a very tiring effort that results in rigid muscles that rebound from the saddle during posting and force the rider into rising strictly from his own effort. (It bears repeating that posting is a movement that results from the motion of the horse, not a movement to avoid that motion. Of course, you will see riders who go through vigorous posting entirely under their own power, but they are completely wrong.)

In order to attain the proper knee contact which will permit the muscles to remain relaxed and workable, the position begins with the angle of the sole in the stirrup. The stirrup bar hangs at a slight upward slant that requires the foot to assume this same tilt with the little toe somewhat higher than the ball of the foot. Now, in order to attain the necessary knee grip, we use the stirrup as a lever, and by swinging the heel slightly down and out, we find that the foot actually pushes the knee into position. This is assured when we realize that the entire leg works as one unit from the hip joint and that the knee and upper leg roll into the flap of the saddle. So many riders try to correct out-turned toes by twisting the ankles. Not only does this weaken the ankle but it actually pulls the knee away from the saddle.

The leg works as a single unit originating at the hip joint. One must be very careful here to watch that there be complete freedom of the knee to bend forward and back during posting. Often this idea of a single leg unit will be misunderstood, and the rider will "lock" the knee at the height of the post, which will result in his feet kicking forward while he is forced into the back of the saddle on the descent. The beauty of the knee grip through the foot position is that it permits the greatest economy of effort with a maximum of control and balance. Bobby Morrow, the great track star, explained his success as his ability to keep his muscles relaxed so that they are free to do their work. This certainly true in riding as it is in any sport.

Just how far the rider should swing his heel to the side must be determined individually. Certainly the foot should swing out only enough to roll the knee and thigh into position. Swinging wider than that is an affectation that results in awkwardness and ugliness. A good personal check for the rider is to glance down the side of his leg and swing the heel down and out until he can see the entire side of the leg down to the sole of the boot. To check the foot for the forward position it is generally practical to say that the stirrup leather

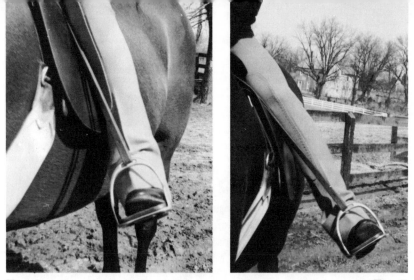

Fig. A   Fig. B

Fig. A   Good foot position, showing even weight distribution on the slanted stirrup iron, which results in close contact of upper calf, knee, and thigh.

Fig. B   Spraddled leg resulting from rotating entire leg too much at the hip socket. This causes tension and stiffness in the upper body and loss of leg control over the horse.

Fig. C   Toeing out. This fault occurs mainly in the ankle itself and should be corrected in the ankle, not in the hip. Rider should maintain hip and leg position, but roll the toe back to forward position shown in A.

Fig. D   Cocked ankle with rider's weight thrown outside to the little toe. Ball of foot is bearing no pressure, and the entire foot position causes the knee to pull away from the saddle and the thigh to roll outward at the hip socket. Of these three major faults—B, C, and D—this cocked ankle is the most serious and should be corrected immediately. Do so by exerting pressure on the ball of the foot and rolling the thigh and knee into the saddle until the position comes back to Figure A. *Photos by author*

Fig. C   Fig. D

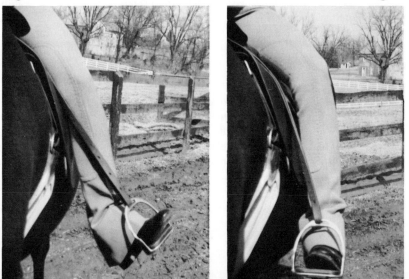

Fig. A

Fig. A "Locked" knee, which will force the lower leg forward to pendulum swing as the rider sits at the post. To correct: Relax and point knee forward on stirrup leather.

Fig. B Fault: Cocked ankle resulting in loose knees. Here we have a perfect example of the cocked ankle at the rise of the post. The knee has pulled back from a flat position on the stirrup leather, because the ankle is rolled out, which loosens the knee contact. In a conscious effort to stabilize this "floating knee," the rider has gripped hard with the inner thigh muscles, causing muscle rigidity throughout the seat and upper legs, resulting in the characteristic swayed back and protruding hips.

Fig. C Corrected position of cocked ankle. This rider is using the foot and ankle (in conjunction with natural body weight and the upward sloping stirrup bar) to give the knee a flat and snug position on the stirrup leather. Thigh and seat muscles are relaxed and pliant, thus allowing the hips to stay well forward. Knee contact must come from the proper position of the foot and ankle, not from knee grip.

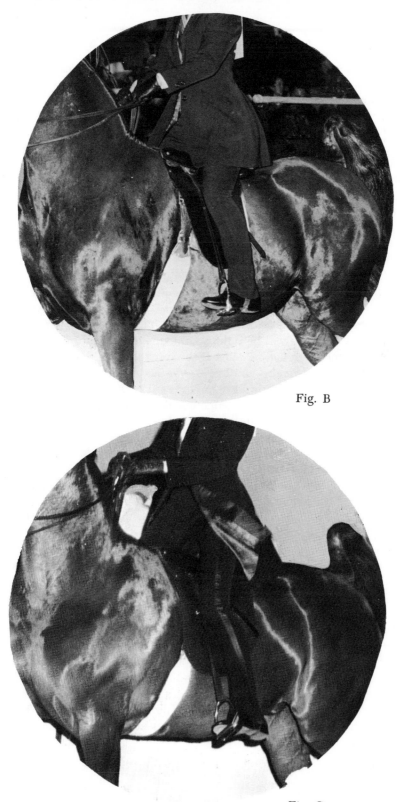

Fig. B

Fig. C

hangs at a right angle to the ground. Feet forward of this line will swing back under the stirrup hook at the height of every posting movement to cause the same swing that a locked knee will cause. There is a well-known phrase in riding, "The seat must be independent of the hands." Certainly this is so, but such a phrase needs a lot of explanation for the young rider. Literally, it means that we must have such good posture and balance in the saddle that no matter what awkward motions the horse may go through we will be able to keep our balance without hanging on to the reins to maintain it. It also means that our hands must be so thoughtful, flexible, and adaptable that any head movement by the horse will be taken care of by the hands and will not pull the body out of position.

It is clear that balance and control, seat and hands, are very dependent upon each other. Balance starts with the foot in the stirrup, and like the old spiritual, "De foot bone connected to de ankle bone, de ankle bone connected to de shin bone, etc.," your entire body balance depends upon the feet in the stirrups. Happily, if the foot is right in the stirrup, the knee will be right. If the knee is correctly placed into the saddle, the thigh will be snug. If the thigh is snug, the seat will be in the right place in the saddle. So, you see, your position is truly built from the foot up. How very important it is that we realize this! I know that I spend many an hour admonishing my riders to develop not only an adequate foot in the stirrup but a positively perfect foot. And the foot must be absolutely perfect at all times.

As has been said so many, many times, we learn by doing, and correct muscular habits must be developed right from the start. The rider who must go through life mentally placing every part of his anatomy on the horse is no rider, because good riding is primarily the work of the mind after we have trained our muscles in the fundamental positions.

The feet must be firm and definite at every gait. The walk is very important and is the primary gait at which the rider may have almost complete mental opportunity to think about his position and start the development of these good habits. Many riders consider the walk a rest period and permit both themselves and their horse to let down. How unreasonable it is to expect that our muscles can loaf during the easy period of the walk (when anyone with a will to learn can look good) and then spring into perfect position when we progress to the more difficult movements of the trot and canter. Oh, no, muscles truly learn by doing, and the rider must spend a great deal of time thinking about his feet in the stirrups and establishing his best position. This will be his character on a horse, his very own style that sets him apart

Although the horse has a hard mouth and is difficult to flex, Kathie Gallagher shows beautiful form. The graceful hand position creates an illusion of ease and beauty, and she has not permitted the horse to pull her out of form. *Photo by Jay A. McClasky*

from the others. One must "jell" into the best figure on a horse that Mother Nature will allow, and this prized position that is "you" begins with your very foundation—your feet in the stirrups.

Did the above-mentioned critique on foot position sound familiar? It should, as it was the major point in the introductory lesson. But you must persist in your expansion and elaboration on this theme in every lesson. If a new skill is learned and the foot position is lost during this learning, then stop right there and analyze what has happened. Someone is doing something wrong, and two wrongs certainly do not make a right.

In the picture we see that the rider has braced out of position with the pulling horse. The knee, instead of remaining firm and in alignment on the stirrup leather, has lost its security. A perfect example of hands *not* remaining independent of the seat.

11

Leg Aids

From time to time we have had visiting riders come to our stable for advanced instruction. It is always an interesting experience to instruct outside riders, because there will be points that invariably arise that do not occur when you deal exclusively with riders whom you have started. It certainly furnishes the teacher with fresh views, from which vantage point both teacher and rider are bound to profit.

Of all the points that I have covered with visiting riders, I do believe that one area in which they agree that they benefited the most is the serious use of the leg aids.

Let me begin by saying that the hind quarters of the horse are the "engine" and the source of power. A horse does not pull himself along by his front legs, but he does push his body forward by the power of the hind quarters while his forelegs are mainly concerned with supporting the front of the body. We must keep in mind that the gaits originate in the hind legs—particularly at the canter. Because a horse does not have a built-in rear-vision mirror, it is very easy for the rider to be concerned only with the part of the horse in front of the saddle, and many people ride with the assumption that, where the front end goes, the back must follow. It is perfectly possible to get from one place to another with only this idea, but for anyone who is interested not only in what a horse does but how he does it, then we must be concerned with the action of the horse's hind quarters.

Very early in the instruction, leg aids are explained. The new rider is advised that the hands control the front of the horse, but the legs control the rear. It is a simple thing to remember that when the right hand turns the horse's head, the right leg draws back and pushes the horse's hind parts. In this way the horse makes a turn with his entire body, more or less on a straight line, and we do not have the awkward twisting of the horse's neck that puts him so off balance.

While it is a simple matter to turn a horse without using the leg aids, we should keep in mind that the horse must be made to obey leg aids and to become accustomed to reacting to them for the later moments when the aids are of very serious use. It must be constantly emphasized that we develop habits in our horse during the most uncomplicated times so that the horse will respond at all times. Certainly it makes sense that we should use strong leg aids to start a canter instead of running a horse into the rail to get the lead. That rail is a long way off when we must perform a figure eight in the center of the ring.

Of all instances where it is important to use leg aids, the most rewarding is at the canter. Keeping in mind that the horse starts his canter with the hind foot diagonal to the leading front foot, we now will see that a strong heel aid to get the horse balanced up on this proper leading hind foot is most important. So many riders make the mistake of being concerned only with the front legs! That is why we get a crossed (or disunited) canter—because the rider has hastened the horse into canter when he has placed the front of the horse in a canter position but has failed to give the horse ample time or opportunity to position his hind quarters and draw up the proper hind foot for the hind lead. When riders are cautioned to take plenty of time in getting set for a lead we mean that they should give the horse time to get his balance on the correct hind foot as well as to angle his leading shoulder forward. Fortunately, when we wish to set up a lead, the rider's leg next to the rail gives the aid. This does three things: it pushes the horse's hind quarters away from the rail, it makes the horse draw forward that hind leg in response to the pressure, and it forces the rider's weight on his inside (next to the center of the ring) stirrup, thus calling the body weight into play, which further tends to make the horse lead out with the proper front foot. How many times we see the misguided rider swing a horse violently at the rail when a canter is called! The horse has three alternatives: he may refuse to canter at all, he may hit the rail, or he can jump into a canter with no preparatory gathering or placement and just take potluck as to the results.

It is surely obvious by now that the preparation for the canter is the most important element of the gait. It takes extreme balance and control for the horse to canter slowly and in form. Most riders find it difficult to collect a horse to a slow canter out of a fast start without drawing the horse into a break. It is much better to do the collecting before the gait starts and have the horse slow from the very beginning.

After the horse is well into the canter, the rider's legs still perform a very necessary function. In order to keep the high, rolling canter, it is necessary to be constantly alert for a change in the speed of the gait.

Many riders have difficulty because they do not realize that their horse has picked up speed. Then they have to take the horse back too much, and he often mistakes that checking for the stop signal and will break gait. If the rider is quite alert to any increase in speed and checks the horse right away while he tightens his legs to keep the horse on the canter, then he will have that desirable slow canter that results from the combination of restraining with the hands and impelling with the legs. It should be obvious that the degree of holding back and the degree of urging ahead depend completely upon the horse and how he is responding at the moment. Even the most anxious horse will tire at the end of a long and grueling ride, so every rider, regardless of his horse's temperament, should learn the immediate use of the aids. I had a very accomplished rider travel many miles to a show and fail badly because her horse, who was always up on the bit, drew back and faltered on a workout. She had never had to urge him on before and was taken completely by surprise. It was a hard lesson, but needless to say, those aids are instantaneous now.

Perhaps even more interesting than the insurance of the proper lead is the extreme collection and obedience that results from attention to the leg aids. When I first became aware that there were such things as aids, I was more interested in horse training than in the teaching of equitation, and the very sound of "leg aids" tended to annoy me. When I finally stopped to analyze the trainer's use of his legs in gaiting a colt and in finishing any show horse, I realized that every saddle-horse trainer worth his salt was using the leg aids that I thought were so flossy and bookish. More than anything else, a very personal experience convinced me that the intelligent use of legs is basic and positively necessary to all riding. We purchased a good horse for use as an equitation horse. He had enjoyed certain success as an open horse, but had slipped into careless habits and mediocre use of his legs. As we trained the horse in figure eights, serpentines, straight-line canter changes, and cantering out of a backward step, we could see a great change occur in the horse. His hocks became placed up under his weight, his head carriage improved, the entire all-round action increased greatly, and in addition to having a wonderful equitation horse, we found that we had a champion open horse, the famous Storm Cloud. Every horse we have trained since then is a better horse for having learned the lesson of leg aids. And without exception, every visiting rider has expressed enthusiasm over his increased control of the horse and looked forward to getting home to teach his own horse better balance, motion, and response through the use of leg aids.

Let us delve a little deeper into the subject and discuss leg aids as they apply at the specific gaits.

So often we are inclined to overlook the importance of the walk. It is one of the acknowledged gaits, and since it precedes and follows all other gaits, it is not only important in itself but also has a tremendous influence upon the other gaits. One of the very first and foremost ideas we must recognize is that when we are dealing with a show horse it is up to the rider to keep the horse at his greatest peak of animation at all times. I often remark that we all have to work for a living, and the horse is no exception. When we ride him, he should work. If we want him to loaf, then we can jog or hand walk him. A state of animation cannot all be gotten through the hands but must be a combination of the hands to keep the horse checked back where he will be "set" (having the neck elevated as high as the horse can carry it while keeping the chin pulled in) and the use of the legs to urge the horse forward so that his hind quarters are well up under him and he is poised and balanced to move into the faster gaits at all times.

Because our lower legs from the knees down move when we use the lower leg aids, many people are unaware that there are "hidden" leg aids that are also of great importance. The firm, tight knee and upper thigh are keenly felt by the horse through the saddle and act as an actual guide to the horse's body. Draw your own arms into your ribs with a firm pressure and you will get some idea of the influence that good, strong upper legs have on the horse. You must remember that the weight of the rider is about one tenth the weight of the horse, and that ratio has a great effect on the animal. If you sit loose and purposeless on him, he is completely at the mercy of the bits for guidance, and many a horse has gotten an unresponsive mouth because the rider tugged so completely on the reins that the horse finally ceased paying any attention at all. A good tight seat in the saddle at the walk will "race the motor" so that the succeeding gaits will be quick and collected. When you see Chat Nichols force his heels down hard in the stirrups at the walk and sit back proudly on the horse, he isn't trying to "show off" for the audience. His only thought is for the horse, and he is a masterful trainer famous for the great balance and lofty carriage of his horses, who get that elevation from his marvelous combined use of legs and hands.

When we move on to the trot, it becomes necessary to use the lower legs more than we use them at the walk. Do not misunderstand and think that there should be a constant "fluttering" of the legs—nothing could be further from the facts. The legs are most used as we begin the trot, and draw into the sides of the horse with the first few strides of the gait. This serves a twofold purpose—to start the horse with the hocks well forward, and to balance the rider so that the stirrups will be in a position to push the rider forward with the first step. If you do not draw the legs back, you will have to lunge forward on the first stride to keep from being behind the motion of the horse, and this is unbalancing to the horse as well as an awkward attitude for the rider. We refer to the leg "aids" as something that benefits the horse, which they actually do, but we must also recognize the fact that they benefit the rider as well.

Aids can be overused, too. We are all familiar with the rider who uses extreme leg movements at the slightest provocation to make sure that the judge realizes that he knows his aids. Certainly this is unnecessary movement on the horse. On the other hand, I have had to be constantly alert for a different fault. One of my riders was being very careful to use her legs, but she did not use them strongly enough or give the horse time to react. She had all cause and no effect. The aids are to be used to get results. If they do not get results, then they are unnecessary affectations. I am sure that everyone agrees that horses are not impressed by the written word. Just because the rider reads that leg aids are important does not make them so unless they are used in a logical manner on the horse to get good results. As a judge, I often see riders deliberately pumping the wrists at the walk and canter to prove to the judge that they have good, sympathetic hands. This is an illustration of the overuse of aids, and one generally finds the rider is a creation of theory and very little fact.

The legs are also important to us at the stand in the lineup. Most of the well-trained show horses know that they are to stand with their heads high. A sharp tap with the heel will generally bring a horse to attention and get his head up. But how many times we see the rider playing the seesaw with the horse's head, yanking up on the curb, staying on the curb until the horse lowers his head, and then jerking away again. This very common fault will be dealt with in much more detail when we discuss the hands, but suffice it to say that a sharp heel, a nip on the reins, and then giving the horse his head will do the trick.

A further refinement in the use of the legs is the teaching of the inside leg aid. Thus far we have discussed the leg, and it has always been drawn back slightly to the hind quarters to force the haunches off a straight line. When your rider has mastered good form at the three gaits and has relatively good control of the horse, then work on circles is very helpful and extremely interesting. Probably now, more than at any other time during elementary riding, will the student appreciate the unity of effort between the hands and the legs: The inside leg aid is the use of the leg directly into the side of the horse near the

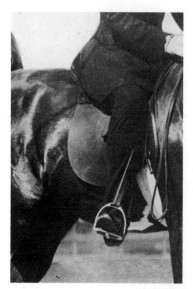

Incorrect use of inside leg aid, showing loss of knee contact and twisting of ankle.

Inside leg aid corrected: Strong calf influence without loss of knee and thigh contact. Used separately, this pressure can help to turn the horse. Used by both legs, the aids force the horse up in the bridle and help to maintain collection.

girth area. The leg is neither drawn back nor forced forward. The sole function of the aid is to exert pressure at the middle of the horse, causing his body to bend concavely so that his actual line from the top of his head to the tail will be a slight arc. We literally "bend the horse around our leg" and make it possible for him to execute a circle or turn in complete balance. Without this bending of his body, a horse will tend to lean to the center of a circle—a movement that invariably degenerates into extreme awkwardness with a low head carriage. Particularly at the canter, the horse loses his collection and balance. The hind quarters drift beyond the pattern of the circle and we have a switch of leads in the rear.

If you are teaching in a rectangular area (our teaching arena is 200 feet × 50 feet), start the rider at a walk, and as he executes his first turn at the end of the arena, call for a complete circle. This circle must be indicated to the horse by pressure of the inside leg aid throughout the circle while the hands restrain and guide the horse on the exact pattern. At first, the rider will exert the major control with the hands, but as time passes he will discover that the effort is more evenly divided between hands and the leg. You will find that this figure is easier for the student at the trot, and as soon as he is sure of the pattern, call for this work at a trot. Circle only once at each end of the ring with emphasis on perfection of pattern through the full use of *both* pairs of reins and the inside leg aid. Watch for overguiding, which will twist the horse's neck, or failure to make a round circle and consequently not returning to the exact same spot on the rail. Only you will know when your student is advanced enough for this work, but it should be used as soon as possible.

A worth-while variation is the serpentine at the walk or trot with emphasis on the inside leg aid. I think that this skill should be saved for the more intense work with advanced riders, but once you have introduced the rider to the inside leg aid, you have to incorporate it into all phases of your teaching. One thing that I would like to make clear is this: If any element of riding is valid, it should be used consistently. New instructors may tend to move from one new skill to the other without maintaining a constant watch that previously introduced fundamentals are still in use. Your main responsibility as a teacher is not just to present the information, but to see that each bit of knowledge is learned and used forever after. Repetition is the very heart of beginning instruction. The rider and the horse both learn by *doing*. If they trot eight times, five badly and three well, then you have succeeded in teaching them how to trot badly.

12

Diagonals

Thus far our instruction has been very elementary, and this is certainly as it should be. The wise teacher will not only study her student's riding form and progress but will be constantly alert to the rider's mental attitude. You may find it difficult to get him to tell you when he does not understand your instruction, and what you may take for inattention or inability is simply the fact that you have not been able to make your instruction clear to that particular student. Since we are dealing with the problems of teaching the individual rider, we have to rule out the very helpful method of this pupil observing other pupils. This is where group instruction has a great advantage over single lessons.

If it is at all possible, try to have an advanced rider ride for the beginner from time to time so that he may see just what sort of picture he is trying to make. It is also most effective to have the experienced rider demonstrate the faults as well. If you do not have another rider available, then you may do the demonstrating yourself. But do be very careful that you are able to demonstrate properly. It can be quite embarrassing to discover that you are reduced to the situation where it is "Do as I say, not as I do." Believe me, it is much more effective to be able to stand with the pupil and comment on someone else's riding. Also, it is much easier to get the observer into discussion when you are not riding. If you, yourself, demonstrate some bad form, the student will rarely be bold enough to comment on it, and you still will not know if the rider can actually distinguish proper from improper form. Actually, the only phase of instruction where I think that observing is absolutely mandatory is for the explanation of diagonals—especially the changing of diagonals.

I have found that pictures serve very well in the explanation of diagonals. Since almost all saddle-horse pictures are taken at the trot, any horse magazine will be filled with good examples.

The mechanics of a trot must be explained once more. A trot is a two-beat, diagonal gait, in which a diagonal pair of feet strike the ground (i.e., right hind and left front) followed by the remaining diagonal pair. The diagonal is identified by the front foot—thus if we are concerned with the diagonal consisting of the right front and left rear, that is the right diagonal.

A diagonal may be recognized by the rider on sight. When he looks at the horse's shoulders, he should be able to tell which shoulder is moving forward and up as he is moving forward and up in the post. Have the rider begin his trot and immediately tell him on which diagonal he is posting. Give him at least half the distance of the ring to look at this shoulder. Most riders will be able to distinguish the diagonal during the lesson period. Occasionally you will have a rider who has a lot of difficulty with this identification. Particularly if the rider is quite young, do not practice this problem to the exclusion of everything else. You will find that the student will start guessing, and instead of learning the diagonals, he will try desperately to guess the right answer. Only time will help such riders, and when you are ready to give up in despair, you will realize that the light has finally dawned.

Only after the rider can positively identify the diagonal should a further explanation be given. During this introduction, use the words "right" and "left." After you have explained about the correct and incorrect diagonals, then always refer to them as either correct or incorrect when the work is on the rail.

A diagonal is "correct" only when a turn at the trot is involved. The correct diagonal to post in a ring is the one to the rail. Very simply, when a horse makes a turn, he shortens the stride of the inside (incorrect) diagonal in order to get around the semicircle. On the straight sides of the ring the strides of both diagonals will be equal and the stride of the outside (correct) diagonal will continue to remain the same on the turn, while the stride of the inside diagonal is shortened. It is obvious that the only way to maintain a consistent posting rhythm and help the horse keep a steady, balanced gait on the turn is to post the outside diagonal.

Only after the student can identify the diagonals consistently should you proceed to the change of diagonals. Remember this: If you teach everything you know in one lesson, the beginner will not only be unable to assimilate all this conversation, but you will have left yourself no new material for succeeding sessions. Keep the lessons fresh, new, and interesting. You will keep yourself stimulated enough to give exciting and inspirational instruction, and such enthusiasm transmits itself to the pupil.

The usual diagonal change is effected by sitting two successive strides. In other words, count for your riders, "Up, down, up, down,

down, up." I have found, if I use the word "Sit," many riders will syn-
copate the rhythm, slouch loosely, and take a double stride which
puts them right back on the same diagonal. Explain that the change is
made in strict cadence and the back should remain arched. Relaxed
seat muscles will take a hard bounce out of the change, but it should
never be done with any skeletal compensation.

As the rider becomes more experienced, insist that he identify the
diagonal with no change in his body position. The beginner may be permitted to lean forward if it is necessary to his learning the diagonals.
However, if you have to permit this, omit it as soon as possible and
enjoin the rider to look down with his eyes, not his head. Further, be
alert to any dropping of the hands, as this almost always accompanies
the bending forward over the shoulder. Not only is this a bad rider
fault, but we find that the horse has been turned completely loose as
the trot starts, and instead of the rider's starting the horse well
collected, he has done the exact opposite, and the horse is momentarily out of control. Collection should precede all gaits. Even for advanced riders it is difficult to start a horse on a loose rein and then
collect him after the gait is established. Diagonals are important, but
nothing is important enough to sacrifice the performance of the horse.
This point must be stressed at all times at all levels of instruction. I
cannot emphasize enough that horsemanship is the riding of the
horse. Many instructors get so involved in seat and hands that they
tend to forget this obvious fact. We have all seen riders who were
pictures of personal perfection whose riding was only "saddle deep." I
have a description for such riders who "equitate" too much. They appear as if—should the horse suddenly drop dead—they would post
right on around the ring and never know that the horse was gone!

A surprising number of horsemen are unaware of the mechanics of
the trot and of the existence of diagonals. We have all seen riders
laboring around a turn with the horse seeming to drop away from the
saddle—all this trouble because the rider was unaware of the importance of diagonals, or even worse, unaware of diagonals. In so many
instances we have purchased horses to train for equitation, and the
horse has been consistently ridden on one diagonal only. He may actually look and feel as though he is lame when you post the other diagonal. Such horses can be corrected, but it takes a long time to get
this animal absolutely even on his trot. Working on circles and at the
serpentine will help, but when you first start to retrain the horse, be
ready to spend many tiring hours on the unpracticed diagonal. I generally ride such horses in only half of the ring, which doubles the
number of turns. It is easier on me, and the horse accepts the new
movement much more readily on the turn, as he can feel his own bal-

ance improve immediately, whereas it is a matter of either accepting or not accepting the change on the straightaway. Be sure that you have corrected this fault in the horse before you get to the explanation of diagonals.

It is almost impossible to teach a novice to ride and understand both diagonals on a horse that is not even-gaited. I recently bought a splendid young gelding for a very reasonable price because he was uneven at his trot. Since he was sound, it seemed obvious that the disparity in strides could be corrected with work on the weak diagonal. Fortunately, this was the case, and the horse is developing into one of the nicest juvenile horses we have had in several years. I certainly do not recommend that the new teacher or trainer set out to buy such a reform candidate, but you should be aware of the importance of diagonals and all of their ramifications.

13

Riding Tournaments

As interest and experience increase in riding, it follows that the quality of both the riding and the horses is bound to improve. Where the children once showed academy horses in the equitation classes, you now have polished little riders showing top-quality horses in the horsemanship and juvenile events. This is all well and good and is the ultimate goal of all who teach and all who learn. However, there is a danger that such perfection will stifle the prospective riders, and instead of encouraging more to join in the fun, we discourage the new rider with our finished products. Here in Kentucky we had a wonderful solution to such a situation. We had early-spring riding tournaments which offered classes designed for the least riders, beginners under eight, up to five-gaited horse classes. Other sections of the country have similar shows, Indianapolis being an excellent example. But more localities should consider the benefits of such events.

In Louisville, the Kentucky Winter Horsemanship Tournaments were held for twelve years and were revived in 1980. A committee of interested adults (generally parents of children in representative stables in the area) set up the class list, arranged for judges, handled entries—in other words, they put on the four shows. These shows were held every other week for four shows, and the intervening Saturdays were available for the show in event of bad weather. Early in January, trainers and instructors of the locality were asked to hand in a list of all prospective riders, listing age and rating as a beginner, intermediate, or advanced. When the list was studied, then the age divisions were broken down into age groups that had approximately equal numbers. For instance, if there were many more intermediate riders than advanced, there were three age divisions for the intermediate and only two divisions of advanced. In other words, the same class list did not necessarily hold from one year to the other.

These tournaments were truly held for the benefit of the riders and their trainers and instructors. While placings must be important to measure achievement, the main function of these tournaments was to give the beginning and novice riders an opportunity to show with equal competition, to give the more advanced riders a chance to try out their new horses at a show where the chips were not down, and to provide the stables with an excellent opportunity to get to work out show-routine practices for a bunch of new horses. There are riders who showed in the tournaments who would not have had the slightest chance for a ribbon in open shows. These were the riders who deserved a chance, for many an expert rider has blossomed from such humble and simple beginnings.

Then, too, these events afforded an opportunity for riders to show who would never again have had a chance to ride in competition for any number of reasons. It is a wonderful thing to be able to present a child with the chance to show a horse, no matter what his future plans may be. Certainly from the standpoint of the trainer the tournaments were a good thing. We had some antipathy from people who did not want the "bother" of initiating a group of novice riders to the show ring, but as Liberace said, "I cried all the way to the bank!" Local shows sell a lot of horses that would never be sold without them. Relatively few people just decide that they want to get in the show business. They "find" themselves in it from some small beginning show on a school horse!

Another benefit that we feel derived from tournaments is the fact that those who intended buying horses for their children bought in the fall of the year to have practice time before the late winter. This is certainly the best time to purchase a horse for a youngster, and all who do so are ahead of the hounds. Still another good lesson to be learned from tournaments is in the practice of good sportsmanship. You know, the older, more experienced riders can sometimes forget some of the thrills that go with just getting the chance to ride in a show. They have perfected their style to such a degree that to them a class is either won or it is lost. It does these children a lot of good to see the radiant excitement of some little youngster who has gotten her first ribbon—no matter the color, just a ribbon is enough. And it doesn't hurt the parents to remember that all thrills are not blue, either. The riders in this locality were known for their wonderful sportsmanship. There were a great number, and they came from various competing stables in this area. Of course, credit is due to the fine parents who foster the right spirit at home. Guidance and supervision in the general policies of the stable managements also count, and, again, the wonderful comradeship gained in competition at the riding meets contributes to this happy fact. Many a disappointed rider has soothed his own wounded pride with the balm of another child's success, and

Practice makes perfect. Elizabeth McBride, eight years old, wins her first blue at the Spring Riding Tournament. Four months later, the same child, mounted on her first equitation horse, shows the results of concentrated work by winning the eight-and-under at the Kentucky State Fair. This is what we mean by the development of "style." From a weak foot and leg the rider has graduated to a forceful, definite body position. The hands bespeak knowledge and empathy between horse and rider. The complete definition of seat and hands can be attained in the very young rider if teacher and pupil strictly adhere to the basic fundamentals of seat and hands. *Top photo by Charles Pence, bottom photo by Sargent*

when you stand at the out-gate and see this wonderful thing happen, it makes you wonder at your own petty smallness.

To continue with more of the advantages of tournament competition, not the least important is the fact that students often are bored with learning after the first of the year. The long and dull winter months generally necessitate riding inside, and while I find that these are the times of the best learning and accomplishment, mere repetition can become very tedious. With tournaments looming in the not-too-distant future, children have a goal to seek, and they enjoy their work. For the new riders it is a great inducement to work. The third or fourth month of instruction for the beginner is a difficult time at best. Since few new riders have seen expert equitation, and since they have already mastered the three gaits, there is a tendency for the child to let down, because he has the feeling that he knows how to ride and that the teacher's instructions are not only boring but unnecessary. When you jolt the beginner with the idea that if he shows sufficient improvement he might be good enough to ride in a show, then you see a resurgence of interest and effort.

I might add here that conduct of the beginner classes was decided upon at each individual show and depended completely upon the recommendations of the instructors. While the classes were set up to provide the most practice for the greatest number, especially in the young beginner classes the greatest care was taken to be certain that every rider could safely canter. If the weather was warm and there had been sufficient outdoor practice and all riders were certainly capable of cantering, then three gaits were called. If there was but one child whose safety was in doubt, then the program was arranged accordingly. The thought that must be uppermost in everyone's mind is that the tournaments function as a service, and the entire point is to run them safely, instructively, and encouragingly.

I would like to use the Kentucky Horsemanship Tournaments for a model. There are several localities that offer such shows, but since we exhibited at these shows for several years, I feel qualified to discuss them in particular.

Ideally, with weather permitting, tournaments should be held every two weeks over a period of four shows. Closer scheduling can become a bit tedious and does not permit enough time between shows for the riders and trainers to work on improvements found necessary in the previous tournaments. To get the most benefit from the shows it must be remembered that the dominant note of the effort is for the experience and betterment of the riders and the horses.

Post entries are permitted in equitation class, but with almost no exceptions, all riders enter all classes for the four tournaments, and refunds are made if the entries do not show. Entries in the horse classes close a week prior to the first show, in order to facilitate the division of these classes. Three must show to establish a class; then once a class has been shown, it may continue with less, since points are awarded towards final trophies. By the same token, post entries are allowed after the first show.

Again, let me make it clear that the following program was drawn up to accommodate best the local rider situation that year. You may vary your program to suit the numbers and ages of the riders each season.

BEGINNER EQUITATION (for riders who have never been in a horse show). (1) Riders 8 and under; (2) Riders 9–10–11; (3) Riders 12–17.

INTERMEDIATE EQUITATION (riders who have won less than four blue ribbons). (1) Riders 10 and under; (2) Riders 11–12–13; (3) Riders 14–17.

ADVANCED EQUITATION (riders who have won four or more blue ribbons). (1) Riders 12 and under; (2) Riders 13–17.

HUNTER EQUITATION (riders under 17).

PLEASURE HORSE (English equipment only). (1) Riders 12 and under; (2) Riders 13–17.

JUVENILE HUNTER

5-GAITED HORSE

5-GAITED PONY

3-GAITED PONY

3-GAITED OVER 15.2

3-GAITED 15.2 AND UNDER

In the above open classes, all riders 17 years and under.

Services of recognized judges were secured for all events, and we found that qualified horsemen were more than generous of their time to assist in the worthy cause of better riding and sportsmanship. Eight ribbons were awarded in all classes, as the encouragement value of a ribbon is well known in such an undertaking. Entry fees were two dollars per class, and admission fifty cents. Beautiful rosette ribbons were given at every session, and an attractive final silver trophy in each division was awarded to the high-point rider or horse at the fourth show. These final awards were based upon the following points: First—20 points, second—15 points, third—10 points, and fourth—5 points. In case of a tie, duplicate awards were made.

While some riders use the tournaments to begin showing their own equitation horses, the beginning rider will be suitably mounted to enter these shows on the instruction horse. In fact, that is really the purpose of this type of competition. There will be plenty of time later for those children who go on into the purchase of their own equitation horse for the better shows. Occasionally, we will luck into that horse everyone dreams of—the beginner's lesson horse that is so great that he can accommodate the progressing rider on into the recognized shows and the "Big Time." But don't count on this. The good old lesson horse generally remains the good old lesson horse, but for these first tournaments or local one-day shows, you can't beat him.

Your clothes do not have to be regulation show habits. You should have regulation jodhpur boots for safety's sake, and be sure that these jod boots are polished and shined. In fact, the keynote of your outfit is that it should be neat and clean. The jodhpurs or jeans must fit trimly or you will not be able to ride comfortably or properly. Unless you have a well-fitting coat and hat, it is better to ride in a neat shirt with button-down collar, necktie secured with a clasp, and bareheaded. Girls should wear nets on their hair and try to fashion a neat, attractive hairdo. I always insist on gloves for showing and instruction. Cloth gloves will slip, so a soft, pliable leather glove that is not too tight is preferable.

Since there is very little difference in the approach to the first show —whether it is on the lesson animal or the student's own mount—I now refer you to the chapter entitled Training Horse and Rider for the First Show, and subsequent chapters, At the First Show and What We Learned at the First Show.

14

Selecting the Rider's First Equitation Horse

Why, when, and what. These are the three words that govern the decision to buy the first equitation horse.

Why buy a horse? There can be only one good answer to this question. We buy a horse when we need one—when the rider has mastered all that the lesson horse can do, when the lessons have become mere repetition for everyone concerned, and when the pupil is obviously capable of meeting the challenge of "more horse." To buy a horse because the Smiths have just bought a horse or because little Emily finally made an A in algebra is a poor reason and the rider finds himself the owner of something that he can manage the first day and will surely outgrow within weeks, or he will be overmounted—which can be a real disaster. Do make sure that the rider is both capable and deserving. Equally as bad is the parent who can readily afford the purchase of a horse, but for a variety of reasons will not follow through when the time has come to take the step. No matter how earnest a student is, he cannot help being bored when he knows that his capabilities are unfulfilled because of the limitations of the horse.

When to buy? Ideally, the time to buy a horse is in the fall of the year. Many good equitation horses are available at the end of the season when riders have reached their eighteenth year. From a learning standpoint it makes sense, as the teacher and rider have the winter months of comparatively uninterrupted lessons to work with the new combination. A horse that is sound at the end of the season is a pretty safe bet. It is possible to buy yourself a bunch of vet bills in the spring, as almost every horse will be sound after a winter's rest. The wise prospective owner will give his order to the agent in plenty of time. You may be lucky and know where the ideal horse is at the very moment you decide to buy, but this seldom happens. It may take months to find the exact horse for your job. This leads us into the most difficult of the three Ws.

What to buy? For every rider there may be more than one possible horse, but there is definitely a certain type of horse that best fits each individual rider. Manners and general suitability are discussed elsewhere in this book, but the "type casting" I mean is the physical and temperamental combination that makes an outstanding pair. There are general categories into which riders may be classed. Short-waisted riders need a high-fronted horse with a good, straight back, so that the naturally low hands may remain fairly low. Put this rider on a low-headed, or short-necked, horse, where they are forced into lifting the horse's head, and the acute angle at the elbow and the overly elevated hands are quite unattractive. Riders with long torsos can use a horse that is somewhat low in the back—otherwise the rider seems to be perched too high on the saddle.

We had an excellent horsewoman, capable of riding anything logical. She was in the older age group, where a commanding appearance is an absolute necessity. She was quite short and of a rather muscular build. What we had to have was a small horse that would act big. He must act big, but be amenable to equitation work and be suitably tempered so that he could be ridden without stirrups. In other words, his size had to be commensurate with that of the rider, but the combination must be so spirited and aggressive that they would appear to be as big as the rest of the entries in the class. While it took nine months of searching to find just the right horse, the successful results justified the effort. Heavy riders should never be mounted on slight-barreled horses, where the contrast would emphasize the riders' size. By the same token, these riders should never have extra-large-barreled horses, as many people think, because the round inner thighs and lower legs will present very wide head-on silhouettes at best, and if you add to this with blocky, wide-bodied horses, the picture will be gross.

Observe the natural movements of your rider. A tall, gliding, graceful girl will need an over-15.2-hand, substantially fine horse with a fairly long stride. A smaller, peppy-acting youngster, quick of motion and reaction, will combine well with a snappy-gaited animal with a pert air about him. Nothing is more attractive than a pretty, petite girl mounted on a fine little mare. The crowd may go for the tiny little moppet on a great big horse, but the judge could cheerfully throttle the genius that put this pair together, because technical perfection is almost impossible for this team, and yet it has crowd appeal. A dependable, aggressive horse can help a rider who lacks force—but be sure that you do not give yourself a real problem by putting a timid rider on a nervous horse. Never confuse nerves with ambition.

The main trick, if you will, about putting together the perfect pair is to take the time to analyze the rider completely and then take the

A handsome little boy and a pony chock-full of personality dramatically demonstrate the idea of co-ordinating rider and mount. Here is truly a "matched pair." *Photo by Jay A. McClasky*

Debbie Basham and Step Aside were always a compelling pair in the ring. She was a small rider mounted on a rather large horse, but represented the fact that unity in a pair can be established by something more than size. Debbie was a firm, aggressive rider, and the horse—although nearly sixteen hands high—was a compact, very collected, sharp-moving animal. You cannot combine a "waltzer" and a "tap dancer" and get a picture like this. *Photo by Sargent*

time to find the type horse that you have concluded is the proper match. Just about the worst thing you can do is to set out to find a horse of a specific color. You will be lucky if you find a suitable horse, whatever his color. Ask yourself if you would like the horse just as much if he were another color, and you will get much closer to a logical appraisal of the horse's suitability. Everyone likes a pretty horse, but the majority of trainers will tell you that the most necessary quality in a horse is attitude. So when you put together your great combinations, just be sure that they will work.

Since the final word in the selection of a first horse for the new rider must rest with the parent who pays the bills, the following is written for the parent. I assume that the instructor is well aware of everything covered in this discussion. He would be wise to have the prospective buyer read this chapter and discuss it with him. It goes without saying that any parent who can afford to buy his child a show horse cannot be a simpleton. But many times parents avoid discussing the actual mechanics of buying a horse, because they are afraid that their questions may be taken as an expression of doubt, and then there may be those who are loath to admit that they do not know everything about the horse business!

It goes without saying that the agent who selects the horse for the child should be the one who teaches it. If this teacher happens to be the parent or another amateur who feels the need for professional help, then by all means, seek out that help. It will be the best investment you ever made.

Let us take a hypothetical case and follow it through: We shall start with the fairly simple problem of buying a horse for a ten-year-old girl who has had a year or so of instruction and desperately wants a horse. You know that she really *needs* a horse, because she has assured you that not only will she never want you to buy her anything else if she can have the horse, but that it will magically improve her grades, table manners, and general health and disposition. That first horse may not do quite all that she claims, but if you make a sensible choice, you will launch your entire family upon one of the most rewarding interests that you will ever have. You will share moments of glory and moments of disappointment, but you will most of all build a fund of family togetherness that you will draw upon the rest of your days.

We will take the problem from the beginning, step by step.

1. Seek competent help from a reputable trainer. You may have talked with several "advisors" before deciding just who your agent will be, but when you have decided, then stick with your selection.

Too many cooks spoil the broth, and certainly too many advisors will only bring confusion.

2. Find a time when you can sit down with your chosen agent and discuss the problem thoroughly without interruption. Trying to give an order to an agent at a show or other busy place just will not give anyone enough time for discussion.

3. Tell the agent what you wish to accomplish with the new horse and ask for his frank appraisal of your child's chances for realizing your goal. You must remember that the horse cannot be the magic ingredient that makes an average rider a champion. Try to shake the stars out of your eyes for a moment and give a very frank analysis of your child's present capabilities and her potential. After you have done all this, then ask the trainer for his frank opinion—and we do mean frank. Certainly you should buy for the future (the fact that you should want to find a horse in the fall of the year proves this wise decision), but buying within the normal expectation of improvement and overmounting a rider are two different things, which only the professional has the experience to recognize.

4. Have your financial arrangements clear. The usual agent fee is 10% of the purchase price. Certainly there are extenuating circumstances—the expenses attendant upon finding prospects, travel to sales, and the like. These expenses can be handled as in any regular business. Your agent is due his commission, and you may request that he buy the animal for the lowest dollar and then pay him his percentage direct, or he may buy with the request that the seller pay him the percentage. There must be mutual trust between you and your agent which both parties will honor. You can expect him to represent your interests just as assiduously as any employee and, by the same token, your part of the bargain is to leave the matter strictly in his hands and not run to every pillar and post seeking advice. You can advertise yourself right into difficulties by asking for too much advice and collecting "agents" along the way. Once you have made up your mind as to whom you want to assist you, then the matter should be settled.

5. About the only preconceived idea of your "dream horse" that you can clutch to the bitter end is to insist upon complete working soundness. To buy color (any color is good as long as there is a good horse under it!) would be pure coincidence. Age is a relative thing in horses as in people. It is important only as it reflects experience. Youth does not preclude soundness, nor does age assure perfection. I can only say that a great majority of the top horses are older horses, and a winner is valuable all his life. Obviously size must be considered, but it must be tested to be true. You may be amazed to discover

that the presence and carriage of the individual horse characterizes his size more than actual measurements. You had better keep an open mind about size until you see the child up on the horse. The sex of the horse matters little. Those mares who are fussy in season are generally shrewish at all times and should not be seriously considered in any event. And there is nothing more annoying than a bullheaded old gelding, so be careful that you do not confuse sex with temperament.

6. When you have decided upon just what type of horse your child needs (and you still have to recognize the fact that the child will be the proud owner and should have some guided opinions in the matter), then you should determine to buy as good a horse as you can possibly afford. In all our years of selecting amateur and juvenile horses, we have never had an owner regret buying a good horse. Recently I saw a card at a car dealer's which went something like this: *Quality is just like buying oats. If you get good, bright, clean oats, it costs; of course, if they have already been through the horse— that comes a little cheaper!* There is no economy in miracles. Perhaps once in a lifetime will you stumble upon a real bargain, but your best bet is to select an agent who is qualified in every respect, frankly discuss your intentions, and authorize him to buy the quality commensurate with your ambitions and pocketbook.

7. Whenever possible, the rider should try the horse. If for any reason you absolutely do not like a horse, be tactful and kind enough to give the seller time to show the horse and then stop before the horse is boiling hot. Above all, do not make a joyriding pest of yourself by climbing on those horses that you definitely do not consider. The seller wants you to be satisfied, and aside from the fact that he is trying to sell high while you're trying to buy low, you are all—yourself, your agent, and the seller—trying to work toward the same goal, the right horse for the right rider. You can be sure that the seller is most anxious to sell right, because his business depends upon the success of his sales. It is a smart buyer who will very frankly ask the seller just what horse he considers the best for his job. You are spending money, but your agent and the seller are putting their judgment and integrity on the line, too.

8. At this point you should stop to consider just what you are doing, and take a good, long look into the future. Examine your real ultimate aims in the horse business and what you hope to acquire of lasting value from this wonderful sport.

First of all, I must make clear that one of the main purposes of this book is to help those riders, parents, and novice teachers whose lack of experience calls for assistance from any quarter. Just as a rider needs to learn his diagonals, so must he and his parents learn the whys and wherefores of the shows. I must preface any of these remarks with the assumption that the trainer or teacher is right. Unfortunately this cannot be the case every time, as we are all human and subject to error. The owner must assume, however, that the trainer is always acting in everyone's best interest. This is a correct assumption, and if the owner will only predicate every opinion on this fact, he will prosper rapidly, as the trainer will have free rein to make the proper decisions without fear of having been misunderstood. Bob Whitney has a wonderful sign in one of his working tack rooms. It reads, *The boss may not always be right, but he is always the boss.* If an owner wants the very best service from his trainer, then he must seek his advice and try to go along with the suggestions whenever at all feasible. This is one of the trainer's services for which you pay, and certainly you are entitled to his suggestions. You must look ahead to both the immediate and distant future for the sake of your child and the well-being of the horse, and only the trainer has the complete knowledge of both horse and rider to chart that long-range program, and the experience to know when to alter the daily plans to advance this program.

Perhaps your child shows unusual promise as a rider, and you are willing and able to go along with this child's horse career to the heights of her capabilities. Naturally you will understand that, in addition to expert instruction, you must mount the rider on one of the best horses. Now, here is where we get into trouble if you do not take that long view. To many uninitiated people the best horse means the finest and most expensive. Not at all! What the best horse means is the best horse for that particular child at that particular time. I know from many years of experience that the child who makes a steady, gratifying, well-earned advancement is the child who goes the furthest and who gets the most out of the horse game.

We can all sit down and eulogize horse shows for what they can do for our children and talk for five minutes before we even mention a horse, so a sermon is not in order here. But those children who go up too fast simply by dint of superior horseflesh too soon have a hard time to keep on an even keel when the "tortoise" catches up. Please understand that I am not against good horses—the best you can get for the job—but do stop and take a long look and see if that child is ready in every way before you hand out the brass ring. Overanxious parents with what we call a "slide rule mind" often conclude that just as soon as Suzy can ride at all well they will do the thing up right and once and for all—the best horse money can buy. In that way, they rationalize, it will take only one horse—it wins now so it will continue to win. But let me put in a word for a rider's "earning"

Tommy Fisher of North Dakota became fascinated with saddle horses when his sister came to us. He inherited Mr. Wonderful from Suzie and a better first horse could not have been found for this particular boy. Mr. Wonderful was perfect. When the gate opened he thought that he was a stake horse and buzzed around the ring with seven-year-old Tommy. This suited the child, who had already ridden cow ponies and bucking calves, a child who would have been bored with the "baby sitter" that we generally associate with a very young beginner. *Photo by Donaldson*

Two years later, after much hard work and many miles in the ring, Tommy was ready for the good mare Starheart Love. After taking second in his first show, he won nothing but blues for the entire year, finishing as World Champion 10 and Under rider at Louisville, quite an accomplishment for the nine-year-old boy and his "teacher," the grand old gelding, Mr. Wonderful. *Photo by Sargent*

the way—perhaps with a beginner's mount, then a better horse, and finally that really good one that he or she has worked so hard to merit.

No matter how good or successful a horse may be, he gets to be a little tiresome to spectators and judges alike after a few years. The steady progression of excellent horses cannot be beaten. By the same token, an owner who has bought a good horse must have the patience to see that horse develop his potential and earn his rating. It takes time to establish a good horse. Just as "one swallow a summer does not make," neither does that first blue ribbon assure anyone that he will never lose. The judges just do not all see alike, but do remember that, while there is only one man who makes the decision in the ring, there are probably dozens of judges in the stands watching that horse perform. If he is truly a good horse and makes good shows, if your rider is truly good and making a flawless ride, then you have started putting bricks in that wall that builds eventual success. You must look

ahead to all this. Those poor, unfortunate people who want everything right now must stop short in their tracks and realize that they
did not advance in business in one stride, and neither can their child
reach his true height in one stride. Life just is not like that, and any
child who finds it temporarily so is in for a cruel awakening.

Not only in the selection of the horse must we look ahead, but also
in the training we must be patient. I certainly am not averse to buying good horses for a rider—far from that. But if you do get something good, do be careful that you allow all the necessary time to get
horse and rider together so that you can keep that horse good. It takes
a lot of foresight to pick just that right horse. We are all familiar with
instances in which a superior horse has been selected, and by the time
it was readied for the young rider it was just another horse. You must
take that long look ahead again and make sure that both the horse
and the rider will reach the peak of perfection together. It simply
takes time, and there are no short cuts.

We frequently receive orders and hear of other orders for the "best"
juvenile horse in the country. Just stop a minute and decide if that is
really what your child has earned yet. Of course you want the best for
him, but do make sure that it is the "best thing" for that child. The
character built by striving, improving, and being rewarded will last a
lifetime through, when the name of the "best horse money can buy" is
forgotten.

9. And finally, when you have bought the horse, do your best to
like him and give him every chance.

15

Training Horse and Rider for the First Show

Let us now assume that the beginning rider has had several months of instruction. He has learned a good basic position, his guiding is adequate, leads and diagonals are second nature by now, and he has his new horse, and you are responsible for getting this novice duo into the ring for the first time.

If you have been working outdoors, your problems will not be so numerous. However, if the new horse and his rider have been training inside, the instructor should get the horse out at every opportunity. Even the most trustworthy mount will want to play the first day you work outside. If possible, drive the horse two or three times before you ride outside for the first time.

When you realize that the rider is sure to be excited and nervous in his first show, you must expect that this tension will be transmitted to the horse. Multiply this by the number of entries in this beginners' class, and you will realize that you must put in a lot of work on the horse to prepare for this first effort in the show ring.

If it is at all possible, have your pupil ride with other horses in the ring. It does not matter if the horses are being ridden or driven, but both horse and rider should get accustomed to traffic. If you do not have other horses around, here is a suggestion that may be an adequate substitute. While instructing the individual rider, I would step into the path of the oncoming student and let him practice passing. Caution the rider to observe the whereabouts of other riders in the show ring so that he will always be in the clear. Whenever you hear from an onlooker that someone crowded a rider or interfered with his showing, just remember that the thinking rider seldom lets himself get into a situation where he can be crowded. Showing is very much like driving a car—ride as if every other rider can be expected to do the worst possible thing. How often we see a new rider blocked on a canter because the rider ahead was having trouble either in getting a lead or stopping to correct a wrong lead! Proper placement at the walk and looking ahead when the canter is called should eliminate any immediate problems.

It is wise to review the mechanics of the canter frequently. I make my riders learn to identify the canter lead on horses ahead of them so that one glance will tell them whether they can expect the leading rider to proceed at the gait or, in case of a wrong lead, to expect a stop and be amply prepared to pull out and around. By all means, practice this pulling out on a canter at home. Because of the very pattern of the gait, a horse will be able to make a sudden move toward the center of the ring in passing a stalled rider; but the return to the rail must be gradual and very collected, otherwise the horse will most surely switch front leads. The transition from one rein to the other in this move must be very smooth, and the beginner must practice. It is a logical idea, but just talking about it is not enough. You must practice.

In training the new horse, practice a lot of weaving on the rail and get the horse very handy. If you ever saw Frank Bradshaw train the great My My, you would see him weave the mare in serpentines at every gait except the canter. She was the World's Champion 5-Gaited Horse and was certainly never called on for a figure eight, but Mr. Bradshaw knows how important maneuverability is to any horse and that it is a thing that must be practiced constantly.

Placement in the ring seems to be one of the most difficult problems for a rider. It is easy to sit on the sidelines with a panoramic view of the ring and know where the advantageous spots are. But it is another thing for the rider to keep himself and his horse in balance, to look ahead and still know what is going on behind him. If saddles had rear-vision mirrors we would have no problem. Teach your rider to vary the rate of speed and learn to ride for the spot in front of the judge, and you will be well on your way to teaching good ring generalship. I have cautioned my riders hundreds of times: "You may be the best rider in the whole world, but if you get covered up and the judge cannot see you, you might as well stay in the barn." Circling on the rail should be used only as a last resort. Imagine the class if everyone used this obvious maneuver. If the riders will utilize the turns to take stock of their positions, then they will have ample time to decide whether to keep their present speed, accelerate, or slow down. Most riders, because they know more about what is occurring in front rather than behind, will want to position themselves by passing and cutting corners. Since the majority of riders tend to do this, it is much better to teach your rider to hold back and let the open rail space catch up with him.

In order to help your pupil as much as possible, train the horse to hold his gaits at various speeds. Occasionally you will get a horse that has just one notch for his trot, and any extension will cause him to get completely out of form. First of all, try not to have such a horse for equitation, but if you do, then teach the rider to work out ring placement by holding back and using extra vigilance on the turns. Such a rider must be told that he will be constantly passed by the other riders, so he must head for the judge with an extra margin of space behind him.

The warm-up period and during the walk are good times to train the horse to be handy. Be sure to use the leg aids every time you move off the rail. Ideally, the finished equitation horse should work mainly off the legs—in close conjunction with the restraining hands. Just make certain that you train the horse the exact way that your student will ride him. You will be pleased to observe how much better any horse is for such complete training. Chat Nichols is one trainer who is a thorough believer in complete aids in the training of show horses, and the beautiful precision of his World's Champion gaited gelding, Rebel Air, was convincing proof of the pudding. It seems to me that the quality of horse training in this country has risen greatly within the last few years. I believe that it is because the majority of professionals are dealing with young amateur riders, and in the teaching they have come to analyze their own problems better. The trainers on top today are the "Thinking Trainers."

Consideration of small details makes for perfection. Every horse must be readied for the show ring individually. You, as trainer and teacher, must "get inside the horse's brain" and know what to expect from that horse. How is he going to react in the ring? Should he be worked extra hard the day before to dull the edge a bit, or should he be rested an extra day to keep him sharp and attentive? For this first time, if you must err, err on the conservative side. A steady, consistent ride is better than the chancy, brilliant ride that is one step from disaster. There will be plenty of time for this later. If the horse will be gingered, try this at home a time or two before your first show. (An amateur who buys a horse with a cut tail should ask the seller to ginger the horse when trying him out. Observe *exactly* how this is done, and then follow the same procedure. Whenever possible, try to buy the tail set with the horse, as suggested in Chapter 2, as it is already fitted to him. Then keep the fleshy part of the tail *very* clean, the cotton padding clean and smooth, and there should be no problems.)

Work your horse on his weakest points. It is a great temptation to ride what the horse does best, but you need to apply your efforts where they are needed. Also—a word of caution—do use discretion in your choice of work. Horses can become very bored and sour quickly

Any coach or trainer will tell you that the greatest component of a competitor is desire. Linda Fischer will always be one of my very favorite students for this reason. Her show record was excellent, in fact unequaled at the Kentucky State Fair, but the thing that will always endear her to me and those who saw her equitation rides is that she never quits riding. This is why I chose this picture of her. She would sit at attention in the lineup and never miss a thing going on in the ring. She could sit there knowing that she was not included in a workout and never be anything but perfect—and she was this way when she came out of the ring, win or lose. She did not win one of the Finals, but as her teacher I have to remember her as one of my all-time winners. *Photo by Sargent*

on work that is drilled too much. The smart trainer is not so much the one who knows what to do as the one who knows when to stop!

Beginning riders will tend to respond to the announcer immediately, with no thought of their relative position in the ring. Explain to the rider that the command "Walk" means to bring the horse to a walk as quickly as he can *after he is in an open spot on the rail.* Most beginners tend to ride in a group, and it looks more like a meeting of the sheriff's posse than a horse show. I like to tell my beginners to think of the class as a parade and that they are the leaders.

Another area that needs careful planning is the lineup. Many times we see riders who wander into the lineup from any spot on the rail, at any gait the horses choose. Those contestants who think that the call to "Line up" marks the end of their efforts are sure to be disappointed. This is where good self-discipline comes in. Instruct your rider to proceed around the ring until he has a good, clear opening to the place he has elected to park and then trot briskly into place. As a judge, I know that one very often does not have the class tied, and this last impression is a very important one. Not only for his own benefit should the rider keep showing every moment that he is in the ring (after all, it is a horse "show" and spectators have spent money to be entertained), but also the horse must never be permitted to cut into the middle of the ring without a signal from his rider.

Parking the horse squarely on his feet is one element of training that is frequently overlooked by trainers themselves. We are all guilty of hurrying from one horse to another in a busy training schedule. However, this is one area of training for both horse and rider that should never be slighted.

We use the voice command "Get out" and a lifting of the horse's head to signal the parked position. Have an assistant on the ground tap the horse's fetlock sharply with a stick. Try to teach the horse to park out by associating this position with voice and rein commands rather than the obvious kick on his elbow. The way you train him to park is the way the rider will get him to park in the show ring, and nothing is more gauche-looking than a rider flailing away with the legs on some unresponsive horse's shoulders. If the horse is slow to respond, the rider may tap the horse sharply with the whip to gain his attention to the signals.

The rider should be further instructed to feel the square alignment of the hind feet with a minimum of twisting around to look. This awareness of proper balance and a consequent leveling of the stirrups must be practiced. It is a habit of the mind—not of the muscles—just as, surprisingly, the best-co-ordinated riders must learn to assess their position; they cannot "sense" it.

One of the most difficult tests a beginning showman may have to face is the workout when a select group is called out to the rail. The horse that has been sharply brought to the lineup and kept at attention during the judge's inspection will be alert for any signal from the rider at any time. It is incongruous to expect a horse that has been drowsing in the companionable group to spring to animated attention and agree to leave the bunch for a workout. The instructor should plan to watch the conduct of the class very closely. If it is obvious that a workout will be called, indicate as much to your rider. Have him shorten his reins into the proper tension of curb and snaffle, tap the horse with the whip, and generally call him to attention. A good rider should expect to be called for the workout, and the psychological impression on the judge is not wasted.

It is best to have the rider take a long approach to the rail, which will give him time to get the horse going before he comes to the judge. The rail rein should be fairly snug—even more so than at the initial part of the class. The horse's desire to pull into the center and cut corners is greatly increased when other horses are in the middle of the ring. If the rider knows that the horse can be expected to want to turn in, then the problem is half solved. There is nothing more disappointing to a judge than to have what looked like a possible winner stalled on the grass. And this could have all been avoided if the instructor had practiced what to do before they ever got to the show. The out-gate and the other horses act as magnets and will attract the horses. If the pupil knows this (and you will find yourself repeating this same thing during the whole career of your rider), then he can generally cope with the problem with little more coaching at the moment.

At the stand, the rider should exert even pressure on the stirrups, heels moderately down, upper leg and knee rolled flatly into the saddle. The seat should be deep in the low back part of the saddle with the coattails smoothed and straightened. Riders must be taught to even the saddle on the horse's back with consistent stirrup pressure. It is amazing that some riders do not know when the saddle is straight, but this is true, and you should stress this point and practice it carefully at home. First of all, the instructor should be absolutely sure that the stirrup leathers are of equal length. It is a good plan to switch sides with the leathers occasionally, as mounting will stretch the left leather. Rein position varies with the conformation of both horse and rider; but, generalizing, we can say that hands at the elbow height or slightly below are good. Very few horses will stand quietly on the curb rein, so it is logical to teach the new show rider to hold the snaffle shorter. Park the horse, slide the hands back on all reins, and then shorten the snaffle to the desired length (in the area above or slightly in front of the pommel). If you do not have the rider lengthen the reins before shortening, the hold will be too short. Also be very careful that the curb stays comparatively loose. With the movement of the horse's head, the curb will tend to tighten up, and then the horse really will fuss with his mouth.

Backing must also be taught. One of the most awkward pictures in the ring is that of a youngster flailing away with his legs to get a horse to move forward out of the stretched park position. I always teach the rider to move the horse forward and slightly to the side with his voice and a touch of the whip. As soon as the horse has moved his hind legs forward, the rider should say "Whoa-back." The pull on the reins should be alternating, and we can imagine that each individual pull draws a front leg back. When the horse has backed two or three steps, again the voice command "Whoa" followed by strong leg pressure and a tap of the whip to return to the original position.

A rider's personality is expressed in every part of his body. Alertness, confidence, and an element of excitement which all competitors should have will contribute to a good position as the judge walks by. Facial expression is another problem. Tension which enhances the rest of the body can contort some faces into an awful sight. The poor child who has all he can do to remember just part of what he has been taught can muster little more than a sickly smirk or a frozen leer when the anxious parent yells at him to "Smile." You may find that you have a rider who actually assumes a very irritating facial expression as he rides, and you will have to correct this at home. Several years ago, when we had a stable in St. Louis, I had an excellent rider who looked like the world's most spoiled brat when she rode. This unfortunate look happened every time she concentrated—and that was all the time, because she was a top competitor. We literally spent days before the Chicago International on this problem and finally solved it by the practice of relaxing the face muscles, and the expression took care of itself. To take a tense visage and force a smile into already overworked muscles will not get the happy, natural look of enthusiasm that you had hoped for.

16

Correct Attire for the Show Ring

In the 1966 Rule Book of the American Horse Shows Association, there appeared an important rule change that clarified the proper dress for the show ring in equitation classes. While a strong plea for conservatism in dress had been made before, it now became mandatory that the riders dress in the following manner:

> Exhibitors and judges should bear in mind that at all times entries are being judged on ability. However, neatness is the first requisite regarding a rider's attire, and the following *requirements* are based on tradition and general present-day customs. *Judges shall eliminate those contestants who do not conform.* (The italics are the author's.)

> INFORMAL: Conservative solid colors are required. Solid colors include a black, blue, gray, green, beige, or brown jacket with matching jodhpurs (white jacket in season) and derby or soft hat.

> FORMAL: Even more conservatism is required for evening wear. Solid colors include a dark gray, dark brown, dark blue, or black tuxedo-type jacket with collar and lapels of the same color, top hat, jodhpurs to match, and gloves, or dark-colored riding habit and accessories.

> MISCELLANEOUS: Spurs of the unroweled type, whips or crops optional.

When the rule for dress became mandatory, the Saddle Seat Equitation Committee knew that there would be some hardship for those riders who had just purchased non-comforming attire, but the trend towards "something different" had reached such dazzling heights, we felt that something had to be done. Certainly good grooming and the exercising of good taste are attributes that we are proud to associate with riding, and the reckless trend towards gaudy clothes had exceeded the bounds of good taste. Good grooming is still a problem that must be dealt with individually. However, there are certain basic principles of grooming that should be observed by every rider.

It is better to have one good suit than a variety of ill-fitting outfits. There are many kinds of material, but nothing looks better, wears better, and tailors better than wool. Coats should measure about at the top of the kneecap. If you want to wear a vest, a one-button coat combines best. The jods should be long. When you are mounted on your horse, the cuff should reach the bottom of the heel. This will mean that the cuffs will drag the ground, so the rider must be careful to keep them turned up until he is on the horse. The bell of the cuff can be a width of your own choosing. I prefer to have the bell wide, measuring forward to the crease of the boot at the instep. If you have the wide bell, caution the tailor to reinforce the lining of the cuff; otherwise it will twist and blow back as you ride.

Consider the whole color panorama when you select your habit. Your greatest consideration must be the color of the horse. Contrast may be striking, but remember that any rider movement is very obvious with the contrasting horse and suit. If you want variation or color, this may be done with the lining of the coat, vest, shirt, and tie. When you decide upon these color notes, do not forget the brow band on the bridle. While there is no ruling against it, I do not personally like anything but dark, matching linings with the formal attire. Boutonnieres are optional. If you use them, keep them small, neat, and well anchored. Nothing is more ridiculous than a large flower (would you believe a chrysanthemum!) bouncing around the ring. For the very small rider, I like a rosebud or button chrysanthemum. Our riders favor a plastic carnation boutonniere that is small, flat to the lapel, and always available. The red color exactly matches the color on the brow band.

It has become popular in the last several years for the girls to wear a small bow at the back of the popular chignon. If you do like a bow, keep it neat, keep it small, keep it secure and in a harmonious color. Large red bows "tacked" on the back side of a hairdo look like taillights. The bow should be close up to the hatbrim and of a width complimentary to the facial features. Like any other part of the riding picture, tone it down when in doubt.

There seems to be much confusion regarding accessories for the formal wear. It is very simple if you consider the original style rules for men's evening wear. With the semiformal (corresponding to the tuxedo), this means, of course, the previously described formal suit, top hat, calf or patent leather jod boots, matching dark bow tie, cummerbund, and gloves. The tuxedo-type shirt is worn and a dark boutonniere. For the strictly formal look, a formal wing collar, white piqué tie, and cummerbund are worn with the complete formal touch of white gloves and boutonniere. Countless times I have been called by puzzled parents or teachers who wanted to know what was the correct attire to be worn in an equitation championship that was held in an afternoon show. Time is your only designation here. If the class is scheduled for morning or afternoon, the dress is informal. Any time after six o'clock, the formal attire is permissible and correct. You will notice that the informal attire is also permitted at night (but formal is never worn during the day). Most riders, particularly at the larger indoor shows, wish to wear either type of formal dress at night. For those lucky riders who might have a conflict with a gaited class, where informal attire must be worn, the informal is necessary. There is a

The formal habit is dark blue or black with matching top hat and black patent boots. Wing collar, bow tie, cummerbund, and boutonniere are always white. The lapels may be full satin or with satin binding, and the jods have the matching seam stripe. Carole Maas is the picture of perfection in this formal outfit. Top hats are never worn except at night performances, but hair nets should be worn at all times. *Photo by Jay A. McClasky*

growing trend for boys to wear informal habits at all times. Professional men trainers almost never wear formal attire, and this style note has been reflected in the boys' equitation fashions. Rain clothes—the jacket and both derby and top hat covers—are wonderful insurance. Keeping an older, spare suit for bad weather makes sense, too.

Now for the matter of hair and make-up. . . . It looks as though pierced ears are here to stay, and if the rider absolutely must wear earrings, keep them tiny and inconspicuous. Girls love to keep up

A perfect example of co-ordinating the clothes and horse. Joe Greathouse, top boy rider of the '50s, chose a light gray to match his mare. Such pale colors would magnify the rider's movements on a dark horse. However, all colors blend here to give a sense of unity and quiet drama. *Photo by John R. Horst*

with every innovation in make-up styles, which change so rapidly that any definite remarks are hard to make. Last year I fought the battle of lipstick. Most riders tend to become pale with excitement. So I would line the riders up and hand each one a lipstick of a lovely, restrained shade of red while the mothers would smile and nod their heads! You must realize how you are going to look in the ring. The hair styles also cause trouble. If you are a girl, please try to look like one. If your hair is long, be sure to wear a net. If it is extremely short, hair pieces will

The daytime habit should be conservative, of a color to complement both horse and rider. Kathie Gallagher wears brown suit, boots, derby, and tie to match her bay horse. An off-white vest and gloves relieve the monotones, while a red carnation and identical red brow band tie in the color scheme of horse and rider. *Photo by Sargent*

Dee Dee Davidson models the semi-formal habit. It differs from the formal only in the accessories. The tie, cummerbund, and gloves are dark—matching the color of the top hat. The flower, also, is dark—generally red, but never white. While the preferred shirt color is white, pale blue is gaining in popularity. The semiformal shirt has the attached tuxedo collar. This habit and accessories may be a dark brown as well as navy or black and is worn only during night classes. *Photo by Sargent*

do wonderfully well under top hat or derby. Hair should really be no problem now, but just remember that classes last a long time, riders do perspire, and what may have been enchanting in the tack-room mirror can be a dripping horror when seen in the ring. Eye make-up should be as tastefully used here as at any time. And avoid it like the plague for the ten-and-unders!

I never cease to be amazed at parents. They spend generous amounts of money on clothes for their children and then arrive at a show with absolutely nothing to keep those clothes neat and clean. Every hatbox should contain the following, besides a hat: Safety pins for pinning down the back number, or for last-minute adjustments to jod straps; straight pins for those eternal tuxedo collar points that refuse to stay down (always wear button-down collars on all informal shirts); a soft brush or velvet pad to clean and tidy the top hat and derby; a sponge to remove the worst of sweat stains when the rider dismounts; needle and thread, including heavy thread to replace jodhpur cuff buttons. A spare button or two can be a lifesaver. Back at the

This rider has satisfied the class requirement as far as dress is concerned, but the entire effect is ruined by lack of proper fit. Good grooming sense will tell you when your clothes fit properly.

hotel, especially if you are attending a weekend show, where they invariably offer no valet service on Saturdays, you should have a traveling steam iron and cleaning fluid. Be sure that the rider removes the coat immediately after dismounting, as wrinkles from sitting on coattails that are sweaty are almost impossible to get out. Take a quick swish with the dampened sponge on the very worst spots and then hang the coat on a hanger to dry. Brush out the dried dirt with a stiff brush, then press the coat. Jods can be touched up in the same way when you return to your rooms. However, you will be wise to purchase two pairs of jods with each suit, as a coat always outlasts the

When Ann Swisher won the UPHA Final, she was the first rider to do so wearing a very light-colored suit. She was sensational, so we ventured the combination again a few years later with Ruth Anne Lewis, who was 13 and Under World's Champion as an eleven- and a twelve-year-old rider in 1979 and 1980.

The success of such a daring move depends upon having a very steady and aggressive rider. There can be no easily detected leg movement, but the rider must be brilliant and outstanding—and this is what Ruth Anne was. Her big mare was explosive, just the right horse to complete this risky combination. It worked but it took a lot of talent to warrant the move. The coat is long, but right by the time of the Finals. Youngsters do grow.
Photos by Sargent

pants, and matching colors is almost impossible. Really smart riders take the coat to the show on a hanger, pin the number to the coat the moment they arrive at the show, and put the coat on just before the class. I know that all this may sound childishly simple to experienced show riders, but new riders need help—and many an experienced rider needs to be reminded of the rudiments of good grooming and proper attire.

As time has passed, the riding coats have gotten longer. Anything below the kneecap may look like a kimono, so try to stay within the bounds of good proportions. For children in the fast-growing stages, a little extra length is practical to keep the suit still fitting in November.

17

Class Divisions and Requirements
at Recognized Shows

In the American Horse Shows Association Rule Book, age-limit divisions for equitation are suggested, and every rider should study these divisions carefully in order to understand exactly what workouts may be called for.

There are thirteen tests from which judges must choose. Tests may be performed either individually or collectively, but no other tests may be used. Instructions must be publicly announced. In Medal and Championship classes, individual workout instructions must be written down by the judge and delivered to the announcer at the beginning of the class, and at the judge's discretion they may be posted if at least twenty minutes is allowed for all competitors to study the instructions or diagrams. However, the posting of workouts is optional.

SEC. 5. TESTS FROM WHICH JUDGES MUST CHOOSE.

Tests may be performed either individually or collectively but no other tests may be used. Instructions must be publicly announced. In Medal and Championship classes individual workout instructions must be written down by the judge and delivered to the announcer at the beginning of the class and at the judge's discretion they may be posted if at least 20 minutes is allowed for all competitors to study the instructions or diagrams.

1. Pick up reins.
2. Back for not more than eight steps.
3. Performance on rail.
4. Performance around ring.
*5. Feet disengaged from stirrups. Feet engaged.
6. Figure eight at trot, demonstrating change of diagonals. Unless specified, it may be started either facing the center or away from the center. If started facing the center, it must be commenced from a halt. At left diagonal, rider should be sitting the saddle when left front leg is on the ground; at right diagonal, rider should be sitting

saddle when right front leg is on the ground. When circling clockwise rider should be on left diagonal, when circling counter clockwise rider should be on right diagonal.

7. Figure eight at canter on correct lead demonstrating simple change of lead. (This is a change whereby the horse is brought back into a walk and restarted into a canter on the opposite lead.) Unless specified, it may be started either facing the center or away from the center. If started facing the center it must be commenced from a halt. Figures commenced in center of two circles so that one lead change is shown.

8. Execute serpentine at a trot and/or canter on correct lead demonstrating simple change of lead. A series of left and right half circles off-center of imaginary line where correct diagonal or lead must be shown.

9. Change leads down center of ring or on the rail demonstrating simple change of lead. Judge to specify exact lead changes to be executed as well as to specify the beginning lead.

10. Ride without stirrups for a brief period of time. No more than one minute at the trotting phase.

11. Demonstration ride of *approximately* one minute on own mount. Movements must be selected from Tests 1–10 above. Rider must advise Judge beforehand what ride he plans to demonstrate. To be used only in championship and/or Medal classes. Riders must have with them two copies (one for judge and one for announcer) of a written one minute workout, in case the judge asks for this test. The test must be stopped at the end of one minute but the rider will not be penalized for not completing it.

*12. Exchange horses, no more than the top six contestants. Saddle may be exchanged. However, should one horse be too large or small to accept this exchange and no horse (among the six) can be found with which to exchange, then no saddles will be exchanged. Riders must have two minutes to be accustomed to the new mount before judging resumes. The attendant for each horse being exchanged must be allowed in the ring.

The usual age divisions at a show where numbers of entries warrant are:

(a) Juniors who have not reached their 11th birthday (Tests 1–3).

(b) Juniors who have reached their 11th birthday but not their 14th birthday (Tests 1–7).

(c) Juniors who have reached their 14th but not their 18th birthday (Tests 1–12).

* Tests 5 and 12 underwent much discussion at the 1981 UPHA and AHSA conventions and the possible changes will be discussed in Chapter 22, "How to Judge Individual Tests."

Other suggested divisions are:

Maiden (riders who have not won a blue ribbon). For riders who have not reached their 18th birthday (Tests 1–5).

Novice (riders who have not won more than three blue ribbons). For riders who have not reached their 18th birthday (Tests 1–6).

Limit (riders who have not won more than six blue ribbons). For riders who have not reached their 18th birthday (Tests 1–8).

It is very difficult for anyone to advise you concerning the number of classes that should be entered in a show. Ring footing, weather extremes, duration of classes, relative soundness of your horse—all of these factors are extenuating circumstances, and they change from show to show. If the rider needs lots of experience, then three classes in one day on a good, sound horse (at a one-day show) can be practical. More advanced riders are smart to keep their maximum to two a day if the class schedule permits. Judges are human (really they are!) and are prone to tire of a rider who appears every time the gate opens. I learned this lesson a long time ago. We were showing horses in front of the highly regarded judge Christian Barham, and I showed a pretty little dappled-gray gelding in every three-gaited class that he could enter. My final effort was in the ladies' class, where I thought that this particular horse would shine. I was stunned and heartbroken to be left out of the money, and finally mustered enough courage to ask Mr. Barham on the following day why I had done so badly. For years I puzzled over his reply. "Why, Miss Helen, I just liked the other horses better." At that time the reasoning escaped me. As everyone else did, I respected Mr. Barham's judgment and I had searched him out not to complain, but to learn. It finally dawned on me years later that I had simply shown the horse too many times at that show and the judge was tired of looking at us.

You must consider the horse and his entire show season. A heavy schedule at the end of the season, when the horse is hard and fit and the winter vacation is upcoming, is very different from overshowing your horse in May, when he is not legged up to heavy work and there is no vacation in sight for him.

Try to keep within your own age limits. Very young riders from the ten-and-under division seldom belong in the Medal and "Good Hands." And for a surprise winner of a Junior Championship to bounce back in the Limit class shows some lack of consideration for the other, less fortunate entrants. Of course, the spacing of events sometimes forces riders into inadvisable classes. When this is apparent and there is a logical rearrangement possible, contact the show man-

Erin Davis and Chantilly Lace were always an eye-catching and successful pair in the show ring. But this beautiful picture was not attained without a lot of thought and practice.

Erin was a quiet, almost retiring child and the selection of the fiery black mare was just right to give her a feeling of drama—real and aesthetic. The mare was comparatively long-backed and the rider was small, so to get the proportions we wanted, I tied her stirrup leathers back to the extended safety snap, moving her back about two inches in the saddle. In order to stay there, she rode her stirrups somewhat shorter than usual because she had a short thigh bone and this was the only way she could stay back. Usually short upper arms can be expected with short thighs, so I permitted Erin to reach somewhat with her hands and carry a very high hand. The high hand aided the youngster in "feeling pretty" and it also assured good control over an ambitious mare.

If you, as the instructor, will take the time to analyze each rider and realize that compromises are wise if they do not destroy balance or sacrifice control, then you will be able to put every rider into the ring looking his or her very best and feeling like a winner. *Photo by Donaldson*

ager as soon as you have received the prize list, and your chances for getting the schedule corrected are very good. If you wait until the day of the show, you will undoubtedly be stuck with the original bad schedule.

Entry fees in equitation classes are generally nominal, so it is advisable to enter all possible classes and select the proper ones as the show progresses. It is much more logical to forfeit a two-dollar entry fee than to pay a twenty-dollar vet bill.

If you have a trainer and are a member of a stable that has numerous entries at the show, try to co-operate and agree to the class selection that your teacher has made for you. The scarcity of good grooms often dictates how many riders will go in the same class. If there seems to be any inequity at a show concerning the classes in which you will ride, consider the difficulties of the trainer and trust that the opportunities will be equalized at the next show. There must be complete mutual trust between the teacher and his rider and family.

When you are not showing or getting prepared for your class, be at ringside. Watch the other riders closely and try to learn all you can. An excellent way to learn is to concentrate on only one phase of riding at a time. For instance, in one class concentrate completely on one rider's hands—their position, relation to the horse and his performance, manipulation on the curb and snaffle reins. During the next class, observe the use of body weight and legs. Five-gaited classes are very interesting from the standpoint of ring generalship and positioning the horse for every gait. Just because you are riding in horsemanship only, do not think that open classes are beyond your comprehension. The junior high school art class has much to gain from a visit to the art museum!

NOTE: In 1980 the AHSA rule change regarding determination of a rider's age was changed to read:

> For horse show purposes the age of an individual on December 1st shall be maintained throughout the entire show year. Persons born on December 1st shall assume the greater age on that date.

18

At the First Show

The young rider going to his first show represents many things to many people. To you, the instructor, he is a part of yourself, a creation, an extension of your own talent and ambition. To the parents he is an entirely different individual—he is "my baby," at that moment the center of the universe, and the entire day revolves around his few moments in the ring. If you think that it is hard for you to be fair and comparative about your pupil in the class, magnify that by ten and you have the typical parents. They may learn to enjoy the classes later, even to watch the other riders a little bit, but this first day—forget it!

Several years back, when the very talented Mary Anne O'Callaghan was starting her show career, we were exhibiting at Harrodsburg, Kentucky. The ring was one of those Kentucky oddities known as a bull ring—completely round, sharply banked, and with spectators seated in the center of the ring. Mrs. O'Callaghan, who was the epitome of the self-possessed, gracious lady we all like to claim as an owner, was very apprehensive over the possibility that Mary Anne would be called on for a figure eight on her new, green mare. Since the ring was so obviously unsuited for this workout, and furthermore since this was a twelve-and-under class, I assured her that no judge would call for figure eights. Imagine our shocked surprise when that is exactly what he did ask for! I don't recall exactly how well Mary Anne did her work, and her mother was no help at all. She had spent the entire time of the workout with eyes tightly closed. When she opened them, she discovered every tiny satin bow that had decorated the bodice of her lovely dress lying at her feet where she had thrown them!

Please be kind—to the child, to the parent, and to the judge. They all have difficult jobs. The instructor should not try to judge. Your time can better be spent analyzing your rider. Start your discussion with the pupil with what he did right, and patiently proceed to the areas of faults and how to improve them. That is what equitation is

all about. It is a means to an end, and every class is a test of how well
you, as the teacher, and the rider himself are advancing to the goal of
complete horsemanship. If there is a cardinal rule, then it has to be:
never publicly condemn a judge! If you must complain, wait until you
get home, and talk only to your own family. We are all human and
need to let off steam, but just don't do it in front of the owners. You
will only make them dissatisfied and yourself unhappy. Learn from
the experience and just put your rider into the ring knowing more and
riding better the next time. You have to believe in yourself. Just give
it time to work. If you have worked with the rider until he is ready to
show, then for that class you must be in complete charge. Parents
should sit in the stands and leave the instructor and child alone. Their
most valuable function that first day is to chauffeur and let the rider
know they were very proud of his efforts.

For the instructor to buzz around before the show asking everyone,
"What does the judge like?" is only to court trouble. We have all seen
some poor child riding around the ring looking as though he were eat-
ing corn on the cob because his apprehensive teacher had discovered
that the judge "likes high hands"! Styles must be individual. I can tell
you what judges like. They like a well-turned-out rider, smart as a
whip, riding every ounce of his horse and looking as though he was
glad to be in the ring. When you can turn your beginning rider out
like that for your first show, then you are ready for the challenge.

If the horse and rider are to make the first show with an instructor
who handles all preparations, then the rider's only concern is to get to
the show on time. How simple this sounds! But hardly a show is held
where at least one instructor is not having a nervous fit because a
rider is late. Several years ago I had taken a rider to Madison Square
Garden for the Medal Final and the "Good Hands." We had entered
her in the ladies' class to have the horse just right for the Medal. It
happened to be the rider's birthday, and a dinner at the hotel for local
relatives was under way. As the meal progressed, it became obvious
that we would have to leave before the final course. Needless to say,
the rider and I were finding it increasingly difficult to swallow, and all
we wanted to do was to get to the show. Finally, we begged their forgiveness and started to leave with only minutes left to make the class.
The mother said, "Oh, you can't go—we haven't had the birthday
cake"! Anyone who has shown at all knows about the many things
that can go wrong at the last minute, so never tempt fate—*be there
on time.*

If this is an amateur production, here are some plans to follow: Arrange your transportation well in advance. In the event that you are
going to be part of a load on a commercial van, have everything

ready to load when the van pulls into your drive. Your saddle and bridle should be clean and in a tack trunk. In this trunk should be an extra halter, two lead ropes or shanks, sweat scraper, hoof pick, rubber currycomb, corn brush, soft finishing brush, four clean rub rags (old Turkish towels are fine for this), shoe polish, safety pins, an extra pair of curb reins, wool cooler, a bottle of ginger, scrim walking sheet, fly sprayer, an extra set of knitted leg bandages, a roll of paper toweling, scissors, a rubber bucket, a plastic container of shampoo, a bar of castile soap, and an electric water heater of the drop variety. All of these articles may be purchased at a tack store. It is a good idea to include a simple first-aid kit—you may not need it, but if you do, there is seldom any place to buy such supplies at a show. Make sure that you have practiced loading your horse in a trailer or van before the day of the show.

Again, get to the show on time. If it is a one-day show, or the first performance of a longer show, get there at least two hours ahead of show time. Late arrivals may have difficulty in finding good parking space for the trailers or van. Inspect your stabling or trailer area carefully. Keep away from wire fences and truck bumpers, and tie your horse securely where he is comfortable, beyond reach of the other horses, and up short enough so that he cannot eat grass. One mouthful, and he will plot and plan all day how to get another. Nothing spoils the finish of a horse more than a bilious green scum all over his bits from a stolen mouthful of grass.

Get your number, pay your fees, and study the ring. Some small shows are put on by committees whose enthusiasm far exceeds their experience. A helpful, practical hint to improve show conditions will probably be appreciated, but do be tactful. Make certain that there will be ample, safe warm-up space. If possible, look over the ring with your rider. Any hazardous spots on the rail can be pointed out and discussed.

It should not be necessary to say that the horse should be absolutely spotless and glowing, but it is a sad commentary to observe how often a judge walks up to a poorly turned-out horse in the ring. A trimming job will not last through more than a two-day show. Manes and tails should be washed and picked out before every class. Some trainers hesitate to pick tails too frequently, as there is danger of breaking the hairs, and such care can certainly be left to the discretion of a capable trainer who will know how to get his horse in the ring in top order. By all means avoid brushing the hairs, as you will certainly wind up with a quarter-horse hairdo very quickly! If tails need tying, leave just a little extra length at the top to obscure the string, but please do not grow the hair to such lengths that the horse looks five-gaited. Unless your equitation horse has an unusually good tail, it is wise to string the tail, since many of your classes are of such duration that the horse is bound to drop his tail to either side. Just remember that most tails do not need to be tied extremely tight at the base, which expands as the tail is raised. Just be sure that the end of the tail is securely held and the string at the root of the tail is merely an anchor for the end of the tail. Sometimes you may tie a horse's tail so tightly that he can scarcely raise it and then use too much ginger to get the tail up, with the result that the horse is fighting and switching his tail and is in a very annoyed state all during the class.

Fig. A   Fig. B

Fig. A   Part the hair at the point where the string will be tied. Make descending wraps around the end of the tail to form a flat, firm band. The string will remain in place in comfort. Never use one single tight wrap, as it will immediately cut off circulation. The second shoestring is tied snugly around the base of the tail exactly opposite the end tie. Knot two or three times and cut the excess string from the base tie.

Fig. B   After the ends have been trimmed from the base tie, thread one end string through the base string and pull the ends tight and tie in a hard knot. The end of the tail will thus be held next to the root of the tail, which will support and keep the entire tail straight and upright. Trim the extra string. The brush of the tail will obscure the ties. *Photos by author*

If your horse has white legs, it is a practical idea to trim the horse in such fashion that you thin down the leg hair so that dust and tanbark will not cling. You do this by using the large clippers and repeatedly trimming down the leg towards the hoof. To cut up towards the knee takes too much hair, makes the hairs stubby, and makes a very difficult "feathering out" at the end of the cut. Some horses have very sensitive skin, especially in the southern states, where the incidence of summer sores is high. In these cases it is unwise to thin the leg hair.

Opinions are divided as to the use of blacking the horse's hooves. Liquid shoe polish is drying, and if used should be followed with a good hoof dressing. If your horse has one white hoof and one dark in front, then we generally feel that no blacking is better on this animal, as it only points out the contrast of the two feet and gives the illusion of an uneven stride. By all means do not blacken a light-colored hoof. Your horse will look as though he forgot to take off his galoshes!

Saddles and bridles should always be shiny clean. New tack should be darkened before use. You should try to match as nearly as possible the darkness of your tack to the depth of the horse's color. Pumpkin-colored new tack distracts from the horse and shows lack of preparation, and nothing in the world can make a horse look coarser-headed than a new, yellow bridle. If possible, all bits and stirrups should be chrome plated, or if you do not choose to do this, be sure that you keep a supply of steel wool and metal polish to care for the metal parts of the tack. Girths should be carefully whitened, but first all old polish should be washed out. Be sure that the whitening is not smeared on the billet attachments, as these areas show up in front of the saddle flap.

There is no substitute for down-to-the-skin cleanliness in a horse, and such a condition comes only from constant good grooming. While it is extremely important to give the horse intense grooming before he goes into the ring, your best results are obtained by good rubbing and brushing as the horse is cooled out after the class, because good hair depends upon good skin condition in a horse, and dried sweat at the hair roots will ruin the skin tone and luster of the hair. This is especially true in winter show seasons, when heavy sweating and scraping do not always occur.

A recent tendency towards artificial coloring of the horse's mane and tail is like any other fad. Used with taste and moderation—generally only to point up or enhance a color that already exists—some aids to beauty for the horse are all right. But do think twice before you get out the paint bucket. It can be very embarrassing to have your horse cast a shoe and leave his white stocking smeared all over the blacksmith's apron! No, there really is no substitute for genuine good looks and good grooming. If you will just go down the list of the top horsemen in the business—Roby, the Bradshaws, Moore, Jordan, the Teaters, just to mention a few—you will find that their horses are conditioned and turned out in immaculate perfection. I don't know whether the horses are turned out this way because they are tops, or they are tops because the horses are perfect, but I do know that good grooming of the horse takes a lot of time and the desire for perfection —and this is within the grasp of all who are willing to put forth not just enough effort, but the best that you have.

The rider will probably have to wear his riding habit to the show, as few shows have dressing rooms. If it can be managed, wear work jods until shortly before the class. If no dressing facilities are provided, then be sure to leave the suit coat on a hanger. Check to see that your hatbox contains the articles listed in the chapter on correct attire. There is a new rule in recognized shows now that all numbers must be worn on the back and must not be obscured by the riders' hair. We always pin the numbers securely in the place on the back that looks the best. The wire hooks on some numbers may not permit this, so we pin the numbers top and bottom. Girl riders should always have a spare hair net or two in their hatboxes. After you have affixed the number to the coat, replace it on the hanger. And as soon as your class is over, hang up the coat again.

Unless you are following a very large class, plan on mounting up about the time the prior class goes into the ring. Most classes average about fifteen minutes, a workable period in which to warm up for your class. You may need to shorten the curb chain one link. Try this in the make-up ring to decide if it is the thing to do. As soon as horse and rider are working smoothly, then walk or wait in the shade until your class enters the ring. Usually, trotting is best to warm up. Never practice your difficulties in the make-up area. If the rider does not know how to ride now, this last-minute, frantic practice is too late and will only serve to upset horse and rider. Decide in what position your rider will enter the ring. Some horses work better when they are first, but for the first show, it is generally better to let your rider follow someone else into the ring. Plan to enter with a good spacing and avoid rushing in with the group. Try to start from some distance back, so that the horse will be established in a firm, even trot and the rider will have already established the proper diagonal.

Send the rider into the ring in a pleasant mood and help him as quietly as you can during the class. Congratulate him (and all others) as he leaves the ring, and *keep it fun for all.*

The greatest lack in the conditioning of a show animal is not in the care before the class, but the care afterwards. So often, at the one-performance show which is heavily patronized by owner-trainer groups, busy parents are anxious to return home, and the care of the horse is slighted. Add to this neglect the breezy trailer that overcools the tired animal, and it should be obvious why the horse makes less and less impressive shows as the season wears on.

One of the greatest misconceptions about caring for a horse is the term "cooling out." To be better understood, it should read "warming out," as the general function of this care is not to see how soon a horse can stop sweating and blowing, but rather to delay this condition so that the circulation and body processes of the horse can simmer down slowly after extreme stress and exercise. Another fault which many commit is to mount the horse much sooner than necessary to warm him up. If he is a little on the fresh side, then it is much better to have given the horse some previous work that morning at home before you ship. To add a long warm-up to a long class is overtaxing to most animals. When the class is over, the horse should be scraped, ragged off very briefly, and put to walking with a cooler or walking sheet. In cases where the weather is extremely warm and the horse is in considerable distress, a very quick tepid bath is helpful. Bandages which have been soaking in cold water during the class may be quickly applied to the horse's front legs as a deterrent to too rapid circulation and as a prevention against founder. Do be sure that the horse is not in a draft, and get him walking as soon as possible. When the weather is unseasonably cool, one must be even more careful to avoid drafts and to cover the horse immediately upon leaving the ring. I cannot stress the importance of the slow cooling-out process too much. Early in my show days, John Hook, a great friend and an unparalleled horseman, impressed me with this, and it has proved true 100% of the time—spend twice as much time walking as you did riding!

19

What We Learned at the First Show

Now that you have gotten your rider into the show ring you should have several good ideas for the succeeding weeks in the training of both the horse and the rider. A good instructor will learn from this first show just what the horse has to do better to help the child and vice versa. It is not too soon to teach the child the rudiments of horse psychology.

My grandmother had a favorite story about the man who carried a salt shaker around all the time. When asked why he did this, he said that if anyone ever gave him a hard-boiled egg, he would be ready! Learning to anticipate your horse's actions and reactions to his surroundings is an art in itself and is the most interesting part of riding and showing. Were a horse automatic and never-changing, we would all soon lose any interest in riding. Yet the very thing that makes for our interest—this individuality of the horse—is so often blamed by a rider when he has made a mistake in the ring that has cost him a placing in a class. There are very few mistakes that the horse makes that cannot be traced to either negligence or lack of judgment on the part of the rider. If a horse is temperamentally unsuited to the degree that he is in constant trouble, then either he needs further training or a new home. We are discussing here the mistakes that occur to an average, well-matched pair of horse and rider.

One of the greatest assets any rider can develop is a good memory. A horse will make a mistake at a certain place in the ring and almost without exception he will repeat this same mistake every time he comes to that place. Being able to recall what your horse has done, and preparing for his probable actions, will eliminate a great many costly mistakes. Let me give an example of a problem that has arisen for countless riders. Perhaps this very thing has happened to your rider at the first show:

Mary has just entered the ring. Quite by accident, a purse falls from one of the front-row boxes directly in front of Mary's horse. He shies badly, but the understanding judge does not condemn the rider for what is obviously an unavoidable misdemeanor. Poor Mary! She is so upset by her awkward entrance into the ring that she cannot think about her horse for wondering if all her friends and neighbors saw her trouble, or she is so irritated at the poor owner of the derelict handbag that she can think of nothing but her "bad break." By this time Mary has circled the ring, and her tension and frustration have been added to the apprehension of the horse, who nearly knocks down the ringmaster in shying away from the box. By the third trip around, Mary has realized that she is in trouble and overcorrects, jerking the horse quickly at the first uncertain step and throwing him into a canter. Alas, a sad story, but how many times have you seen it happen?

Let us take this same situation and remedy the mistakes. The horse has shied away from the purse. Mary returns to the rail as soon as possible, using a strong heel and a firm hand on the reins. She does this to correct the horse and remind him that she is the boss and that she is there to help him. She keeps an extra-firm rein toward the rail to hold her place there. When she is several lengths from the box, Mary tightens her legs into the horse's sides, clucks to him, and urges him gradually into a stronger gait. She is very careful not to jerk the horse or make any sudden or extreme moves, as she will only excite him more and make an even greater hullabaloo—for the horse will not only be reminded of his previous fright, but his rider's excited handling will certainly confirm the horse's suspicions that something dreadful is about to happen. If Mary is very clever, she may have rated her progress around the rail so that she is in the process of passing another horse just at the time she reaches the box. In that way she has obscured the trouble spot, and even more important, has distracted the horse and prevented his making a habit of shying at that place. A judge will be the first to see this evidence of smart horse-

This picture is an excellent example of a very small rider in total control of her horse. What does not show is that the night before I had ridden this horse for over an hour to teach him to walk along the exact spot where this picture was taken. Under ideal circumstances, it would have been a good lesson to let the rider participate in this correction but there was no time for this during a show. The horse had been frightened during the preceding evening's class and had found that he could misbehave with his tiny rider. There was only one thing to do, and I was the one to do it. Severe punishment would have compounded the problem for the next performance so I worked him back and forth over this one area time after time, slightly jabbing his mouth when he sidled off the rail and praising him when he stayed in line. It took a long time but it was worth it. Not just for the ribbon which you see, but the horse did learn to walk the second way of the ring. If he had not been corrected and had repeated his mistake the next night we might have had a permanent fault. It is not always convenient to train horses but if you are conscientious and not afraid of work, then you will go that extra mile whenever necessary.

I cannot resist telling an amusing incident about this little girl when she showed Bonfire her first time. It was two months prior to this picture and she was doing remarkably well, considering that it was also the horse's first show with a juvenile rider. When the canter at the reverse was called, nerves had taken over and Heidi was too tense to let the horse move out of his lead. The entire audience got in the act and the shouted advice and resultant clucking sounded like a plague of locusts. When she came out of the ring, the little youngster's eyes were as big as saucers and she said, "Mrs. Crabtree, I never knew there were so many ways to canter a horse." *Photo by Inman*

manship, and very often what a rider fears may be a fatal error can be turned into a winning ride.

You may discover that the horse has learned some bad tricks at the show. Mistakes at home can be corrected repeatedly until the horse forgets his transgressions, but in the show ring we have to settle for the smoothest handling of a bad situation. Very often the horse will assume that the rider is unable to enforce his demands, and the seeds of disobedience have been sown. This is why the riders of jumpers are permitted to take another jump after a horse has been blown out of the ring on refusals. Unfortunately, there is no comparable handling of disobedience in equitation classes.

If the horse would only learn his lessons correctly, maintain what he has learned, and never vary, horse training would be so simple.

Although the horse has shied from the photographer, Janet Henry has maintained good control of her mount through the action of her wrists, with no loss in form of horse or rider. Perfect balance in the saddle has kept the hands quiet and made this subtle correction possible. *Photo by George Axt*

But, of course, such is not the case. Even the most perfectly trained horse will have his off days, and from such unimportant beginnings real trouble starts. I believe that, of all important aspects of horse training and riding, it is not so much knowing what to do, but *when* to do it. This is where we separate the men from the boys. Enough common sense and time spent in plain, old-fashioned logic can generally tell a trainer (and I use the term here to embrace all persons who consistently ride a horse) what to do for his horse, but where we must develop our talents is in the split-second judgments that tell us when it is time to quit.

Let us take a hypothetical case and see it through. I want to select a problem that is a common worry with many who are introducing their horses to equitation routines for the first time. I refer to the canter.

Most canter trouble comes from a horse's anxiety about the proper lead. Generally, the horse that bolts into his lead or frets and dog-tracks on the walk preceding a canter is worrying about one of two things—each the fault of his rider. Either the rider has been giving incorrect signals or has been severely punishing the horse for his mistakes. In either event, he is in trouble. Either the horse will try to dive into a lead before he can be wrestled around with a confusion of conflicting signals, or he will refuse to canter on the conclusion that he will not be yanked for a wrong lead if he has taken none at all. I know many trainers who will let a green horse continue to cross-canter on the assumption that, since it is such an ungainly gait for the horse to execute, his own discomfort will tell him not to do it.

Here we are at the state of decision. Do we stop the horse immediately or do we let him go on? Perhaps the best solution for the novice trainer in this predicament is to ignore the mistake the first few times. However, if we continue to ignore it, the horse may actually teach himself to cross-lead and develop a bad habit. Immediately analyze your canter preparation and make sure that you are taking sufficient time to position the horse at a bias to the rail so that he is balanced to take the correct lead. If you are not at fault, if the horse continues to cross-canter, then you must stop him, but do it smoothly. A disunited horse is a great aggravation, but the worst thing in the world you can do is to jerk a horse's mouth at this time. You have never ridden anything until you have ridden a mouth-shy horse that throws his head straight up and swaps canter leads. And this is just what you will get if you punish the horse for either a disunited canter or shifting of leads. Take your time, keep a low and very sympathetic hand on the reins, use your leg aids very gradually and only to position the horse, not to kick him into the stride, and when you have cantered success-

I love these two pictures because they show the beginning of equitation experience and what six short summers of instruction can do when you are dealing with a bright child and a parent who is willing and able to mount the child according to her progress.

In 1972 Mary Lou Gallagher was a determined eight-year-old rider who was avid to learn. Her times for instruction were intermittent, so she had to think more than she actually rode, and think she did.

We return to the Cincinnati show ring —this time in 1978—and Mary Lou Gallagher had learned the true meaning of equitation. This fourteen-year-old child rode her explosive five-gaited gelding, Lad O'Shea, to victory, a prelude to the World's Championship in the Juvenile 5-Gaited at Louisville. This would have been impossible without a thorough grounding in the fundamentals of equitation and an understanding of the psychology of her horses through the years. No one gets a horse to do this much by wishing. *1st photo by Gloria Axt, 2nd photo by Jamie Donaldson*

fully, then *quit*. If your analysis of the fault has been right, if the correction has worked, it will work again the next day. No matter how right a thing may be, if we drill a horse too much on any one thing at a time, he will build up an intense dislike for the routine and you will be back where you started. One of the hardest things to learn in riding, to repeat, is just when the horse has had enough. Good training consists of daily repetition, in moderate doses, of the right things. You cannot rush the process in any way.

The practical application of equitation cannot be tested too soon, and nowhere is it better served than in the Saddle Pony division.

Ruth Anne Lewis won the World's Championship with Chablis Premier when she was only twelve.

Equitation made this possible and the open competition stimulated the aggression that enhances equitation—clearly a reciprocal advantage. *Photo by Sargent*

There are several "exercises" that you may need to practice with your horse to get him to relax and wait for the complete canter signal. To review, we begin the canter by slowing and collecting the horse, then still checking him back, we use the outside leg aid to push the horse's hind quarters away from the rail. Many horses who rush a canter do so at this particular moment because they have been kicked into a lead prematurely and have the idea that they are supposed to canter when they feel the leg aid, instead of positioning themselves from the leg aid and then cantering after they are in position. If this is the case, then drill the horse on a sort of serpentine walk pattern along the rail. Turn him to the rail at a walk, then walk away from the rail, then back again, etc., until the horse is aware that he can turn to the rail without breaking into a canter. This is a very simple remedy and is the best remedy for bolting I know. Frequently horses that are so aid-shy as this have been severely spurred, so it is a good idea to use leg aids at every opportunity to accustom the horse to leg movements that are not severe. Frequent halts and petting of the horse's neck when he responds quietly will work wonders. I know this sounds like the "Flicka school" of riding, and many trainers avoid any such overt displays; but the amateur owner needs to use every advantage he can muster, and such unmistakable rewards for good behavior are helpful. If you have an indoor aisle in your barn, this is an excellent place to work this serpentine walk and it is a very worth-while winter improvement exercise. It has the added advantage of making the horse more responsive to guiding and will do a great deal to improve the rider's facility with his hands.

For any horse that rushes into his canter, one must be careful about clucking to the horse as well as kicking him into his lead. I have a rider now who has a mare that wants to rush her leads. His main trouble has come from the habit of clucking to the mare, who is already too anxious to go—and he is not even aware that he is making the sound. You may be amazed to find yourself doing something similar to cause your difficulties. As in all cases of over-anxiety in horses, the rider must analyze himself extremely carefully. And it goes without saying that you absolutely must hold your temper. Even if you restrain your actions, you may get mad or excited and inadvertently tense up. The horse feels this immediately and then he is off in a frenzy of indecision. It may be difficult to control yourself when the horse makes repeated mistakes, and you must not expect a miraculous change overnight, but if you will persist in your sensible routine of rehabilitation, you will get results, and that is the only way you will get them.

20

Beauty in Rider and Horse

There is something of importance to every rider and the teacher who is responsible for putting a rider in the ring. And that important matter is beauty. We have a great many young riders who come to us for instruction from out of the state, and one of the main considerations is not only to correct and perfect the riding style, but to do it in such a manner that those lessons learned will be retained from that time on, and not be just something that the rider can do for a short period of very critical surveillance while he is here. Of course, those fundamental principles that involve weight and balance are so obviously right that the riders will retain those corrections forever, because they are the natural and the easy way to ride. However, the points that go beyond those basic factors are the stuff of which blue ribbons are made. This applies to every phase of showing, from ten-and-under equitation right on to the amateur gaited stake. These points have to do with beauty—beauty of the horse and beauty of the rider.

Some people are endowed with a great sense of beauty. It is evident in their very appearance and manner of movement. Others are not so fortunate, and these are the ones who will have the most difficult problems, but by the same token, these are the very riders who will benefit the most from mastering the ways of beauty. As a teacher, and one who is genuinely interested in young people, I know that there is no greater sense of attainment for a teacher or parent than to see a gawky, unsure, and untidy youngster develop into a creature of neatness, poise, and grace. Perhaps I am too prejudiced when I maintain that riding a show horse is the quickest and happiest way to effect these changes, but the thousands of parents who have watched the transformation (and have enjoyed the process) can attest to this pleasant fact.

Now, we are all aware that there must be beauty, but how to attain it in every facet of riding is another point. Let me begin by urging the rider simply to consider the fact of beauty. I learned long ago that there was a short cut to a good basic seat in the saddle by asking the rider to assume what he thought was a beautiful posture. With very few exceptions the rider was fundamentally right as well as aesthetically attractive.

Let us dissect the rider, so to speak, and analyze each part of the body:

We must begin with the foot in the stirrup. Your foot position on the stirrup bar is your literal foundation for all riding and, as I have said before, if your feet are wrong you are wrong all over. I like to use the word "character" in describing a foot on the stirrup. It must be firm, supple, sloped to match the upward slant of the stirrup bar, and it must establish a good position and keep it. The complete weight of the rider must be distributed comfortably from the stirrups up through the seat to permit the entire portions of the rider's body that contact the horse to absorb the weight of the rider and to permit his total area to react to the movement of the horse. We *must* have weight in the stirrups to snug the thighs to the saddle. When viewed from the front, there will be a more or less straight silhouette from the rider's hip to the stirrup. This is beauty of line—not the parenthesis look of the bowed leg or the rigid look of legs outthrust too far—but a definite look of function, grace, and power.

Now let us consider the head and shoulders. Because, if the foundation of foot in stirrup is right and the carriage and attitude of the upper body is right, the hips and seat in the saddle will have to be right.

We must all consider the literal weight of the rider's head in relation to his balance. A head generally weighs slightly more than one tenth of an adolescent's total body weight. Where that rider holds his head is of extreme importance not only to his appearance but to the functional balance of the entire body. If we can get a rider to lift his head and pull his ribs up out of his belt while keeping his shoulders low and relaxed, we will have a beautiful rider and a balanced one.

It does a great deal of good to remind a rider that he should be proud. Pride of accomplishment and pride in the wonderful opportunity to show should be reflected in every rider's attitude. Barbra Streisand is not the most beautiful woman in the world, but when she steps upon the stage she has such pride and presence that we are all attracted. A rider should enter the ring with that inner feeling of "Happy day, here I am and I am going to ride so well that these other riders will know that they have been to a horse show." If a rider wanders into the ring, uncertain and almost apologetic, he presents a very unattractive picture to the judge, and his own self-confidence will shrink away, leaving him with nothing but worries. You may not have all the confidence in the world, but if you attain an attitude of assurance and present a picture of beauty, the battle is half won. A pleasant countenance comes from within, and it can be developed with mental effort and training. So many riders are admonished to "Smile," when nothing is sadder than a pathetic effort to smile when the entire body is reflecting anxiety. If you smile, smile all over. Make yourself beautiful in every portion of your body. You must think of beauty and grace.

Now, the part played here by the teacher or parent is to stand on the ground and observe what slight alterations in the position of the head, torso, and arms are the most attractive. Sometimes an unusual

When Colleen Donahue bought the World's Champion 3-Gaited Pony, Crimsonette, she was our shortest rider. Two years and eight inches later this picture was possible because we could make some logical alterations to the usual style of this rider. Her length was mainly in her legs, so we shortened her stirrups and had Colleen carry the pony high in front. Her solid equitation background made it possible for her to maintain control and balance while making these rather extreme adjustments. So when we ask the question, "Where should the hands be?" the answer is, "Where they need to be." *Photo by Donaldson*

length of hand and arm, a horse who carries either an extremely low or high head, an extreme length or shortness of the rider's torso—in other words, any problem of unusual proportions of horse or rider should be dealt with individually on the basis of what is the most attractive position from the judge's view that will permit maximum balance and control of the horse. Riders with extra-long arms and hands generally look better with considerable bending of the wrists towards each other to foreshorten the appearance and position of the forearm. By the same token, short-armed riders can carry a more parallel position of hands to give a longer look. Riders with long necks need to pull the chin and push the neck back on the shoulders, while short-necked riders should try to sit as tall as possible and may even extend the neck very slightly forward. Certainly it is elementary that regardless of the build of the rider or of any problems with the horse, the wrists must be in a sloping position not only for the sake of beauty but to facilitate and encourage an elasticity of the hand on the reins.

Beauty in the rider is not a trick. It is merely making the most of the good points, and minimizing the bad.

It is a foregone conclusion that any show or equitation horse will have at least a minimum of beauty and conformation, but the beauty I refer to is that quality of finish and training that can be controlled by the rider and trainer. We have previously discussed the importance of grooming and regular training as it applies to the horse's condition. What mainly concerns us here are those little "extra" considerations that spell complete perfection and beauty.

I would like to begin with the tack. New equipment is fine, but it should be dyed a dark color so that it will not attract undue attention away from the horse or make his head look big. All keepers should be in place, reins should be held smoothly. How often we see a rider with twisted reins that look like a handful of spaghetti! Brow bands should be well up on the horse's head, but be sure that they are not too tight or too wide for comfort. Especially with a short-headed horse, the cheeks will be taken up in the last notch and those buckles will force the brow band too high and it will irritate the ears and make the horse bad-eared. If this is the case, one should have the cheeks cut down in length. The end loops on the brow band should be wide enough so that, where the headstalls pass through, there is room for the leathers to lie flat, rather than stacked upon each other. I will always be grateful for the advice of a wonderful veterinarian friend in St. Louis, Dr. Kammerer, who pointed out the many "head and mouth" troubles that arise from nothing more than ill-fitting crownpieces on bridles. It is especially true with a horse that goes almost exclusively on the curb. We become very concerned about the

Kathy Ethredge presents a picture of perfect balance and harmony between horse and rider. This is a striking example of the proper choice and elevation of the reins to collect the horse so handsomely while maintaining perfect "equitation" seat and hands. The beautiful form is the result of hours of practice and showing in equitation classes. Here Kathy is riding her equitation mount, Stonewall Emblem, to reserve in the Amateur Under 12 at Lexington. Beauty of horse and rider must come from the unified perfection attained through the training of the entire combination. *Photo by Sargent*

horse's mouth and chin with the bit and the curb chain, but tend to neglect the real fact that, since the curb works on a lever principle, the top of the horse's head receives a great deal of pressure and much head fussing can come from the top of the head even more than from the mouth.

In addition to the possible discomfort from curb-bit leverage, even more usual is undue pressure caused by the habit of pulling the bridle down into place by the cheeks after it has been put on the horse. We try to insist that the grooms carefully adjust the snaffle bit and caveson to their proper alignment *before* the bridle is put on the horse. Generally one can detect poll soreness by touch, but if there is any doubt that it does exist, it is wise to take a piece of sheepskin (oftentimes a crown covering from a halter will do) and cover the bridle crown for work use.

Another area that is often unknowingly abused is the corner of the horse's mouth, which may be pinched or bruised between the curb hook and the mouthpiece. A change of hooks or the elevation of the bit in the mouth generally takes care of this problem. A horse with unusually large or fat lips will sometimes have trouble as well as look unsightly. Use a shoestring to tie comfortably around the jaw, under the tongue, to hold the lip in place. Never pull this string tight, however.

Perhaps you are wondering what this discourse on proper bridle fit has to do with beauty, but the first aid to beauty in a horse is comfort. We have a family joke about one of our horses. Several times we have been asked what we did to this particular horse that he should be so much more attractive and animated than previously, and we say that it is a secret ingredient known as "TLC." Of course it is not a secret, and it is used by all trainers and riders; it is "tender, loving care." A horse cannot be animated and beautiful if something is hurting him, and one must exert constant watchfulness to see that nothing is causing the horse discomfort. The matter of tying tails merits some thought, also. A double wrap around the end of the tail will keep the string in place without too much tightness, and only a snug wrap around the base of the tail is needed because we must realize that the root of the tail enlarges as the horse raises his tail. Many an animal has become a sour, restless tail-switcher because someone tied the string so tight that it was almost impossible for the horse to raise his tail. Perhaps these hints may seem out of place in articles on equitation, but not all riders and their "assistants" have the advantages of a professional trainer who undoubtedly knows all of these facts. As we have said many times, you cannot ride perfectly on a horse that is not working perfectly.

One last word about comfort: check to see that your saddle fits properly back of the horse's withers and shoulders. What can be a constant irritation, up to the point of lameness, is a saddle (especially a cut-back saddle) that rides deep and forward behind the horse's shoulders and butts into his high shoulder muscles when the leg stride is back. Be sure that the saddle is set far enough back to allow for maximum stride. Taking care to slip the hand down under the final tightened girth will keep the girth from pinching.

When we think of beauty in a horse, too often we have a mental picture of some thrilling champion that we have seen before, and we do everything in our power to make our own horse fit that same mold. Part of this idea is fine; we must try every moment that we ride a show horse to be aware of the appearance of the horse and to present him at his most beautiful position and motion. Where we may get into trouble, however, is to try to make every horse look alike, when his potential of beauty is dictated strictly by his natural conformation. Many a horse has been spoiled and made sour by the rider's attempt to force him into a position that is physically impossible for the horse to attain. Certainly we all like a big-fronted horse that raises up, sets himself like a peacock, and looks miles ahead; and we must try to present this sort of picture, but only within the physical limits of our own horse. The greatest help we can have in deciding just what is the best position for our mount is to have a good horseman on the ground to tell us when the horse looks his best. It is better to get some experienced outsider to decide this important factor, as decisions within families make for too much uncertainty.

When the proper position is reached, the rider must make every effort to memorize this head and neck position and practice every step to maintain it. The greatest error a rider can commit is to generalize too much and ride strictly by the gait. (By this I mean that a rider will align his curb and snaffle at the proper tensions and height to get the desired head carriage and then just freeze there.) We must ride not just the gait, but every stride. There will be at least ten minor adjustments and corrections in every circle of the ring to maintain a constant position of your horse's head. Riders who hang on to one hand position until the horse has made an obvious mistake with his head must, in turn, make very obvious corrections which spoil the whole picture of both horse and rider. When the rider can learn to anticipate the slightest movement of his horse and make a minute correction before the act, then he is a real horseman and is fulfilling every requirement of equitation, "the art of riding a horse." The rider who can do this and keep his own form and perfect balance to help him do it is a finished product.

While this head position is the most important single element of perfection in the style, presence, and way of going in the horse, we must analyze our own respective mounts to find just how near to perfection we can come.

Condition and practice will do more for your problem than anything else. Driving a horse in a combination bridle and gradually working up to the best arch and elevation is a great help. Proper practice will develop those neck muscles that will enhance the arched position. We all know that colts brought up from pasture have stretched the crest muscles and shortened the upper chest and throttle, so that grazing animals are inclined to be turkey-necked when first checked up. After a time, however, we see muscular changes occur that permit and aid the arched and elevated look so coveted in the show horse. We cannot count on the added excitement of the show ring to work all the miracles of animation. Our horse will animate if we have worked him in such a fashion that habit places him in the proper form, and we can leave his mind and mouth relatively free to respond to the added stimulus of the show ring.

You cannot wait until you get to the ring to train your horse and expect to get any kind of a show out of him. Horses that are constantly being yanked and jerked, whipped and spurred in the ring are not suited for the juvenile or amateur and they should either have additional training or a new home.

Thus far in this discussion of beauty, we have touched only upon the beauty of position. Of equal importance and unconditionally linked with position is speed. It is a common error to consider speed as related to form only in the five-gaited division. There are some horses that are capable of staying in form at a variance of speeds, but almost every horse has the speed at which he is the most attractive and the most comfortable (and this is a great consideration in the equitation horse).

A phrase that has helped me with riders a great deal is to tell them that they should pretend that they are climbing the stairs. To think upward, not go down to the basement. So many riders substitute speed for animation unknowingly. They will cluck to a horse and urge him on to get animation, but forget to hold the horse back to keep the balance and collection. A collected, well-balanced, graceful horse comes from that combination of urging on and holding back that gives him the appearance and potential of a coiled spring. The German Olympic team at New York in 1959 had the most perfectly balanced horses I have ever seen. Dressage utilizes control at the highest level, and the American Saddle horse should be ridden at extreme collection to show the elegance and action that are the trademarks of the Saddle horse. It goes without saying that there are basic elements of training and riding that apply to any type of horse and any style of riding, and the fundamental law of balance is foremost. It changes in breed and style only to accommodate the variations in conformation of the horse and the job that each individual horse has to do. Some of the most valuable help that I ever received was from a young Austrian, Albert Ostermaier, who stabled his wonderful dressage horse, Florian, with us one winter. His hours of patient practice in the saddle and on the lines were all pointed at the collection and balance of his horse. Certainly he was gorgeous, that Florian, and his beauty came from his collected hocks that carried the heavier weight of his body so as to free his forehand for the lofty head and neck carriage. If every rider could only see such a horse, what a help it would be!

Yes, we must have an idea of beauty and strive for it at every step. You will make your own decisions as to how you accomplish it with your own horse, but an honest analysis of your horse and how near he can physically approach this ideal is your start. You may not make a silk purse from a sow's ear, but at least you can make it a pretty ear!

21

Saddle Seat Tests 1–12

PICK UP REINS—TEST ※1

Since this is considered the simplest individual test that can be asked by a judge, we find it called for most often in the younger age groups. The term "Address reins" is frequently used, and the young rider must be apprised of this terminology in practice, so that there will never be any chance of his failing to understand the judge's commands. Because addressing reins is relatively easy to do, many riders fail to practice this test enough. What we should always remember is that we are dealing with a live animal, and his performance during these tests greatly affects the performance of the child. Horses who are not literally taught to stand still with a quiet head position during the moment of freedom when the reins are laid on the withers tend to move about or turn their heads from side to side when suddenly given complete rein freedom. During the training year, when our riders are at school and the training of the horse is done entirely by us, I always place the reins on the horse's withers immediately after mounting and address the reins exactly as the student would do. This accomplishes two things: it accustoms the horse to the rein manipulations, and also teaches him that he is to remain quiet and at the parked position after mounting and to stay there until a signal is given to move out.

The proper fit of the bridle has been discussed previously, so now it is time to discuss the proper fit of the bridle again—this time to the rider. It goes without saying that reins should be narrow, supple, and clean. They should also be the proper length to suit the combined conformation of both horse and rider. Small riders are generally mounted on relatively small horses. This being the case, you will probably find that the reins should be shortened. The bight hangs to the right side of the horse's shoulder, and when the rider is at a stand or in motion, the end of the reins should never hang lower than slightly below the knee of the rider. Longer reins can catch under the foot or become entangled in the billet straps and girth buckles. To avoid any rein entanglement, use a Humane Girth with the split-Y straps. Fasten the front buckle high and the back buckle low. (Do not use the center billet.) Now tuck the end of the front billet under the back billet. This will keep the strap from moving forward ahead of the flap to catch on the reins. The placement of the buckles in an uneven position will provide a comfortable hollow for the knee, whereas even buckles make a bad lump under the flap and frequently cause knee chafing. The length of the girth is extremely important. It must be short enough to permit the low fastening of the rear buckle. The same harness repairman who can shorten your reins can also cut down the length of the girth.

I wish to make it very clear that attention to detail cannot be overemphasized. This chapter concerns addressing reins, yet we are well into the discussion and do not yet have the rider on the horse! Previous references to tack have preceded the first entry in a show, but the ultimate attention to detail must be made at this juncture when we are striving for utter perfection in every facet of riding.

It should go without saying that all reins should be held flat and not twisted. You will find that the snaffle reins are buckled together (so that they may be used with a martingale) and the curb reins, never being employed with the martingale, are sewn together. The difference in the attachments of the reins together makes for easier identification when they are sorted, so this difference should be noted. To lay the reins on the horse's withers, first make certain that the horse is well stretched on his park (he will stand quieter if he is well balanced). Now, with very relaxed grip, slide the hands back to the end of the reins at a height just clearing the pommel of the saddle. As the end of the reins is approached, widen the hands until the reins are taut and making a straight line directly across the withers. Carefully place the reins on the withers, and release. The snaffle rein should be lying directly behind the curb rein. If it does not come out of your hands this way, place the reins in this juxtaposition with the right hand. To pick up, first grasp the two reins at the center points (buckle and stitching) with the first two fingers of the right hand and lift them about two inches above the withers. Beginning with the little finger of the left hand, place each succeeding finger around the reins in this order—snaffle, curb, curb, snaffle. The thumb goes under the four reins to complete the grip. With this proper assortment of the reins, draw the right hand back and slide the left forward to the usual riding length on the reins. As you release the bight, release the curb rein first and tighten slightly more on the snaffle before you release it. In this way you will avoid jabbing the horse on the curb and causing him to lower his head out of position. As soon as the bight has been

Picture showing the hand positions on the four reins: The right hand draws the reins while the left hand slides forward. The right hand is shown here at an exaggerated height in order to clarify the finger positions for the camera. Normally, the right hand would remain about the same elevation as the left. *Photo by author*

released, grasp the two right reins with the right hand as they are released by the left fingers. Keep the hands low at all times and avoid aggravating the horse with fumbling movements.

If you will place the reins in careful position before picking them up, your actions will be graceful and workmanlike. Should the horse root his head down as you pick up the reins, a sharp nip on the snaffle with your right hand as your left hand moves forward will raise his head with no added motion or delay. To quote the AHSA Rule Book, "The method of holding the reins is optional, except that both hands shall be used and all reins must be picked up at one time." Since the above-described procedure has worked for our riders for years, I have had no reason to change. Alacrity, smoothness, control—these are the points of judgment in this first test. Only practice will develop these points, and only attention to detail will make them possible.

BACK FOR NOT MORE THAN EIGHT STEPS—TEST #2

Whereas most of the exercises we teach the horse must be practiced a great deal, backing is one basic movement that should be well taught, then infrequently drilled. How many times we have seen equitation horses become confused or just plain mad during a difficult individual workout and start backing out of the desired position!

If you are working with a horse that backs poorly or not at all, try the following procedure: Stand squarely in front of the horse holding the reins close up to the bits on each side of his mouth. At the word command "Back," push the horse backwards with even pressure of both hands. As the horse takes the initial step, quickly ease the pressure on his mouth and immediately push back again. In this way, you will teach the horse to back from a signal (pulling on the reins and a release as the horse moves back), a distinct pull for each step moved. For this ground work it is helpful to have the horse lined up on a straight wall so that the wall will keep the horse in line. If the horse is difficult to back from this first ground training, use the blunt end of a whip to jab the horse in the breast as you push on the bits.

Now, place the reins on the horse's withers and step to the side of the horse facing his head. Practice the backing lesson from this position, picking up the reins as the seated rider would, and working the horse back a step at a time. You may now start guiding if the horse wants to cramp his neck and back in an arc. Keep his head straight with his chin dropped in but not down. Now mount up, and you should be able to back the horse promptly.

Each horse responds to the bits in his own way, so it is impossible to determine exactly how much pull the rider should be dividing between the curb and snaffle. As stated before, the horse should relax his neck and jaws to be responsive, and this is best gained with a combined use of both bits. Full snaffle tends to raise the horse's head and to cause him to throw excessive weight on his hind quarters, from which position he will either refuse to back at all, or spraddle badly behind and move convulsively. Too much curb will lower the head greatly, causing the horse to drag his front feet, rather than to take deliberate steps. Abusive handling of the horse's mouth can easily teach him to rear. Backing is not difficult for the horse to learn if you take his lesson in logical sequence, but because it is simple, it is often overlooked until the rider is in a class and everyone remembers at once that they had neglected to teach the horse to back!

In the lineup always park with ample space between horses. Not only should you do this for the benefit of the judge, but the adjacent horse can back into your horse and force you out of good position just as the judge approaches. Your horse may need the reins changed somewhat from the hold used during the park, so this adjustment for the back should be made before the judge arrives at your place in line.

The ring procedure for backing has been discussed in a previous chapter, so we will review only briefly: Move the horse one step forward from the stretch. As you feel him move, say, "Whoa, back," and back three steps. Again, "Whoa," and move the horse back into position with leg pressure, voice, and whip if necessary. Be sure that you use leg *pressure*. Three strict rules to obey are: do not cluck to the horse as you are backing, do not jerk his mouth, and use only leg pressure or whip to guide and control, never kicking.

PERFORMANCE ON THE RAIL (A)—TEST ♯3

As a judge, and as a teacher also, I am constantly aware that the simpler the workout, the more demanding one should be. At no time may we have the opportunity to so impress the rider with the importance of doing something well as in this very simple test of individual performance on the rail. I am referring to the most elementary work one can call for—trot down and back, canter down and back. There is hardly a rider anywhere who is incapable of this simple test, and yet —by its very simplicity—it can be one of the most revealing tests of horsemanship that we have. In some of the more intricate workouts— figure eights, for example—the talent of the horse for close work and the amount of expert training can sometimes cloud the issue of just how much is rider and how much is horse. On the other hand, any horse is capable of trotting down and back the long side of the rail and cantering down and back. I have heard riders complain that they were "only" asked for this easy workout and have seen them display the utmost disregard for perfection. Quality of what one does always counts, but when such a simple workout is called, it must be *perfect*. Every step should reflect complete control and demonstrate the depth of the knowledge of the rider.

Let us begin at the beginning: The preparation in the lineup is the start. The rider must know his horse. Will the horse leave the group willingly? Is he tired or fresh? Where should the whip be held to hold the horse to the rail? Exactly where does the rider plan to make the reverse? How soon should the rider begin his stop in order to reverse at the exact spot chosen? What speed is the best at the trot going down? How will this speed affect the stop and the reverse? How long should one hesitate before making the reverse so as to assure a smooth flow of control and guarantee a trot out of the reverse instead of a broken gait? How strong should the first canter signals be? How much will the horse be attracted to the group in the lineup—both at the departure and the return? Should the reverse and canter be more deliberate on the return than on the departure? These are the searching questions that each rider should ask himself before he ever leaves the group. And the rider is never too young or inexperienced to have these points brought up. The mere fact of going through the workout on both correct diagonals and both correct leads is not enough—it is the *quality* of each step that we are looking for. The real value of any figure work is not in the work itself, but the opportunity it gives the rider to anticipate his horse's mental and physical reactions to an exercise in control.

Let us study the anatomy of a perfect work down the rail. The horse is well collected, head up and set, firm and even in his trot, with strength forward through the rider's knees. By the time the rider has made a long approach to the rail, the horse is in this form and positioned *on the rail*. If the horse wavers as he leaves the lineup and fails to stay close to the rail, you may surely expect that the rest of the ride will go from bad to worse—because the rider will have ignored the initial moment of control that establishes the tenor of the entire work. The halt is gradual but definite, employing the voice, the hands, weight to the rear, and a firming of the hips. In this way, the horse will balance himself to the rear into a smooth, co-ordinated stop. The reverse will originate in the rider's leg next to the rail while the hands restrain the horse and keep his head and neck straight and in balance.

The horse will be kept quiet and relaxed so that the primary stride of the trot will be of normal length and cadence, permitting the rider to rise smoothly with the correct diagonal, thus assuring the trot instead of the canter. The trot will be brilliant, taking advantage of the natural animation engendered by the approach to the other horses in the line, with care taken not to slip over the razor's edge into a broken gait and loss of control. The stop will be easy. The reverse should be strong to overcome the "homing" tendency of the horse and to avoid his being distracted by the closeness of the other mounts. The leg aids will continue strong until the horse is well established in this new gait. Weak aids here would probably result in the resumption of the trot, as the horse tends to repeat what he has just done. The halt will be the same as the prior halt at this same spot on the rail. However, even more deliberation should accompany this return. At three quarters of the reverse, the aid is alternated to the other leg, which sets up the canter so that we have the pure reverse and canter, as opposed to the careless reverse, walk, and canter. The transition from one leg aid to the other will be so subtle as to blend the horse's reverse into the canter, as opposed to a sudden impulse that will bolt the horse into a charging gallop or disunited gait. Extra collection must be employed here, as the horse will have anticipated that the return will be at the canter, since he has gone down the rail at that gait.

The halt is called for at least four strides ahead of the stopping point at the trot. This allows for the extra "pull" of the lineup on the horse who senses that the workout is over. After a brief halt, the horse is walked into position in line.

Have you noticed anything missing in this description of a workout? Not one word has been said about the "form" of the rider. It must be assumed that the rider has applied himself so studiously to his elementary lessons that his seat and hands will be correct. If they are not, he will not be able to make the perfectly controlled ride that we have just described. The rider who goes to the rail with his concentration divided between his and his horse's performance will fail to deliver the convincing ride of that entrant whose entire performance reflects a knowledge of the inside of the horse's head as well as of his body.

PERFORMANCE ON THE RAIL (B)—TEST #3

While riding on the rail may be basic, as described in Performance on the Rail (A), it may be as difficult as any judge wishes to make it. Change of lead on the rail is generally conceded to be one of the most difficult skills of all. The primary elements of (A) always apply. To these we add the preparation for and the departure on the incorrect lead.

The rider must have the complete attention of his horse for this change. If it has not occurred to the rider before, it must now become quite evident that the horse should have been taught to take his canter leads completely from the aids. Whenever my students are working on the rail individually, or as a group, I always admonish them to start the canter without any help from the rail whatsoever. Horses that canter only because their forehand is jammed at the rail, and they may canter or bump the rail, soon learn to depend upon the rail as part of the canter signal. When the incorrect lead is desired, there will be no rail to lean on, and the horse will fail to get the canter at all, or he will arc away from the rail. Quite obviously, the rider who can take the canter change parallel to the rail is fulfilling the instructions, while the rider who veers away from the rail risks a switch of leads in a quick attempt to get back to the rail, or finds himself working half of his workout off the rail entirely.

Ideally the horse will have learned to hold the parallel position and determine the desired lead primarily from the rider's body weight, which has shifted to the rail side. There will be a subtle use of the inside (next to the center of the ring) leg aid to hold the haunches to the rail. The bearing rein will cause the horse to lean his leading shoulder forward, and the direct rein will hold the horse "on course," so to speak. When a horse first learns to do this, his tendency is to move away from the rail as he starts the lead. With more practice, the aids may become increasingly subtle, the arc away from the rail should diminish, and the day that the horse holds his position and leans into the rail is the day we have been waiting for. The horse recognizes the work, reacts to the aids, and has definitely learned to do this difficult exercise.

It may seem tedious to the instructor and student to practice changes of lead down the center of the ring for weeks and months until the horse is letter perfect before ever starting this change of lead on the rail, but one will certainly be far ahead in the long run. If you start this rail work too soon and without the necessary preparation, your horse will surely spend too much time literally practicing the wrong thing, and you will find that instead of teaching him to take the lead close to the rail, you have taught him to get the lead change by cantering in a half circle off the rail. It seems unnecessary to bring out this point, yet I have seen so many riders persist in a basic error like this under the misapprehension that they must struggle on until the horse "does it right," when what they were actually teaching the horse was to "do it wrong," simply because the horse did not have the elementary background to understand the work.

We have found that the following routine practiced for three or four revolutions around the ring is good training. Starting at the end of the long side farthest from the gate, canter the horse on the incorrect lead to the end of the ring, walk the turn, canter the long side, and walk the turn. In this way the horse is getting practice in starting this lead both away from and towards the natural pull of the gate. Most horses respond to affection, and a complimentary pat on the neck as the horse comes to each end of the ring is a great teaching aid. We have a mare now who is inclined to be overanxious and very reluctant to wait for the signals from the rider. Rather than argue with the mare at the expense of her mouth and my disposition, I learned to fill in the time between a halt in one gait and the beginning of the succeeding movement with caressing her on the neck. Now, every time that I do this, she immediately arches her neck, pops her ears forward and gives every indication that she is pleased as can be with her accomplishments. I may be reading too much into her actions, but I do know that you can catch more flies with sugar than vinegar!

Obviously, there are many variations of individual railwork that the judge may call for. Generally, plain common sense and an unhurried approach will see the rider through any instruction from the announcer. However, make it a practice to be absolutely certain that the rider understands the instruction. This is the duty of the judge—to make the instructions very clear. Should there be any doubt, the rider may ask for clarification from the judge (never ask the ringmaster), but most of the time this is unnecessary if the rider has taught himself to pay strict attention to every word of the workout instruction. If the work is on the rail, then be certain that is where you do it. I am sure that every judge has his own "pet peeve," and mine happens to be the contestant who does not keep to the rail when it has been specified.

The command to precede the canter change on the rail with a few steps at the back should be discussed briefly. In addition to the material covered in the section on backing, we should underline the use of the aids in holding the horse's haunches close to the rail. Primarily, this is the duty of the legs, yet there is no place where it is more apparent that there is always interaction of all aids than with this particular control. The leg aid towards the center of the ring must be used to hold the parallel position, but since this is also the identical aid used to get the more familiar canter, then we see that the guiding aid must be very subtle as we rein back. When the required number of steps have been backed, then the aid is increased to halt the backward movement and to signal the departure at the canter. At this rein-back remember that the hands and voice are the primary aids.

PERFORMANCE AROUND THE RING—TEST ⚡4

Performance around the ring usually embraces the execution of several gaits. This test is not used as frequently as some of the others, but it offers unlimited scrutiny of the rider and can be very demanding. Personally I like this workout, as we see the horse ridden under the influence of the varying factors that exist in a complete circuit around the rail.

A typical Test ⚡4 might be:

Trot down the length of the east rail. Halt at the center of the turn. Back three steps, then move into the left canter lead and describe a circle. Halt on the rail, remove your feet from the irons, and trot back to the lineup on the west rail.

Now, right away, someone is going to be in trouble. When the rider arrived at the show he was to have gone to the ring to look it over and acquaint himself with the entire show area. This he did, but he forgot one important thing, and that was to orient himself and establish the directions in the ring. Some rings have the directions lettered on the rail, but not all. Some announcers and judges will make the directions clear, but do not count on this. Know your directions, so—in the event that you are called first—you can proceed with impressive authority to follow the instructions. If you are one of the better riders in the class, or your back number is the lowest number or the first in the program, chances are very strong that you may be called first. And despite your position in order, you should know what you are doing and never count upon following what the preceding riders have done.

One of the main hazards of this particular test is that it will generally contain very involved instructions. You must pay strict attention and never take anything for granted. Frequently, riders will hear the beginning of what sounds like a very familiar workout and then stop listening. This is pure tragedy, because if you don't shoot yourself for this stupid carelessness, your instructor will!

On the trot down the rail you should be technically perfect in every facet of seat and hands. This may be one of the few times when the rider can concentrate more on himself than on the horse, but very little. The best rider will still be able to get that forceful performance out of his horse without sacrificing his own form.

Pick out the exact center of the end of the ring and stop there. To go beyond or short of this point will put some part of your canter circle near the rail, which could interfere with your pattern as well as present a very gauche appearance. The circle should be round—make an orange, not a banana—and be certain that you terminate the circle at the exact point at which you left the rail. Horses that have been drilled a great deal on canter serpentines will tend to canter half of the circle and stop, so use strong leg aids and plan ahead for this eventuality. Every individual work has one particular point that I call the "booby trap." This trap occurs now, when the feet are withdrawn from the stirrups and you begin the trot down the rail back to the lineup. If you are not very careful, the horse will jump into a canter, and he can do this in one split second to ruin the entire workout. Move into the trot with firm control and smoothness. Your best cure here is the ounce of prevention.

An ever-present factor in performance around the rail is the tendency of the horse to pull off the rail. How well the rider can keep a close rail position should be the primary consideration, because the success of the entire exhibition is predicated on this elementary show of control.

The variations that may be called for in this test are unlimited. The best preparation, therefore, is to master every basic individual test in the book, and practice differing combinations. If you have empathy for your horse—the ability to feel things as he does—so that none of his actions can surprise you, then you should welcome this test as an opportunity to show the true extent of your horsemanship.

FEET DISENGAGED FROM STIRRUPS. FEET ENGAGED—
TEST ⅍5

For the first two years after this new test was added to the list several judges called for the test at a trot. It even appeared in the Medal Finals. Unfortunately, the test was printed erroneously and was intended for use only in the lineup and, as should have been apparent, only for the ten-and-under age group. It is a good test for the very young as we need to insist from the very first that the correct usage of the tack is mandatory.

In teaching the youngsters to do this exercise, the point to stress is that the foot must reach for the stirrup from the horse's side outward in order for the stirrup leather to be properly turned. This seems a very simple thing, but perhaps because it is so simple we instructors had not been giving it the proper emphasis. It is a good test and a valid test. It is easy to do, but just as easy to miss, so teach it well.

FIGURE EIGHT AT TROT—TEST ⅍6

The description of this test in the rule book is "Figure eight at the trot, demonstrating change of diagonals." Of course diagonals are important, but many riders become so unnecessarily concerned with them that they feel they are the feature attraction of the figure eight. True, no matter how good the eight is, if the diagonals are wrong, the test is a failure. But the important thing to remember is that the easiest part of the figure is the diagonal. If the rider is at all wary of his identification of the diagonals, then he should make sure that he secures the proper one and proceeds directly into the figure eight from his approach, with no stop at the center. What is most valuable in this test is the opportunity to display perfect control. The pattern is *everything* in the figure eights and at the serpentines. Surely, anyone beyond the first thirty days of instruction can be counted upon for diagonals or leads, but it takes a top rider to make two matched circles beginning in the exact center of the area provided, with the horse and rider in perfect balance while maintaining the exact same rate of speed for both circles. It came as a surprise to me that some people do not have a sense of pattern, nor are they capable of returning to the intersection. What I had interpreted as poor control of the horse was actually an inability to describe a figure eight at all.

The riders were playing "statue" on the lawn one evening after dinner, and it dawned on me that it would be fun to have them demonstrate their one-minute workouts on foot. At first it was a hilarious exhibition, with sidesplitting versions of cross-canters, missed leads, and balky "horses," but then the girls overcame their self-consciousness and we got down to the serious business of perfecting figure eights on foot. I had already had the riders counting the number of strides in the first circle and then matching this number to make the next circle equal, but with the students who had a lot of trouble getting absolute perfection, this did not seem to be enough help. So, instead of counting the strides and matching them (which called for very quick mathematics if the riders checked their steps at the halfway point), we decided upon a test circle to determine the number of strides that each horse averaged on a logical-sized circle. When we found that the range was from fourteen to twenty, depending on the gait and agility of each horse, and since we wanted numbers divisible by four, we established either sixteen or twenty as the number of strides in each circle, and instead of aiming for the total, we would aim for four marks, each one a quarter of the way around the circle. For instance, let us say that at the intersection the rider is facing north. In a sixteen-stride circle, he would be facing west on the fourth stride, south on the eighth, east on the twelfth, and back to north and the intersection on the sixteenth stride. The results were remarkable, and riders who theretofore had wandered around in limbo were able to find the intersection and go on to the next circle and match it in size, as well as to return to the central point. According to this scheme, our riders should always make perfect eights! I still have not succeeded in getting the riders to count every time, but when they do, the improvement in the patterns always shows up. Counting the figures must be done repeatedly, so that the mind will count automatically while it is simultaneously dealing with the other elements of control.

Some judges prefer that riders move directly into the eight without a stop at the center. I generally teach my riders to identify the intersection by halting and then proceed to execute the eight. This is more difficult, as there is danger of the horse's breaking into the canter at the beginning, but I firmly believe that the figures serve a purpose and that there is so much more to learn from beginning the eight from a standstill. As a judge, I never penalize a rider who takes the easy way, but merely ask the harder way of my students because I want them to learn everything there is to be gained from the individual workouts. If you have your rider halt before commencing the circles, do be brief. It annoys a judge to have the rider halt, park, and pose or otherwise deliberately delay the class. Certainly, workouts should never be hurried, but do remember that time is important in a horse show, and judges become very impatient with grandstanding riders. Another point: *do not* back when the figure is completed unless it has been called for. Never do more, or less, than is instructed.

Rein handling attains its greatest sophistication at the figure eight, especially at the trot. If a horse were like a car, and, setting the steering wheel at a certain pull, we would be assured of returning to the point of origin, the execution of a circle would be delightfully simple. However, such is not the case, and astute rein work is necessary to accomplish the perfection required. The most common faults in the circles are as follows:

Failure to trot from a standing start. Generally this is caused because the rider overlooks the fact that the horse is anxious to return to the group and, unless well contained by the calming voice and very gradual release of the reins, will hop into the canter and head for home.

Breaking the trot during the first circle. This generally occurs at the specific point in the circle where the horse turns away from the group. If the rider uses the strong inside leg aid and equally strong bearing rein with firm guidance in the direct rein, the advance around the circle will be smooth and controlled. Failure to realize that the horse will be drawn rapidly to the group and retarded as he turns away will cause trouble, since the rider will have permitted the horse to increase his speed toward the other horses, thus teasing him into thinking that he is actually going back to the lineup. When the rider discovers this error, either it is too late and the pattern is lost, or such a strong, direct rein correction is made that the horse is thrown off balance and into a canter. The horse must feel constant pressure on each side of his mouth, and this contact must be sufficient so that any transition from one rein to the other will merely be an increase in pressure, never a series of full pulls or full releases.

Breaking the trot at the intersection. This can occur as we approach the intersection, and most often results from severe overguiding at the last moment, when the rider discovers that he is going to miss his point. The correction is obvious: more careful control, and planning ahead for the intersection. The quarter plan for executing the circle can avoid this trouble. Even more frequent is the jump into the canter as the diagonal is changed and the direction reversed. Too much speed, a rough diagonal change which bounces the hands, or both, can result in this mistake. Too, the horse will again be turning toward the lineup and naturally tend to increase his speed.

There will be a tendency for the rider to trot forward on a straight line at the start of the first circle (while searching for the proper diagonal). Conversely, the horse will be inclined to cut back too soon at the top of the second circle. For this reason, the matching of the two top halves of the circles will be especially difficult. The outside rein must hold the horse to the pattern, and then the transition to the direct rein with help from the bearing rein occurs again at the halfway mark. There are no straight lines in a circle.

During practice, halt the horse for at least ten seconds upon completion of the eight. Increasingly, as the horse becomes better trained at this test, he will realize when the test is over and will want to dash back to the group. Some horses have a more pronounced herd instinct than others. For those horses that have a real problem, working in blinkers and holding the horse's head quite low so that he is not given such a good look at his companions at the opposite end of the ring may keep him from developing a control problem. It absolutely will not work to whip or spur the horse for this fault. You will only add hysteria to a problem that already has nervous overtones. We must distract the horse, make him feel secure in the rider's complete control, and be clever enough to outthink him and make early corrections before bad habits have become engraved upon his reactions.

FIGURE EIGHT AT CANTER—TEST #7

Our discussion of the figure eight at the canter is predicated upon the study and mastery of the figure eight at the trot. The greatest aid to perfection at the canter is a complete understanding of the outside influences that draw or retard your horse as he makes the circle pattern.

We must assume that the rider will get his leads. Failure to do this should be handled much earlier. What we have to learn here is the extremely adroit use of the aids. As the trot eight required superior rein work, the canter adds to this the most understanding application of the legs. Not that the legs were ignored at the trot, but they do play a more vital part at the canter.

Particularly in riders who have depended too much upon the rail to get a lead, we find a tendency to get the canter leads by leaning strongly over the shoulder while turning the horse's head in the opposite direction. A well-trained horse will follow his head; thus, such handling is almost certain to result in the improper lead. The hands should be used to keep the head and foreparts completely "on course" while the combined leg aids drive the horse ahead on this course, or, individually used, indicate the chosen lead and control the position of his hind quarters and his entire body. Frequently we see a rider literally throw his weight over the leading shoulder and keep it there. Too much speed and a tendency for the horse to lean to the inside of the circle are the results. Most of the time, such a circle is uncontrolled and the rider fails to make the point of departure, thus overlapping the circles badly. The inside leg aid, which bends the horse's entire body around the leg to fit the curve of the circle, will allow the horse to execute the turn in balance and collection and return to the exact point of intersection.

I feel compelled to say something about judging here. We have all seen judges who were busy writing on the scorecard at this very moment and who missed the fact that there was a woeful lack of control and a missed intersection. In large classes it behooves a judge to mark the leads on a card, but it should be done at the completion of the figure so that full scrutiny of all phases of the eight may be possible. I consider the failure to close the circles properly the cardinal sin of this test, even more so than a momentary failure to start on the proper lead. The audience generally recognizes only lead faults and is not adequately educated to appreciate all the subtle nuances of superior control, but the judge should either educate himself to this point, or—knowing the comparative values—have the intestinal fortitude to give the proper credit to the quality of the pattern and the control that made it possible. There are times when a horse will fumble for a lead and the top rider will restrain the horse until he is properly aligned to ensure the lead. Undoubtedly, this is horsemanship. This brings us to one of the highest skills demanded by this test—timing.

You will notice that the change is now referred to as a simple change of lead—"This is a change whereby the horse is brought into a walk and restarted into a canter on the opposite lead." This rewriting of terminology was to make certain that a flying change is not used. Further, it forces the rider to employ the only practice that ensures the change of lead. When the horse stops his canter, he must realign his feet so that the transition to the other lead is possible. To jam the horse into an abrupt halt and make a standing start into the canter from this foot pattern is full of obvious pitfalls. We must give the horse an opportunity to get set up for the change. Ideally, the halt, followed by one step at the walk, which will permit realignment, is graceful and workmanlike. The innate sense of timing with which some riders are gifted tells them when to strike off in the canter. For those less fortunately endowed, practice with good instruction can give the rider this tremendously important sense of timing.

SERPENTINE AT TROT AND / OR CANTER—TEST #8

Work at the serpentine is relatively easy if the rider has mastered the basic principles of the figure eights at the two gaits. Just as it is extremely easy to make careless eights, so it is at the serpentines. In the first place, we must be reminded that change of diagonal or lead becomes necessary (and logical) when a change of direction occurs.

Therefore, the pattern of the serpentine should be precisely what is described in the rule book—"a series of left and right *half circles. . . .*" In other words, at the moment the rider's body crosses the imaginary center line, the horse should be (for that one stride) exactly at right angles to the line. The diagonal is changed on this stride, and the arc into the next half circle begins at that instant. Unless the arena is unusually small, the space allotted will permit from four to five half circles. Should the instructions call for a show of at least four diagonal changes, remember that this will mean at least five semicircles, as the first half circle is merely the beginning and we are counting the changes, not the half circles. This being the case, make sure that the figure is started as far from the lineup as possible. It is always better to have room to spare than to discover halfway down that there is not enough space to finish the work. It is not only necessary to make the changes on the imaginary center line, but the half circles should be identical in size and speed. Again, we utilize the counting of strides to help maintain equal proportions.

Frequently, we will see riders crossing the center line on a bias line and then making an abrupt turn to cut back and slant again across the imaginary line. It is obvious that these are not half circles and that it makes absolutely no sense to change the diagonals in the center when there is no change of direction at that point. Such mistakes are pure carelessness, as the description in the rule book could not be more explicit. In fact, most poor demonstrations of these tests are simply caused by failure to think and analyze.

Again, just how strong the aids will be is determined by the direction in which the horse is moving. Going away, the forcing aids— strong, general aggression and extra care that the horse does not lag and try to turn back each time he crosses the center line—will generally produce a strong enough trot so that the horse can be held firmly. The firmness of touch is vital, since a horse that is "loose on the bits" is hard to hold on a specific course, despite the help of all the aids. On the return at the trot, there is much less forcing necessary, as the natural attraction of the other horses will provide the incentive. Constant and greater collection, with a lessening of the leg aids, should produce a serpentine that will match the first one in speed and stride. With these two elements being equal, pattern is simply a matter of concentration and counting. The use of the inside leg aid becomes very delicate here. Generally, the mere indication of this aid during the diagonal change is enough to start the next half circle, while continued pressure may tend to reduce the desired size of the arc and force the use of the outside rein. This in turn may fool the horse into thinking that he is to trot down the rail. In other words, overuse of

SADDLE SEAT TESTS 1-12

Running through the posted workouts is an invaluable aid. I always ask my riders to do this, going through the motions of the aids as much as possible and making mental preparation for the work by trying to anticipate their mount's acceptance or resistance to all phases of the workout. Karen Fischer's upraised hand indicating a diagonal and her intense concentration, as well as that of her fellow riders, illustrate the seriousness of this practice. Each run-through will vary, as each horse reacts differently, but every rider benefits. *Photo by Donaldson*

aids demands counter aids—all of which would be no problem if the aids were not overused in the beginning.

The execution of the serpentine at the canter is almost identical with that at the trot. Basic elements of control, reaction of the horse to his surroundings, counting, etc., are ever present. The best word of advice that I can give about canter serpentines is that they should be practiced sparingly. The best practice for the canter serpentine is the straight-line canter change. If your horse and rider can change leads on a straight line, then changing at right angles is very easy. Serpentine practice in itself is not bad, but it tends to cause the horse to "fishtail" on the line change. So, for the sake of precision on the line change, keep your serpentine canter practice to a minimum.

In the average-size ring, eight to ten strides at both the trot and the canter produce good, workmanlike serpentines. Very large loops show great lack of imagination and control, and the small, wavering line is equally unimpressive. The keynote of success is pattern. Equally important is the underlying quality of empathy between horse and rider that permits the attainment of pattern. The rider who senses that his horse is so tensed up that eight strides will be disaster while ten will be manageable, will truly exemplify good teaching and good riding.

CHANGE LEADS DOWN CENTER OF RING—TEST #9

In practicing the center-line change, one must have a strong sense of balance and direction. The immediate establishment of the straight line is a must. Remember, you should let the horse know that you are going to proceed in a straight line—not a serpentine. To inform him of your intentions, proceed directly from the lineup to the center start, and walk a step or two to identify this line to the horse as well as to the judge. Almost anyone can get from here to there and change leads a couple of times. What is difficult is to do this in a *straight line*. In order to accomplish this, imagine that there is a taut wire strung down the center of the arena and that there is a ring at the top of the bridle, through which this wire is run. The horse must keep his head straight.

Now, hold the horse so that his head remains pointing exactly forward. Use the outside aid to move the horse's haunches one stride off the line. At this moment the horse should feel some direct rein influence on his mouth, but this must be countered by an almost equal restraint with the bearing rein—otherwise the horse will take a stride or two off the line. Immediately divide the line into the proper-length segments to accommodate the requested number of changes.

Stop firmly with a steady hand and a definite deepening in the saddle. Never grab your horse on the stop, as he will surely move sideways off the line if you do. The simple change is called for here, so make certain that the walk step is either on the line or is an immediate correction of any deviation from the line. Going away, the horse will tend to waver from side to side, and coming back, the pull of the group will straighten and strengthen the forward pull but the horse will want to rush, so the rider must anticipate this and plan for it.

The horse should be taught to reverse on the forehand. In other words, the head should still remain on the line and the body should make the turn. This is accomplished by holding at the stop and turning mainly by use of the outside leg aid and the combined restraint and action of the bearing rein and the direct rein. Do this slowly. Particularly in practice, make the horse remain standing several seconds before moving down the line and beginning the canter.

If you find that there is a tendency to rush into the next lead, try alternating ten strides of canter, then ten at a walk. This may also be done at the trot and is discussed extensively in the section on Demonstration Ride—Test ✗11. Since there is a possibility that this alternating change may be called for or that the rider might choose to use this in a demonstration ride, it is a good practice routine.

When you are introducing the new horse to canter changes, it is best to do this in an aisleway, where the confines of your working area influence the horse to keep the straight line. At first there will be considerable use of the reins, but as the animal begins to realize that the changes are correct and that he is not being stopped for having committed an error, then the rider should begin to minimize the aids —particularly the hands. This refinement continues on into the work in the arena where the leg has moved the haunches a step to the side of the line. In time, the rider will become so subtle that there will be almost no visible reaction to the aids other than a fluid movement into the desired lead. The line change should be practiced every time the horse is worked, making certain that you do it only enough to polish the maneuver but never to the extent that the horse becomes sour. Since it is work on a straight line, we do not need to be too concerned about making the horse unsound (which may happen with exercises that require a great deal of turning), but the greatest danger here is temperamental, not physical. Know your horse and rider, and try to keep them both learning and happy in the learning.

RIDE WITHOUT STIRRUPS—TEST ✗ 10

(No more than one minute at the trotting phase)

Of all of the tests called for, riding without irons is one of the most popular. Because it is called for so frequently, I can only conclude that it is considered worth while by many. Because I am so firmly convinced that leg and knee contact should originate in the use of the stirrup irons rather than a gripping in of the knees, the value of riding the saddle seat without irons escapes me. As it appears very difficult, however, it is a crowd pleaser.

This is one test that, more than any of the others, depends for its success upon the compatibility of build between horse and rider. Short, slender riders have a definite advantage in this workout.

How often we have seen spectators unduly impressed with the superior appearance of the small rider, when they were unaware that such a child had no problem in keeping the knees on the top half of the horse where they would provide some support for the posting motion. Knees that drop below the width of the horse do not have any mooring and are responsible for the clutching around the horse that is so disastrous. Clutching will prevent the rider from elevating at the post and, at the same time, will goad the horse into more speed than is desired. The only solution that the long-legged rider has is to pull the knee up until it reaches the area just above the widest part of the horse's barrel. If the rider has a long thighbone, which most tall people have, the knee will be quite forward of the rider's seat. The knee that is drawn to the top of the horse will not only fail to help the rider post, it will be an actual obstacle that must be "jumped over" each time the rider attempts to post. Not so with the more fortunate, short-legged rider. He will have the knee up on top of the horse, and because of the shorter thigh, will naturally have the knee dropped under his hips, where it can hoist him aloft at the post in the same relative position that he has when riding with stirrups. Some long-legged riders are able to post not from the knee but from that point of the thigh that grips the wide side of the horse. This is certainly a position that more closely approximates the look of using the stirrups, which is what we are aiming for. Edward Lumia, winner of both Finals, was the best rider without stirrups I have ever seen. But he was a very strong seventeen-year-old boy.

With constant practice the muscles can become developed enough to permit any rider to accomplish this feat. But I always wonder if this time could not be put to so much better use in the practice and understanding of equitation. Still, I must be fair and admit that this test does have some merit. The confidence that comes with mastering anything difficult cannot be overlooked. There is the added security in the knowledge that the rider can ride without stirrups should he ever lose them during a class. Devotees of this test will point out that riders develop balance—which they most certainly do in all phases of riding, not just without irons.

There are many instructors who share my aversion to this ride, and certainly there are just as many or more who would disagree with this opinion. To make this a fair test, however, I do think that the judge should be very careful in his analysis of the various combinations of horses and riders, and if there appears to be a gross inequality within these combinations, then, perhaps, this test is not applicable. Certainly it is up to the instructor and all concerned to mount a rider suitably. We are assuming that this is always the case and are not building in excuses for badly suited, trained, or gaited mounts.

Now, facing the eventuality that riding without stirrups can be called for, the teacher must prepare both horse and rider for this test. Start with the walk. The position in the saddle should be identical with the normal style of the rider with irons. The knee should be on the stirrup leather, shin perpendicular, and heels moderately down. Shorten the reins up to the crest and use almost complete snaffle. Start the trot very slowly and permit the rider to balance on his knuckles at the horse's neck if absolutely necessary. This may be done only if the rider's arms are long enough to permit this without any leaning forward. There will be a strong tendency in the beginner to lean forward, pull the heels up, and draw the legs back. There is absolutely no way that a rider can post without stirrups in this position. The knees *must* be kept forward in place and the heels forced down. Only in this way will the knees stay atop the width of the horse and the entire muscular system of the thighs be brought into use. The rider must maintain such a position that he will roll into the saddle from the knee back to the seat, via the back of the thigh. If the legs have slipped back, the vertical forked position will result in the rider who does not post at all, but merely rebounds to the motion of the trot. By all means, sitting well back to get the greatest saddle thrust is very helpful.

Riding without stirrups at the canter is almost as simple as the walk, and it is best to use this gait to begin the practice of this test, as it acquaints the horse with the movement of the free stirrups without the added confusion of the unskilled rider attempting the trot.

The horse, as well as the rider, must learn to accommodate himself to this test. If you have a horse that is extremely sensitive to the loose stirrups, you might try trotting the horse on a long line with the empty saddle and stirrups free. But be very careful that this is done gradually or you may—instead of teaching the horse tolerance—teach him how to be a bucker. The logical way to break a horse to riding without stirrups is for the teacher to practice this. I do have a feeling that each instructor will hastily figure out his own way to accomplish the task from the ground!

DEMONSTRATION RIDE—TEST ⅍11

The demonstration ride should be sufficiently daring to be distinctive; but by the same token, it should surely be something that the rider has every confidence of doing perfectly. Obviously, the road to perfection is practice. However, this is not enough. Before the practice should come some very deep analysis of the work to be done. Since this is an elective workout, exceeding care should be taken to choose the best possible arrangement of the elements of the work to assure the most success.

To illustrate: In an alternating straight line, showing both leads and both diagonals, it is possible to so arrange the sequence of the work that the transition from one gait to another is easily possible. I spend hours at this sort of analysis, and it is one of the most stimulating aspects of instruction. For instance, analyze the halt out of the canter; the horse stops with the leading foot in the forward, braced position, which means that the very next step that he takes will be with the opposite foreleg. If a horse stops his right-lead canter into a trot, it means that he will stop the canter with the right front foot and will start his trot with the left front foot, thus causing the rider to pick up the immediate trot on the left diagonal. Knowing this, it becomes obvious in planning an alternating line change that the pattern should be: right lead, left diagonal; left lead, and right diagonal. In this pattern, you have arranged the sequence in such a manner that the very mechanics of the gaits in their transitions have aided the rider in the immediate changes without any searching for diagonals.

In instances of individual rides that call for a succession of changes or a specific number of strides, one must be aware of the possibility of the rider's forgetting just where he is in the workout. We have all agonized for some unfortunate rider who has had a sudden lapse of memory at such a time. Rather than berate the rider for this "black-out," it is better to face the fact that such a mistake is very likely to occur. It is easy to sit on the sideline and criticize such a blunder, but anyone who has ever had to execute a complicated individual work under the great stress of an important class can sympathize and understand how this can easily happen. As an instructor, I have tried to invent phrases or words which are very descriptive (the shorter the better) and which will help a rider "stay on course." I describe this alternating line change as a "sandwich." In other words, left lead, right diagonal, right lead, left diagonal. The two lefts are the "bread" and the two rights are the "meat." After a rider has done this sequence a time or two, he will always know what comes next.

Another element that should be planned ahead with extreme attention to clarity is the rider's description of his intended workout. There is nothing more frustrating to a judge than to have some rider fumble incoherently for words to describe his ride or, even worse, state one intention and then proceed deliberately to do something else. One of our intermediate riders was showing at Dayton a few years ago. She was very anxious to get to do a one-minute workout and was quite thrilled to be included in this test in the Medal Class. Imagine her consternation when she realized that she had ridden up to the judge and said, "I will trot to the far end of the ring and execate a figure oot"!

At advancing periods during the show season, I have my riders write down their one-minute routine, and we discuss it, and if it is clear, concise, and something that the rider can do with confidence and flair, then it is decided upon. Thereafter, that is the workout that the rider will do until it is time to change to something more demanding. Never leave the decision as to what the workout will be until the class. At one show, I had a frantic rider ask me (the judge) what I thought she should do! And this was a good little rider who was capable of doing everything in the book!

In practice, the instructor should point out that there are varying sorts of rings, and the workouts should be planned with this in mind. Generally speaking, if we discuss the fact that some rings have the judge's stand in the center and other rings are completely open, minor changes to suit these physical ring differences are all that will be necessary. It was stated very early in this book that the rider should study the show ring as soon as he arrives at the show and be well acquainted with the setup before he enters the ring. To fail to do this is pure negligence. Everything that can be planned, organized, and practiced about the elective workout should be done. There are certain elements of horse reaction that are always constant. Remember, he is a "herd animal," and work done on a line away from the other horses will be slow, whereas work on a line coming back to the group will be quick. Therefore, the rider should be reminded that he should determine the sequence of his work with his horse's nervous and physical capacity at that particular moment. If the horse is too aggressive and on the bit, all lines should be worked away from the group. If the horse is very tired and the rider feels that there is danger of the horse's breaking gait downward, then work the line changes towards the group. Such variations are only common sense, and since this one-minute workout is generally called only in the final classes of the show, a quick directive or suggestion as to how each horse should be worked before the class will take care of this point. I like to think that my advanced riders are thorough enough students of their horse that I will not have to advise them, but I generally do—which is probably a disservice to the thinking riders.

Not to be overlooked is the choice of a workout that will fit into sixty seconds. Time your practices very carefully. It is better to have your work short. You may find yourself rushing and making mistakes if you choose too much to do. You can always stop and park your horse smartly to add a few seconds at the end.

EXCHANGE HORSES—TEST ✗ 12

Change of horse is one of the most misunderstood and misused individual tests that we have. It has even come to the point where a motion was made several years ago at the national convention of the American Horse Shows Association to drop this test from the rule book. Fortunately, the motion was almost unanimously defeated, but there still remains much discussion about the fairness of this test.

First of all, let me say that I am wholeheartedly in favor of this change of horse, and it has been my experience that every qualified equitation instructor that I have discussed this with feels the same. The main dissenters seem to be those professional trainers or parents-who-teach who fear that the fine horse they have selected for their rider will be given to another contestant, while their rider may get an inferior horse in the exchange. The problem here is not in the test but in the judging. While this book is primarily for the student and the instructor (and I have avoided discussing judging as much as possible), this is a problem in judging and must be faced as such.

To return to the point of dissent—that the change of horse may be unfair to the rider of the better horse—this is an invalid point if the judging is conducted in the manner in which the test is intended. This should be a *comparative* test. The judge has already seen the competitors ride their own horses (it is stated in the rule that the judge must never call for anything in the change that the riders have not done previously in the class on their own horses), and the judge must remember very clearly just how the riders handled their own mounts. For this reason, changes of mount should never involve more than six riders at a time, as a memory comparison for more than that number is extremely difficult, if not impossible.

After the change has been made, then, the judge must compare the two rides—does rider B ride the horse as well as rider A rode him? If our critics of the change are right, then they have based their conclusions on bad judging that makes an entirely new class after the change of mounts and judges the contestants as they compare *at that moment,* rather than a comparison of the two rides. If the class is judged this way, then of course it is wrong—the rider who gives up her superior horse is in the agonizing position of being defeated by her own horse. Horses are not judged in equitation, but one would have to be blind not to recognize the fact that a rider can show more and better horsemanship on a horse whose temperament and conformation permit him to co-operate in the execution of the required figures and rail work.

The riders welcome change of horse, and the question most often asked me before a class is "Do you think we will get to change horses?" They feel, and so do I, that there is so much to be learned by the change. I would love to do this at home, when the riders are here practicing before the show season opens, but it would hardly be fair, as there are generally several in the same championship, and any value they may derive from a change in the ring would be lessened by their having practiced this at home. Moreover, it would certainly not be fair to the other riders in the class.

A judge must also be very careful in selection of the horses for a change. Horses with severe temperamental problems should never be used, as there is a real danger here. The first question the judge must ask himself is "Is it safe?" Then "Is it fair—are the two changing riders in close contention for the same ribbon?" For these reasons, an indiscriminate change makes absolutely no sense at all. Several years ago, when Lynne Girdler and Storm Cloud were right at the top in equitation classes, the judge lined the riders up in the older age group and had each rider dismount and then change to the horse immediately to his right. Of course the change proved nothing, as there was no basis for comparison at all. This class turned into a travesty, for obvious reasons. But the real trouble came in the championship! Storm Cloud was tremendously popular, and when the command "Line up" came over the speaker, the Charge of the Light Brigade looked like a pony ring compared to the mass descent of horses and riders upon Lynne and Storm Cloud. It should have been a class in musical chairs! By this time the judge realized what trouble had been triggered by the previous class, and change of mounts was not called for.

Here is a perfect example of the need for a judge to have an alternate workout in mind.

For the rider who is preparing for the championships or the older classes, where this change may be called, the best preparation is to learn as much about all horses at all times as you can. One of my best riders displayed a keen interest in every horse in every class from the very first. The other children might have been out riding on the Ferris wheel during the three-gaited stake, but not Debbie—she was right at railside, taking in every move of every rider and horse. She watched each individual workout like a hawk in her own classes. I know that she was capable of riding every horse in the class should she have been called upon to do so. And now that she is out of equitation, she is frequently invited to catch ride in the amateur division. She exemplifies those riders who harvest the rewards of equitation if they will only apply what has been taught, and change of mount is one of the most valuable and interesting individual tests that we have.

22

How to Judge Individual Tests

The following chapter is the text of a talk given by the author to the participants in the AHSA Judges Forum in October 1980.

Begun in 1978 as a mandatory clinic for all licensed AHSA equitation judges, this annual presentation was designed to reinforce the judges' understanding of the skills and responsibilities of recognized judging.

In this book I have deliberately confined myself to teaching the horse and rider. Time has revealed that a majority of instructors as well as judges use the book from time to time for reference. With this knowledge in mind and being a judge myself, I am aware that there is much for the riders and instructors, as well as the judges, to learn from looking at the other side of the coin.

In the opening remarks I thanked those in the audience for their attendance and added that, sadly, the judges who needed the most help were the ones who had not bothered to attend. The talk was most attentively received and I felt that a medal should have been given to anyone who would listen to a one-hour speech. We *must* have good judges. Nineteen-eighty saw a disturbing situation in which many judges simply were not qualified. If this chapter can aid in the judging of individual workouts and make just one careless judge improve, then my time was not ill spent.

Why do we have workouts? To answer this, we must go back to the very foundation of equitation and remind ourselves that equitation is horse training, nothing more—and certainly nothing less. And no place has a judge a better opportunity to evaluate a rider's ability to understand, anticipate, and control the horse than at the individual workout. But a workout must never under any circumstance be a cop-out or a crutch. You, as judges, must be intelligent enough, experienced enough, and—yes, I will say it—just plain interested enough to be able to evaluate a class in a positive manner. By this I mean that the judge can pick his placings because of his positive impressions—

how well can the rider actually ride, not who was the last to make an overt mistake? If we look at workouts with a positive attitude, then the manner in which a rider executes a figure eight, for example, assumes almost as much importance as the figure itself. My idea of a cop-out is a judge who is unwilling to tie a class on what he sees before him and, instead, calls for a workout, hoping that someone will miss a diagonal or hunt for a canter lead. In such judging we do not need judges—a computer will do. Because what we are then doing is overlooking the worst fault of all—the fault of not riding the horse to his best performance. In its place we are encouraging riders to become so fearful of "making a mistake" that we will never let competition improve our young riders—and that is what we should be judging: equitation as a means, not an end.

I certainly do not advocate forgiving a sloppy performance from a rider who appears to be badly mounted simply because the horse appears to be causing trouble. A judge must mark his card on what he sees, not on what he assumes. This is dangerous territory because the judge cannot be sure that the so-called "unsuitable" mount is not the result of a slow-thinking rider who fails to use the aids in time to get results and the poor horse gets the blame. However, we are all aware that a rider can do everything exactly right and still have a horse step off on the wrong foot or hesitate in getting into a canter. If the rider is smart enough to see this coming and waits until the horse sets up properly—to me this is superb horsemanship and should be rewarded. If the flow of the work is erratic because of the rider's bad timing, that constitutes a major fault of the rider, not the horse. I think judges must be good trainers, good instructors—preferably both—to be able to evaluate quality riding.

Now we begin to see where a background of good horse training is an absolute prerequisite for the judge. This is why very few equitation parents make adequate judges. They evaluate only the finished product and do not understand the multifaceted horse handling that made the picture possible. You must have the intestinal fortitude to evaluate these situations and place the blame or the credit where it lies. We have all seen judges pounce on one step of a wrong diagonal to tie a good rider down below a rider who had gotten every lead, every diagonal, and had ridden the entire workout with such self-conscious caution that he was about as exciting as a church picnic. The quality of the three gaits and the demonstration of positive as opposed to negative control at the figures—this is what we should be judging in individual workout. The mere absence of culpable mistakes does not make a good ride.

When you accept the invitation to judge equitation you should go to your rule book immediately and study every aspect of the rules. It is hard to remember, for instance, that workouts 1 through 4 are all that are permitted for ten-and-under, etc. Know the percentages of credit for all breeds, as some rules supersede.

Make certain that you are technically correct in your choices of workouts. Be sure to give your copy to the announcer prior to the class. Make certain that it is clear and concise and that the announcer is to read it verbatim—never adding or deleting anything. It is well to caution ringmasters who may want to communicate with riders. If you work very hard to make your instructions clear, workable, and fair to all, you will have very few questions, if any at all.

Posted workouts—and they are optional, not required as some believe—must be posted at least twenty minutes prior to the session. If you have any doubt about getting back to the show on time, it would be wise to have the office post the workout at the end of the prior session and make the necessary announcements to inform everyone.

I think we need to mention complexity of workouts. This may be sensitive territory, but in view of the alarming frequency of workouts that are literally impossible to do, I think this discussion is justified. Study your written or diagramed instructions carefully, then get on your own two feet and literally trot and canter your way through what you request. That will tell you if you are logical. Do what your instructions say, not what you "mean." Workouts should never be guessing games. Above all, never let someone else write or diagram your workout for you. Do it yourself. As the sausage man says, "Down on the farm, we do it right or we don't do it."

The ideal workout should test the rider's ability to control his horse at the various gaits on lines, circles, and variations of these two elements, both going towards the group and away from it. Sixteen-part workouts that test and retest a rider's ability to show any of the above-mentioned controls are not only meaningless (as the rider has proved himself the first time) but again lead to the negative control that stultifies the rider and deadens the horse's performance. You, as judge, can get yourself into a peck of trouble with overlong workouts just as the open judges can do with overworking stake classes. Workouts have only part of the judging percentile, and when a judge calls for something too complicated or overlong, then the balance of judging is distorted or appears to be so. If you are really hooked on very involved and tedious workouts, search yourself and make sure that you have not given in to the dangerous temptation to "be different," to prove your own worthiness as a judge. If you truly believe that twenty- or twenty-five-part individual workouts are justified, then perhaps we should add a class for workouts only.

Study the ring. Know what is practical for the working area and, above all, be fair. I cannot recall ever seeing a deliberately unfair equitation judge, but I have seen countless unfair ring conditions that vary from rider to rider as the workouts progress, because of the judges' negligence. Give ample thought to the placement of the lineup so that under no condition will it interfere with the workouts. Never let the lineup change position or do anything that would make unequal conditions from one rider to the next. To be avoided at all costs is the idea of excusing riders after they have done their individuals. If there are fifteen horses in the lineup when the first rider works, then there should be fifteen when the last rider works.

Never permit riders to repeat workouts (this generally refers to the first called). If your instructions are faultless, as they should be, then a mistake belongs to the rider. In the rare case that something catastrophic happens in the ring or stands to blow a workout, immediately halt the rider, return him to the lineup, and wait until the disturbance is rectified. Then let the rider start again from the beginning.

Since workouts count 50% in AHSA classes, 40% in UPHA competition, and may vary according to local shows and breeds other than Saddle horses—specifically Arabian, Morgan, and now Walking horses —it is only logical that you must judge and mark on a score sheet your placings of the riders at the three gaits both ways of the ring. It is from this evaluation that you decide what riders will participate in individual work, if any. And in the case of specialty classes or championships that demand a minimum number of riders for the workout, again you choose how many riders will work.

A good system is to set up a work sheet graphed out for your particular workout. List your riders according to their placings based on the rail work—it seems to obviate the public's and the riders' conclusion that the order in which the riders are called is significant if you call riders to work in numerical order. However, be very careful that you keep the right scoring with the proper back numbers.

Now let us look at the twelve individual workouts:

PICK UP REINS—TEST #1

The primary point of judgment here is the knowledge of and the demonstrated ability to sort the reins in the proper sequence. This is all we should expect of the ten-and-unders. For the other two age groups, add deftness of rein handling, control of the horse, and possible correction of the horse's head and neck position. Therefore, the faults to look for:

Rein Alignment

Horse Backing Up

Incorrect Neck and Head Positions of the Horse

BACK FOR NOT MORE THAN EIGHT STEPS—TEST ⚓2

I do not believe that we can nail down an exact "proper" way to back a horse. One common denominator, however, is that the horse should move forward with at least the hind feet out of the stretched position. (This will not apply to the Arabians or to those Morgans who are not stretched.) Any combined use of snaffle and curb along with a voluntary use of the voice is acceptable if it gets results and is comfortable to the horse. Ten-and-unders should know how to do this. Older-age-group riders should be able to guide the horse with hands and legs to get a straight line back and to return to the exact original position. Faults to look for:

Failure to Move out of Stretch

Failure to Back

Dangerous or Cruel Use of the Bits

Failure to Back Straight

Failure to Use Voice or Whip, When Necessary,
    to Return to Original Position

PERFORMANCE ON THE RAIL—TEST ⚓3

Since Test 4 states performance around the ring, we have to assume that this test is confined to a straightaway.

For any age group, it seems only fair and logical to line the horses up along one side of the ring for the line inspection, then reverse to face the center so that the riders will be looking at the opposite rail where the work will occur.

For the ten-and-unders, we must avoid asking for anything beyond a simple walk-trot and/or canter down the rail. Halt, reverse, and return to the lineup. Any version of any or all of the three gaits is up to the judge and really seldom needs to occur in ten-and-unders. However, if you have a group of top riders who you feel can handle this rail work, you will make many friends by allowing these youngsters to experience the thrill of a workout. At this level, the ability to execute the gaits called for with proper diagonals and leads, plus the rudimentary aids in instituting the gaits, halting, and reversing, are really all we should expect.

For the next age group (11–13) the options are more varied. However, if we stick to the letter of the law, then our choices are quite limited, adding only Test 4 (Performance Around the Ring), which quite obviously does not fit a straight line on the rail, Test 5 to disengage and engage feet in stirrups, and then the sixth and seventh tests, which complete the allowed tests for the eleven-to-thirteen riders—those of figure eights at trot and canter—again, nothing that qualifies as work on the rail. This then is a gray area and I will not bore you with Tests 8, 9, 10, 11, and 12, which are also not applicable with the exception of 10, Ride Without Stirrups.

This rail work is pretty much dealer's choice and a good judge will analyze his riders and select work that is demanding mainly in expecting total perfection of execution. These riders should be perfect—coming up on the original diagonal, using body as well as hands and voice for flat stops parallel to the rail, consistent speed, which is attained by aggression going away from the starting point, and sensitive restraint on the return. Again, we are back at square one, which is our quest for perfection . . . the quality of the work or pattern is of prime importance.

Now, right here, I would like to attempt to clear up once and for all the ongoing confusion regarding changes of diagonals at a specified stride.

We all agree that the stride is counted from the first time the rider's seat hits the saddle at the full stride (as opposed to sitting the trot prior to starting to post)—that first stride is "one." For example, let us say we are going to change diagonals every three strides. The rider starts posting and each time his seat hits the saddle that is one stride. Therefore, the count would be one, two, three-three, one, two, three-three. Changing every four would be one, two, three, four-four. You see, counting strides is just like birthdays . . . we are not one year old on the day of birth, we are one year old at the end of the first year. We have posted our stride when the diagonal front foot we are moving with strikes the ground. To judge the changes is easy. Merely keep in mind the number of strides you have called for and count with the rider. The diagonal change (the repeat count) is not a stride, it is a half count that puts the rider on the opposite diagonal. The posting count resumes immediately after the double count. Again, the illustration—one, two, three, four-four . . . one, two, three, four-four. I believe that the specified change should be clarified and spelled out in the rule books to forever clear up this obvious state of confusion.

Another movement that is frequently called for is the individual circle. Nowhere in the rules is there an allusion to single circles—so we have carte blanche here, too. Any time a circle is called for that originates on the rail, the judge must be very alert and mentally mark the exact point of origin so that he can assess the perfection of the pattern. Anyone can turn around and continue on down the rail—what we, as judges, expect to see is a completely round circle whose size is commensurate with the strides of the horse. This circle is centered— that is, one half of the circle is ahead of the point of origin and the final half is of the exact same size and comes in behind the departure point. This can only be accomplished when the rider has firm control on both sides of the horse's mouth and can deal smoothly with varying moments of the horse's compliance or resistance as the rider circles.

Major faults are erratic speed, breaking gait, failure to use the aids (especially the inside leg), and letting the rail turn the horse. Any one of these faults will result in an imperfect circle. So you must see that the circle, like any other maneuver, is a demonstration of rider mentality as well as physicality—and that is important.

PERFORMANCE AROUND THE RING—TEST ⅜4

Here we reach the final test that may be required of the ten-and-under riders. And here we have a wide-open opportunity to see just how much our so-called baby riders can do with a horse. I think it is a living tribute to Saddle Seat Equitation, and the tremendous strides it has made, when we see the level of training and ability demonstrated by these youngsters. As the AHSA Rule Book states in the subheading, tests may be performed individually or collectively. Obviously this is the first of the tests that permits recalling to the rail your selection of a group of riders to compete again with their peers. It permits a closer comparative look at your top riders. This being so, I would like to suggest that in an eight-place class, if you choose four riders to go back to the rail, then try to tie your fifth, sixth, seventh, eighth, and reserve numbers before you send the four out. This will speed your judging and almost totally reduce any margin for error in listing numbers on your judge's card. With this done, your mind is totally free to evaluate your workout.

Forcefulness, technical correctness, style and balance, ring generalship—these are the points to consider. Be wary of confusing speed with animation, or excessive cutting of the ring with showmanship. Look at every rider. We have all seen the sharpest rider, who kept entirely to himself, get overlooked. Make sure if you send four riders out that you look at four riders. Faults to look for are:

Failure to Get the Horse out of the Lineup and on the Rail to Work
Freezing Up Under Pressure and Riding Only the Tack, Not the Horse

With horses lined up in the middle, we can test the rider's ability to cope with the horse's natural desire to rejoin the lineup. Be your own person, do not let your judgment be influenced by the crowd's natural love affair with the tiniest rider out there. If he or she is the best, then that child should win, size notwithstanding, but do not give in to any unjustified desire to be a popular judge. You are there as a fair, qualified adjudicator, not a person out to win a popularity contest.

Everything that has just been said regarding the test around the ring for the ten-and-unders applies to the older age groups, but you can go steps further in asking for reverse and canter, for instance. Reverse and canter, not reverse, walk, and then canter. The canter must originate in the final segment of the turn.

Halting and walking may also be interjected into your commands. However, the most deserved popular work around the rail is simply at the walk, trot, and canter where pure horsemanship and talented judging meet.

Be careful that you do not ask for riding without stirrups in any under-fourteen age group. That is allowable only in the fourteen-to-seventeen, or specialty or championship classes, of course where the classification is seventeen-and-under. Try to be thorough enough to recognize top performances from horses of varying levels of ability. Here we are again at the horse-trainer-oriented judge, but to be fair and keep our judging zeroed in on the rider and not the horse, then we must credit maximum results of the rider's ability, not maximum performance of the horse. Only in this way will we, as judges, be able to truly demonstrate the meaning of the sentence "Only the rider shall be judged, not the horse." If you know enough to recognize the good rider who can ride a mediocre horse to be better than anyone ever thought he could be, then truly you will be judging equitation at its highest level, and you will be the judge that our thousands of dedicated and talented riders deserve.

FEET DISENGAGED FROM STIRRUPS. FEET ENGAGED— TEST #5

I believe that this test originated as an outgrowth of the ongoing, perennial discussion regarding riding without stirrups. To answer the proposition that practice in riding without stirrups is necessary to keep from falling off should a rider lose a stirrup, the obvious outgrowth was Test #5, in which a stirrup (or stirrups) is lost and then retrieved. It is a new test and is being tried with open minds and mixed reactions. At the standstill, it can only be recognized as a test of two things—can the rider get his feet back in the stirrups and, most importantly, does the rider recognize when his feet are in the stirrups

properly, that is, with stirrups and leather turned from front to back?
This is very easy to judge as riders who go between the stirrup and
the horse with the toe are going to be wrong and those who enter the
stirrup from the outside are going to be right.

When we get to the test in motion at the trot (I have never seen it
called at the canter, but it could be, I suppose), this is an entirely
different ball game. Look at your riders. Do you think you are maintaining equality of opportunity when a stirrup hangs one or two
inches below the width of the horse's belly? This stirrup is rather im-
mobile and yet far enough below the width of the horse to hang just
free enough to remain at right angles to the horse, giving that fortunately built rider easy access to this stirrup. Now let us consider the
5' 10" rider whose stirrups hang down five to eight inches longer and
by their very length are a definite moving target, even on a very
smooth-moving horse.

I am not here to advocate or criticize any workout. But you, as
judge, should consider variations such as I have described. Then it is
up to you whether you use such a test; but if you do, then you should
be aware of the built-in inequities of some tests and make proper al-
lowances for those differences.

Test 5 was changed at the 1981 convention of the AHSA to read:
"Feet disengaged from the stirrups. Feet engaged. To be done at the
lineup, only." This change was made for the 1981 season as it was determined that the original wording was in error in not including the
restriction to the lineup.

FIGURE EIGHT AT TROT—TEST #6

Figure eight at trot, demonstrating change of diagonals. Unless
specified, it may be started either facing the center or away from the
center. If started facing the center it must be commenced from a halt. At
left diagonal, rider should be sitting the saddle when left front leg is on
the ground: At right diagonal, rider should be sitting saddle when right
front leg is on the ground. When circling clockwise, rider should be on
left diagonal, when circling counter-clockwise rider should be on right diagonal.

Figure eights are also very useful and revealing workouts. Almost
any green-to-equitation show horse can do a figure eight, even at the
canter, so we judges should be most demanding of the rider's entire
ride, not just a demonstration of two "somewhat" circles at the correct
diagonals. The diagonals are the easiest part of this work and should
almost be taken for granted—for this reason, an incorrect diagonal is
purely and simply a careless mistake for which there is no forgiveness

and it should be treated severely. What we as judges are looking for is the purity of pattern and, to me, the most important part of all—the approach to the figure eight. A good judge can tell you halfway down the approach whether the rider is going to have a successful eight. The sluggish horse must be aggressively set up so that the rider holds the horse's attention and keeps him responsive throughout the figure. The anxious horse must be ridden with quiet control, to allay his fears and make him likewise responsive. If the start of the eight is not designated, you will see some riders trot right into the eight. Others may walk into it and others may stop and park. Any one of these interpretations is good if it is executed perfectly. Therefore, when you graph your score sheet, do begin with a space for approach and mark up or down the obvious psychology that each rider uses to set up a good eight on his particular horse. Needless to say, the circles should be round, preferably free from the rail, but never under any circumstance influenced by the rail. The horse should maintain perfect balance and consistent speed throughout, and the halt should be exactly on the point of departure at an exact right angle to the facing rail or center line. Only by the subtle use of all aids, hands and legs, voice and body weight, can a perfect eight be accomplished. It is permissible for the rider to look for the intersection if, in looking, he is able to maintain perfect balance in the saddle and not interfere with the aids. I do not think that any of us like riders who are so afraid to risk a mistake that they turn into automata . . . glassy, staring eyes and every muscle a captive. Ann LaMonte had a saying years ago for such kids: she called them "constipated riders" and I still think of it whenever I see one.

Now on your score sheet leave a place for return to lineup. This is the frosting on the cake and can demonstrate great skill in heading back to the lineup on the designated gait (generally a trot), showing great flair but not overriding or dogging along under the false assumption that the judging is over.

FIGURE EIGHT AT CANTER—TEST #7

Figure eight at canter on correct lead demonstrating simple change of lead. (This is a change whereby the horse is brought back into a walk and restarted into a canter on the opposite lead.) Unless specified, it may be started either facing the center or away from the center. If started facing the center it must be commenced from a halt. Figures commenced in center of two circles so that one lead change is shown.

Almost without exception, everything that has been said about the figure eight at the trot applies to the figure eight at the canter. Do remember that eights originating facing the center must begin from the halt at both gaits.

I suppose anything that gets results is admissible to a degree, but proper use of leg aids has to be rewarded. Since horses respond to pressure by leaning into it, not away from it, the inside leg aid not only wraps the horse around the circle but encourages the horse to make the full circle on the proper lead without switching. Of doubtful value is the kicking outside leg to try to hold the pattern and keep the horse cantering. More often than not this awkward flailing of the rider's legs will result in a cross-canter.

If the horse is running out of gas, then a rhythmic tap with the whip can keep him going and the inside leg pressure will get the circle completed. A smooth stop and immediate progression into the next lead is generally in rhythm, giving a stop for the horse to change leads. Either direction, unless designated otherwise, is permissible. What is not to be rewarded is the rider who institutes aids for the left lead, mistakenly gets the right lead, and circles right. You, as a judge, should not be taken in by this, even though the audience probably will. Again, be of stout heart and judge what you know is correct.

SERPENTINE AT TROT AND/OR CANTER—TEST #8

Execute serpentine at a trot and/or canter on correct lead demonstrating simple change of lead. A series of left and right half circles off-center of imaginary line where correct diagonal or lead must be shown.

The serpentine is one of the most popular tests, and rightly so. It encapsulates in one maneuver just about every element of normal horse control, and it is a workout that depends very greatly on the rider's ability to guide. I only wish that trot serpentines were included in the ten-and-under tests. At the 1981 UPHA Convention and the AHSA Convention it was unanimously agreed to include the serpentine trot as one of the individual tests for riders under 11 years.

This is a pure test of control and should be judged as such. It may be a surprise to some of you who are not active equitation instructors to hear that many riders, even successful regional winners, truly cannot guide a horse. The rider may look like a dream of perfection on the rail, where friend horse is playing follow the leader, but when we ask for the serpentine at the trot, the rider is forced to demonstrate control. Right here, I would like to define control. It is not merely negative—that is, the ability to restrain the horse, keep him from running off or cantering too fast, and other extreme behavior faults. Rather, control is the always-with-us need to see the rider anticipate and therefore handle the horse at a logical pattern, to force when necessary, to restrain when necessary.

At the serpentine with the lineup at the end of the ring, the horse's natural inclination is to turn back towards the group at every crossing of the imaginary line. This can result in a bad pattern. Instead of the required half circle, which is exactly what it should be, the half circles turn into what we call paper clips and the horse trots several steps on a straight line across the imaginary long line, turns around, and does the same thing in the other direction. There are no straight lines in the serpentine, and such a performance indicates that the rider is mentally behind the horse instead of preceding the horse. This is a series of corrections, not directions. Such patterns, even though they may be consistent and fulfill the required number of line crossings and diagonal changes, have not demonstrated understanding of a horse's mind or control of his body.

If you are comfortable with drawings or diagrams, it is very easy to draw the exact pattern the rider executes and this will give you a quick résumé before you mark your card by telling you all you need to remember about every rider. You will have an actual picture of each ride. Look for snug but comfortable rein pressure, use of the inside leg aid to help the horse literally bend his body around the arc, perfection of pattern. There we have the whole hub of the workout . . . diagonals count, of course, because the horse is changing directions and the proper diagonal is not only required but physically aids the horse in making his turns rhythmic. But control is everything.

Now on the return serpentine we must keep in mind all of the elements of control we have just evaluated, but add to them the positive control of keeping the pattern the full half circle and a consistent rate of speed. Whereas the horse wanted to turn back at every crossing going down, on the return he will want to rush back to the group on the shortest line possible and resist making the full half circles. It delights me to see a smart rider on a hot horse know enough to set up extreme control of the horse and position that horse's head so that he will not jump off his feet or lose his rhythm at every direction change, because that is exactly what that horse will want to do.

Keep your eye on the rider at every phase; these workouts go fast and if you make notes about diagonals you can very easily miss a mistake that should lose a class or a great demonstration of brainy control that could win it.

One of the most frequent and frustrating judging errors we see—and to be avoided at all costs—is a workout that does not fit the ring.

As the judge, make certain that you know whether the judges' stand will be in or out of the ring. If it is permanent and large, then obviously the area in which to work will be long and narrow. It should be evident that a three- or four-segment serpentine will not go from one end of the ring to the other. It cannot fit. There will have to be more elements to go the full distance since the half circles will be small. You must be logical and study the ring very carefully to avoid asking riders to compromise a pattern to fit an illogical working area.

Consider the use of aids. You should be able to evaluate the necessity for aids. They are exactly what the word means . . . help in attaining control. Aids are the most obvious and most necessary, certainly. But hands alone tend to control only the front half of the horse; since the motor is in the rear, body and leg controls assume extreme importance. Do not hunt for "obvious" aids because the temperament of the horse will dictate the strength or even minimal use of legs in particular. Whereas a sluggish horse may require strong leg pressures, a nervous horse will provide his own impetus and an overt leg aid could blow his mind. Think about aids studiously so that you will be instantly aware of their logical application. The old dictum, "Where the horse's head goes, the body is sure to follow," is not equitation.

Voice commands are great aids, especially in halts, stops, transitions of gaits. They should be subtle, and intercommunication between horse and rider. Many people are not sure that voice aids are legal. Of course they are but, like anything else, they should be subtle, workable, and logical. Clucking and use of the whip are also aids and should get results. We have all judged riders who were so afraid to move that we would have bought the horse just for the privilege of hitting him when he needed it. Constant clucking like a lonesome cricket is meaningless and can be distracting. Pecking at a horse with the whip is a demonstration of futility. If use of whip is necessary, then credit it and mark down the rider who fails to use it.

Most of the foregoing about serpentines at the trot obviously applies to the serpentine at the canter. Add the importance of the outside leg aid to set up the canter (if the horse is of the proper temperament to require it) and you will have the analysis of a good canter serpentine well in mind. Again, do consider your lineup and try to place it where there will be the very least distraction for the individual rider. A good tactic is to ask the rider to halt at the end of the work and address the judge. This will give you time to make a conclusive note, if necessary, and it will keep the next rider from jumping the gun and possibly interfering with the performing rider.

You may also ask the rider to park out, but be sure that all horses are of the breeds that park out if you do this.

In all probability, the canter serpentine away from the start is the

easiest test for the judge to evaluate and for the spectators to understand and yet it is demanding enough to make it extremely worth
while for the contestant. If you have an open ring and choose to work
the horses on a straight line down the center, it is best to line up your
riders at the end of the ring. This applies to all serpentines. In this
way, we will not have a double magnet for the horses . . . the drawing power of the horses lined up on the left rail, for instance, which
will surely draw the horses off the pattern when setting up the right
lead. It is not the province of a judge to deliberately build in booby
traps—there are enough of them in an excellent workout to test the
riders. If you are judging Finals classes, or even championships, and it
is feasible to do, excusing all riders prior to the work and letting them
ride in the empty ring individually has to be the fairest setup of all.
Even this is not foolproof. I recall the Medal Finals in the old ring at
the Royal. My rider was waiting to enter next and the entire Canadian
Mounted Police Team, bits jangling and thirty-six flags flying, passed
in formation ten feet behind my rider. Needless to say, it was all
downhill from there . . . full speed ahead.

As at the trot, rhythm at the canter serpentine has to attain considerable importance. Once the first lead is begun, the halt and change
should be as nearly rhythmic as possible—that is, canter, change
canter—not canter, chaaaaange, canter. If, however, a rider has a
horse who is obviously aggressive or nervous, this rider who can get
his leads and patterns with a rhythm suited to the temperament of his
mount should never be counted down. Again we come back to the
point that it is the rider who is being judged, not the horse.

We cannot allow moving off course or false starts, but the matter of
timing a canter departure to ensure success from a difficult horse must
be rewarded, not penalized. Ask yourself two questions: Is this a perfect pattern? and Would this rider make a horse trainer in the future?
You will know what to do. We are looking for perfection, but we
must never overlook extraordinary talent and horse handling.

CHANGE LEADS DOWN CENTER OF RING—Test #9

Change leads down center of ring or on the rail demonstrating simple
change of lead. Judge to specify exact lead changes to be executed as
well as to specify the beginning lead.

This is one of the easiest tests to judge and one of the more difficult
to do. So much of the success of the lead change demands extreme
control. The judge should be keenly observant in order to evaluate
every nuance of what goes into the entire performance.

A top performance demands an absolutely straight line. In order for this to happen, a horse must stop quickly, comfortably, in a state of relaxation, and walk one step into the change. The proportions should be equal—for instance, the direction to begin with the left lead and execute two changes would mean that the ring is divided into thirds. The most foolproof way to explain and keep your own understanding straight is to say, for example: "Begin with the left lead and then make three changes of lead." This would mean left, right, left, right. This is an alternating change. When alternating, it is trot, canter, trot, canter, or the reverse—canter, trot, canter, trot.

For several years I have used the word "sandwich." Perhaps you can think of a better word, but it is descriptive. The examples are trot, canter, canter, trot; or canter, trot, trot, canter. This is to give a quick recognition of the test and also to keep a judge from referring to such a change as alternating, which it certainly is not. This same designation may also be used at the figure eight.

I was not aware until I had written this discussion that this Test 9 referred only to canter changes on the center line. Nowhere is there a reference to trotting with diagonal changes on the center line. Perhaps this should be added, with the same specifics for diagonals as are spelled out for leads.

When changing leads on the rail, extreme tact must be demonstrated to halt the horse either perfectly parallel to the rail or with influence to the rear towards the rail in order to set up the change. To be credited is the rider who can maintain a straight course. To be severely penalized is the rider who uses too much hand and turns the horse's head towards the center of the ring with the resulting mistake of bowing off the rail or, even worse, cantering diagonally into the middle. The skill here is for the rider to influence the neck and body parallel to the rail. Again, hands and timing are the two factors to look for.

I think that the sandwich change is a very good test as it somewhat rules out the extra-smart horse that will take a "do nothing" rider through a series of canter changes. A horse will not make the transitions to the different gaits on his own. However, in your instructions, please be sure to mark stops where you want them. Obviously, from the trot to the canter we must have a stop. From the canter to the trot one may ask for either a halt before the trot, or no halt, with the rider getting a direct transition from the canter into the trot. This is a good demanding test, testing the rider's ability not only to stay on the line, but to get a trot when the horse's natural inclination is to switch back into another canter change.

In a sandwich straight-line change we can get almost every element of control . . . the immediate departure on a specified diagonal, a halt, canter on a specified lead, halt and change leads, and finally a direct transition to a specified diagonal at the trot. We have in one package the skills of a standing start, a stop on the line, a direct departure, a change of lead, and a transition from canter to trot . . . all on specified leads and diagonals. If a rider can do this and add a return on a serpentine, the judge has seen about every control that can be demonstrated by a rider.

RIDE WITHOUT STIRRUPS—TEST ☆10

Ride without stirrups for a brief period of time. No more than one minute at the trotting phase.

We have here a very controversial test, and if it is fair to say that a test can be used as crutch by an indecisive judge, then this is the culprit. A good, conscientious judge will care enough about equitation to have actually ridden, or attempted to ride, every test that he will call for. I am not being facetious . . . I truly feel that in order to evaluate a workout one must have experienced it to understand enough to judge it.

You will find, everything else being equal (and it never is), that if you call for riding without stirrups it should be with a small group so that you can view all riders at the same time. If not, then the rider just advancing to the judge and passing while still fresh and not tired will look fine. Pity the poor rider who has just passed the judge and will have ridden five hundred feet before being judged. There is nothing fair about this. It has nothing to do with horse handling, and I cannot believe that any judge would want to ask for a workout that is not fair.

The only way for a rider to post well without stirrups is to have the horse trot strongly so that the boost of the saddle and the lesser posting time in the air will make posting without stirrups possible, as it must be a combined movement of horse and rider. Heels must be down and the shin bone vertical, even slightly forward, but never clutching back. This will put the rider too far forward in the saddle and consequently lose the lifting motion of the horse's hocks.

If you are going to use this test, then you must be able to analyze each rider's build, weight, and length of leg (especially the thigh) and then make your decision. It may be argued that the same proportions work for or against a rider at any time, but the intelligent use of stirrups makes good riding possible for everyone and the lack of stirrups takes away this opportunity for some.

I do believe that teachers' objections to this test, based on variances in the horses' gaits, are not well founded. After all, we do know the test is there and suitability of mount is not the responsibility of the judge.

Short riders, especially short-legged riders whose knees hang naturally on the top half of the horse's back, should post very well without stirrups. They actually fit the test and the hanging stirrups are not low enough to bang into the horse and disrupt his performance. But do consider that the tall riders do not have any of these advantages. If a rider asks to cross the leathers over the pommel, I think he should be allowed to do so and that one should never suspect the rider of a bid for extra attention or credit. This is a very legitimate request.

I had a young rider at the Arabian Nationals who came to the farm and he asked if such a request was permissible. In his case, the stirrups actually flew forward and repeatedly hit the horse in the breast and shoulders.

In this test there are more do's and don'ts for the judge than for the riders.

1. Consider, after having tried the test yourself, whether you really want to use it.
2. Do not fail to realize that riders' builds have a great deal to do with this skill, and modify your analyses accordingly.
3. Try to observe all riders at the same time. Exhausted muscles should not be any part of your decision.
4. One "do" I have to mention. You will be smart to step behind your riders. I did not see it, but everyone on the grandstand side at a big show one year saw a championship won with riding without stirrup . . . singular.

DEMONSTRATION RIDE—TEST #11

Demonstration ride of approximately one minute on own mount. Movements must be selected from Tests 1–9 above. Rider must advise judge beforehand what ride he plans to demonstrate. To be used only in Championship and/or Medal classes. Riders must have with them two copies (one for judge and one for announcer) of a written one minute work-out, in case the judge asks for this test. The test must be stopped at the end of one minute but the rider will not be penalized for not completing it.

First of all, I think that everyone should know why this test originated. We AHSA Equitation Committee members wanted to get rid of a very impractical test that called for selected riders to ride a horse supplied by the show committee. It did not work because the rider following a bad rider was unfairly penalized in inheriting an annoyed, if not downright infuriated, horse.

Also, we must all remember that these rules cover the entire country. In many areas we have a mixture of breeds for mounts. For that reason, we devised the one-minute test to help equalize the class in which we had Morgans and Arabians as well as Saddle horses.

Since I dreamed this one up, I feel very free to criticize the test.

Number one . . . you have to be a very quick learner to be able to judge a workout that you have rapidly scanned in a few seconds.

Secondly . . . this is not a good test unless you have the variety of various types of mounts to justify it.

There are several other aspects that show this to be a bad test, except in the situation just mentioned. I called for the test at the Syracuse Morgan Show last fall and was dumfounded when the steward came to me after the class and said I had tied a rider who had done an illegal part in her workout. Since I always believe stewards, I thought fast and said it would not have affected the outcome under any circumstances. The alleged infraction was Test 10, Riding Without Stirrups. When I got back to my rule book, I saw where it said Tests 1–9. The 1980 rules say Tests 1–10. What had happened was that the numbers of the tests had been changed that year and it was not intended to keep riding without stirrups out, only to exclude the final test, change of horse.

As a judge it was my duty to really know those rules—which I thought I did—but it was a lesson to study the rules, mistakes and all. As Joan Farris always said, "If you can't be good, be technical."

EXCHANGE OF HORSES—TEST ⚹12

Exchange horses, no more than the top six contestants. Saddle may be exchanged. However, should one horse be too large or small to accept this exchange and no horse (among the six) can be found with which to exchange, then no saddles will be exchanged. Riders must have two minutes to be accustomed to the new mount before judging resumes. The attendant for each horse being exchanged must be allowed in the ring.

Well, here we are . . . we could talk a full hour about this test. The pros and the cons—both have validity. Let us address ourselves to the intended use of this test. It was written to mean that rider A and rider B exchange horses. The judging is based *only* on the way rider B rode A's horse as compared to the way rider A had ridden him, and vice versa. That is the only way that quality of horse does not enter the picture. For years, trainers have screamed that their customers were buying good horses, only to be bested by them on an exchange. For years, instructors have argued back that this does not happen because the judging is based on comparison of how both riders rode two horses, not as a new class where the rider lucky enough to trade to the better horse had an insurmountable advantage.

Now, I was invited to speak by the AHSA committee today on all these workouts, so I feel that a discussion has to precede the judging techniques. Our basic idea was right—a simple comparative change. What I am finally having to admit after holding out for many years is this sad fact—the test is all right, but we do not have enough judges analytical enough to understand it and judge it.

Now, with this new version, we are in real trouble and like the song in *Music Man,* "I mean trouble with a capital T"! Let us dissect the new rule, sentence by sentence: The first sentence is fine: "Exchange horses, no more than the top six contestants." This was limited as it was felt that it was almost impossible for a judge to compare (and I emphasize compare) a larger number. I had always felt that the changes were deliberate between first and second, third and fourth, up to fifth and sixth. Only once in all these years have I seen other switches that were fair to all.

Now comes the most incredible thing ever put in the rule book: "Saddle may be exchanged. However, should one horse be too large or too small to accept this exchange and no horse (among the six) can be found with which to exchange, then no saddles will be exchanged"! Right there we have canceled the whole idea of the test— *comparison*—and have opened a can of worms that evokes situations that Johnny Carson couldn't even dream up. I have a feeling that Warlock or Missy's Flying Genius would strangely wind up being the only horses to fit all six saddles (it does not have to be six, that is just the maximum). The judge is supposed to designate with whom each rider exchanges (that is what the "E-X" means on the front of the word). If a judge calls for more than two riders to get off of a horse and change to potluck, this is change of horse and can only be construed as a six-way tie for first. That judge is already in trouble, and trying to arrive at a justifiable conclusion by exchanging horses is only going to confound his difficulty.

Now we come to another addition: "Riders must have two minutes to be accustomed to the new mount before judging resumes," and the final sentence, "The attendant for each horse being exchanged must be allowed in the ring."

We may already have had a saddling contest. Now the dust has barely settled and for two minutes the audience (who will need a road map by this time) will be treated to a very exciting equitation lesson. Two minutes is a long time and there are not two, four, or six instructors living who can keep quiet for two minutes, myself included.

Now I am certainly not an attorney, but you could graduate at the bottom of the law school class and know that the last two sentences of the test are gilt-edged invitations to sue the judge for liability. "Riders must have two minutes to practice." Why? It is dangerous to ride a strange horse. "Attendants must be allowed in the ring." Why? Because it is dangerous. Now I have never felt that selective exchanges by very competent judges are dangerous and I have loved to call for this test and the riders like it when it is properly done. But the sad truth of the matter now stands, and those trainers who said it was unfair are right under the present rule. Those folks who said it was dangerous have just had their fears put in writing and those judges who have feared that they would be liable in case of accident . . . move over, here comes "Chicken Little." Test 12 was widely discussed at the UPHA convention and the following revisions were unanimously adopted for presentation to the AHSA, at which meeting the AHSA also agreed to the revision. However, under the rules no changes could be made before the expiration of the then current rule book, which covered 1981.

The revisions: "Saddles and / or stirrups may be exchanged at the discretion of the rider and / or trainer." The two-minute trial after change was deleted and the attendants were limited to two per horse and allowed in the ring only during the actual exchange.

In summation, I can only voice what every rider, instructor, parent, and lover of horses and children feels. Any judging is an honor and an obligation, but you judges must search your souls and answer the obvious questions: Am I qualified? Do I know as much as or more than the riders I am judging? Or have I applied for my card not through competence but to assure myself of judging jobs? For the sake of everyone here I hope all of your reasons for wanting to judge equitation are right.

23

AHSA *Medal*

While there are a few worth-while horse shows in the country that are not affiliated members, most of our better shows belong to the American Horse Shows Association. Any rider who wishes to understand the class requirements of a recognized member show should join the Association and carefully study the rule book. This may be done by applying at the following address:

American Horse Shows Association, Inc.
598 Madison Avenue
New York, New York 10022

If you intend entering the Medal classes, membership is mandatory and you will be wise to apply early, as shows are required to demand proof of membership for the Medal classes. Apply in January and keep your card at hand so that you may list your membership number on the entry blanks when entering the Medal. The Medal class sponsored by the AHSA may be held at any Association show that requests permission from the home office and offers three additional classes under AHSA rules suitable for those competitors who are eligible to compete in the Medal. These classes do not have to be equitation classes. There is no prescribed workout for Medal classes.

Medal-class winners become eligible to ride in the Medal Final, which is currently held at the American Royal Horse Show in Kansas City late in the fall. In both the preliminary classes and the Final, judges may call for any of the rule book "Tests From Which Judges Must Choose." The number of Medal-class wins to qualify for the Final changes occasionally. For this reason, it is always wise to read the rule book each year so that you may plan your schedule early. This flexibility is a good thing, as it is felt that the number of riders in the Final should represent the cream of the crop, so to speak, and yet the qualifications should not be so many that there are not enough classes open to riders who deserve the chance to be in the Finals. Back in 1959, when Joan Hill and I judged both the Medal and "Good

Hands" Finals at Madison Square Garden, there were seventy-five riders competing. Many of them were not of championship caliber. Since all officials felt that the Finals should contain only the best, it was decided at that time to increase the number of wins to qualify. This did result in fewer riders and more quality, and disposed of those riders who made the Finals only because all the good riders had already qualified and the remaining classes at the very end of the season were up for grabs. In the past few years, since the Medal Finals have been moved to the Midwest and the cost of showing horses has continued to rise, the qualification has been reduced to one again. It will probably continue to remain that way unless the number of finalists again becomes unwieldy.

Since both Finals are in the fall, after school has resumed, the horses and riders will have let up a bit from the strenuous regimen of shows during the summer months. We must consider this fact—in the Finals, figure work is extremely important and the horse should be at his most dependable and responsive best. Therefore, the training of the horse takes on special overtones, as the rider may not be able to practice as much as usual. The teacher, thus, takes over more of the training, and he should be very concerned with the soundness and the mental attitude of the horse. We generally find that we have from a month to six weeks between our last summer show and the Medal Finals at the American Royal. For two or three weeks, depending on the individual horse, we let the horse down a bit. Jogging is the order of the day. It freshens the horse, relieves him of the tedium of routine, and is probably therapeutically advisable, as most horses show the wear of a heavy show season. Once or twice a week is plenty for the rider to practice during this time. He will be busy in school the first few weeks and, too, the rider often needs a little rest to refresh for the big test ahead. This is a time to know your rider, and the teacher certainly should understand the motivation of each rider by now, so plan your practice sessions individually and almost from day to day or week to week. Overrule any sweeping, last-minute changes, and while it is only smart to know as much as possible about the judging habits of your Final judge, do not change any of your basic teaching to suit some reported foibles of the judges. Riding in the Final is a bit like getting married. If you were good enough to get there in the first place, don't change the pattern now.

Two judges are selected by the members of the AHSA Equitation Committee to officiate at the Medal Final. Whenever possible, the riders should enter the open classes to get a feeling of the show and the physical setup there. The warm-up area is woefully inadequate, and the horse should be prepared for the morning preliminary with this in mind. There is some working space outside but the footing is very bad and, in case of rain, very muddy.

Clothes should be checked before you go. Many a rider has outgrown habits during the summer. Being properly attired is a must—especially for those seventeen-year-olds. For them, there is no tomorrow. Have two good habits, or one good valet!

Arrange to arrive at the show at least one hour ahead. Plan on even more time if you make the final ride-off in the afternoon. In the past, there have been monumental traffic jams, and one frantic, two-block run was all it took to convince me of the need to be early.

It has become customary to have the contestants ride as a group on the rail, select some of the group (or groups) to return, and then perform an individual workout. The individual work is done very fairly, as the riders enter the ring one at a time. From twelve to sixteen riders are chosen to return for the ride-off in the afternoon. This group enters the ring together and works the three gaits both ways of the ring, and then each one is individually tested. Such a procedure is eminently fair, as all riders have identical ring conditions in which to work. At the 1968 afternoon Final, the contestants were lined up on one side of the ring and faced out, being cautioned to look ahead and not observe the preceding riders' work. Since there were over a dozen riders, those last in line were at a real disadvantage, as their horses had to stand absolutely motionless for a long period of time. It is best to have identical conditions for every contestant.

24

NHS Saddle Seat Event—the "Good Hands"

The National Horse Show Saddle Seat Event is "For Junior riders who have not reached their eighteenth birthday. To be judged as a group at a walk, trot, and canter. A minimum of four riders are required to individually execute a figure 8 at the canter, trot back to the judge, stop, and back." (One should know that the age of the rider is determined by the rider's age as of December 1 and will remain that same age for the entire show year.)

This test, unlike the judge's choice of tests in the Medal, is always the same and is printed annually in the AHSA Rule Book, as well as appearing in its entirety in the show premium list. The "Good Hands" differs from the Medal in another respect, in that it is sponsored by the National Horse Show Association, not the AHSA, and consequently, the Final is always held at the National Horse Show—a constant fixture at Madison Square Garden in New York City. To be eligible to compete in the Final, the contestant must have won two firsts in this event at recognized shows in Zones 1 and 2, or one first at a recognized show in Zones 3 to 10. Just as the qualifying classes over the country always specify the above-noted workout, so is this workout held for every final rider in the morning elimination ride at the Garden.

Let us analyze the working of the workout and clear up any misapprehensions over the content. Canter a figure eight. About all the latitude the judge may be permitted here is to specify in which direction the eight must be started. Unless specified, the rider is left to his own interpretation. The trot to the judge indicates a direct line from the finish of the eight to the judge. The rider should be particularly careful of the angle of the feet, as this one factor is very apparent during this head-on approach. The halt should be planned and practiced so that the horse can be counted upon to stop and stand quietly. If the horse is not parked out, there is no necessity for moving forward to step out of the parked position. In case the horse has been parked out, then the rider should move forward the step. However, even though the park is not called for, it has become a popular option.

As stated before, the morning ride-off for all qualifiers is held on the weekend at Madison Square Garden. Unlike the preliminaries, in which only four contestants are required to be individually tested, all riders do the prescribed workout after the class has worked on the rail and has been lined up. Then, upon completion of this work, the horses are returned to the stables, and the agonizing wait for "the list" begins. In the old Garden, this list was always posted on a certain wall that early gained the sobriquet "The Wailing Wall."

In the afternoon class, when the selected finalists ride, the workouts are completely the choice of the judge (or judges, as the case may be). The New York audience is a very sophisticated and critical group, and the tension is tremendous. The rider should be prepared for this, and, whenever possible, it is wise to enter the horse and rider in a previous class at the show. Not that the spectators are rude or un-

The moment of truth: riders are lined up in the old Madison Square Garden, preparatory to the individual workout in the "Good Hands" Final. *Photo by Steve Bechtel*

sympathetic, but so many in attendance are very knowledgeable, and this critical—and appreciative—appraisal presents a real mental hazard to the riders.

The winning of the "Good Hands" is a memorable experience, from the red-carpet presentation ceremony, through the many photographers following back to the stable with the request for "Just one more picture, please," to the dizzying climb to the press box, where the Big City papers are ready to interview the breathless winner. It is a long way from that first lesson years before, but this crowning victory is worth every moment of the climb to the top. Because—as Charlie Brown replied when Linus said, "Winning isn't everything"— "That's true, but losing isn't *anything*."

25

UPHA *Challenge Cup Equitation*

In 1967 a group of dedicated professional horsemen and horsewomen founded a group to be known as the United Professional Horsemen's Association. Since there was no regulatory organization other than the American Horse Shows Association, it is obvious by the very name that this new organization was founded with the main purpose of bettering the horse business for the professional and the owners that he represented. One of the primary verities that was apparent to all trainers was the fact that much of the continuing success of the show horse industry depended upon the juvenile riders. Emphasis upon equitation was automatic.

In setting up a specific equitation class that would be distinctive and simply not another type of Medal class, the UPHA Challenge Cup competitions were originated in 1972. The defining feature of these classes was that 60% for rail work and 40% for workouts was the judging basis. In evolving such a class, we felt that we would not only have the distinction necessary but that the UPHA was the logical group to recognize that Finals judged so heavily on workouts could be a stifling influence on the real aim of equitation—the art of riding a horse.

Following are the specifications as determined after the 1981 Annual Convention:

Open to all Saddle Seat Equitation riders, 17 years of age and under, on any type of horse (mares and geldings only).

No minimum number of entries required.

Rider must qualify in the chapter in which he lives. Parent's legal voting residence to determine chapter. Horse may be stabled anywhere.

One win will qualify for the Final. The first four places will entitle a rider to ride in a Chapter Championship and the winner and reserve in a Chapter Championship will qualify for the Finals, also.

At the 1979 Annual Convention it was decided to offer a Junior Championship for riders 13 years of age or under. Such riders might ride in the Open National Championship, but they could not ride in both. Winners of the Junior Championship would be ineligible to ride again in the Junior Finals but would be eligible for the Open Finals.

Since the UPHA Challenge Class is rated as a "local" show, pleasure horses will be acceptable mounts.

The show must have two other equitation classes to be permitted to offer the UPHA Challenge Cup class.

In the qualifying classes and chapter championships, the top four riders must be worked individually, more at the judge's discretion.

Showmanship is paramount throughout the class.

In the National Finals, which have been held at The American Royal for several years, all qualifiers will ride in groups not to exceed 20, first on the rail and then execute an individual workout. A minimum number of 15 riders will be chosen for Phase 2, in which the same horse must be used.

No individual workouts will be permitted in Phase 2. However, selected riders may work again as a group on the rail. A champion and reserve champion in both Junior and National Finals shall be named with the next eight riders called in numerical order.

Needless to say, the UPHA classes have been great factors in encouraging riders in all chapters to compete. The chapter championships are of excellent caliber and the Finals competitors are the best in the country. The quality of riding has improved tremendously with the emphasis on the showing of the horse—confirming the wisdom of originating such a class.

While the UPHA Challenge Cup class may be offered at a non-recognized (by the AHSA) show, the age of riders follows the AHSA requirements, which changed in 1979 to read that the age of a rider would be determined on December 1 preceding the birth month instead of the previous date, January 1 in the year of birth.

As in almost any other class at a horse show, there has been laxity on the judges' part in studying the rules of this particular class. The fault obtains not only in this class but is a universal fault, but since the UPHA classes differ in emphasis it is most important that stricter control over the judges' preparation and qualification be observed.

Since the emphasis is on showmanship, some overanxious riders tend to override their horses and to cut the ring severely. Instructors must be on the lookout for such inclinations in the competitors because the competition is extreme and it is easy for all concerned to place too much stress on winning the Finals. There was a tendency at one time to ask incredibly long workouts of the riders, turning the Finals into more of a memory test than a riding test. Then the pendulum swung the other way and stunningly simple workouts were called that were not a true test of control (in the Junior Final). By the time this book is published, it is the author's hope that moderation will have prevailed and we can have individual workouts that test a rider's control and showmanship without becoming either too involved or too simple.

The fact that some of the children are showing and winning juvenile three-gaited classes with the horses that they are placing in the Challenge Cup Finals is proof that the UPHA classes have done what was planned for them to accomplish when they were started nine years ago.

26

AHSA Medal Final Winners 1958–1980

RIDER		INSTRUCTOR
Lynne Girdler	1958	Helen K. Crabtree
Brienne Jorgensen	1959	M. Robert Mannix
Mary Anne O'Callaghan	1960	Helen K. Crabtree
Gloria Green	1961	Joe Vanorio
Lindy Patrick	1962	Helen K. Crabtree
Randi Stuart	1963	Helen K. Crabtree
Julianne Schmutz	1964	Jim B. Robertson
Edward Lumia	1965	Helen K. Crabtree
Andrea Walton	1966	Helen K. Crabtree
Judy Fisher	1967	Marcella Lahr
Janet Henry	1968	Helen K. Crabtree
Barbara Hoffman	1969	Marion Brown
Julee Lampkin	1970	Harold Adams
Susie Maccari	1971	Dick Gray
Judy Maccari	1972	Dick Gray
Dana Lyon	1973	Helen K. Crabtree
Mary Lib De Nure	1974	Jan Lukens
Kate Williams	1975	Helen K. Crabtree
Virginia Cable	1976	Jim B. Robertson
Carol Reams	1977	Jim B. Robertson & Jimmy Robertson
Dabney Cubbage	1978	Jane Bennett
Ashley Tway	1979	Harold Adams
Janice Christensen	1980	Jane Bennett

27

NHS *"Good Hands" Final Winners 1958–1980*

RIDERS		INSTRUCTORS
Linda Frankel	1958	M. Robert Mannix & Jim B. Robertson
Jan Casler	1959	Maynard Casler
Victoria Reiter	1960	Richard Lavery, Sr.
Sarah Nutting	1961	Helen K. Crabtree
Nancy Ripa	1962	Joe Vanorio
Sue Ellen Marshall	1963	Jim B. Robertson
Randi Stuart	1964	Helen K. Crabtree
Edward Lumia	1965	Helen K. Crabtree
Judy Fisher	1966	Marcella Lahr
Andrea Walton	1967	Helen K. Crabtree
Jennifer Miller	1968	Helen K. Crabtree
Janet Henry	1969	Helen K. Crabtree
Susie Maccari	1970	Dick Gray
Judy Maccari	1971	Dick Gray
Mary Lib De Nure	1972	Jan Lukens
Dana Lyon	1973	Helen K. Crabtree
Linda Lowary	1974	Helen K. Crabtree
Kate Williams	1975	Helen K. Crabtree
Virginia Cable	1976	Jim B. Robertson
Carol Reams	1977	Jim B. Robertson & Jimmy Robertson
Mary Lou Gallagher	1978	Helen K. Crabtree & Redd Crabtree
Shauna Schoonmaker	1979	Helen K. Crabtree
Janice Christensen	1980	Jane Bennett

28

UPHA Challenge Cup Finals 1972–1980

RIDER		INSTRUCTOR
Judy Maccari	1972	Dick Gray
Sherrie Phelps	1973	Ruth Palmer
Mary Lib De Nure	1974	Jan Lukens
Elizabeth Finch	1975	Dorothy Dukes
Ann Swisher	1976	Helen K. Crabtree
Shauna Schoonmaker	1977	Helen K. Crabtree
Todd Buchanan	1978	Ann Judd
Diane Caldemeyer	1979	Lillian Shively
Janice Christensen	1980	Jane Bennett

UPHA CHALLENGE CUP JUNIOR FINALS 1979–1980

Kendy Almeida	1979	Debbie Wathen
Jama Hedden	1980	Lillian Shively

29
Finals Winners 1958–1980

Lynne Girdler, Louisville, Ky., won the AHSA Medal Final in 1958. At the same time, she was demonstrating the depth of her horsemanship by showing her World's Champion five-gaited pony, Everlasting Joy, to an undefeated season and by garnering another World's Championship with her equitation and juvenile mount, Storm Cloud. Lynne's outstanding characteristic was her great ability to change mounts.

Instructor, Helen K. Crabtree. *Rider photo by John R. Horst, Instructor photo by Sargent*

Linda Frankel, Huntington, W. Va., won the "Good Hands" Final in 1958. Linda was blessed with remarkable co-ordination, and this—along with cool poise and precise form—keeps her memorable in the minds of horsemanship devotees.

Instructors, M. Robert Mannix and Jim B. Robertson. *Photo by Freudy*

The youngest rider ever to win the AHSA Medal Final was Brienne Jorgensen, Kendall, Fla. This twelve-year-old was small but mighty, and those who saw her outride a huge class of the best in the country will never forget her. The year was 1959.

Instructor, M. Robert Mannix. *Rider photo by Freudy, Instructor photo by Shen-Courtney Studio*

Jan Casler, Troy, N.Y., won the "Good Hands" in 1959. She was a rider of great natural ability and ably demonstrated a thorough knowledge of real equitation. In 1969 the author wrote, "She will surely have a student duplicate her important win someday." How prophetic! As Jan Lukens, operator of her own successful stable in Ravenna, N.Y., Jan produced Mary Lib De Nure, a Final winner in both 1972 and 1974.

Instructor, Maynard Casler. *Rider photo by Budd, Instructor photo by Boice Studio*

In 1960, Mary Anne O'Callaghan, Louisville, Ky., won the AHSA Medal
Final. She was a flawless rider and was defeated only once that year.
She went on to show her Starheart Montgomery to become World's Champion Juvenile Three-Gaited Horse. Her most outstanding trait was an
elegance in competition that few ever attain.

Instructor, Helen K. Crabtree. *Photo by Jay A. McClasky*

Victoria Reiter, Akron, Ohio, was one of the prettiest girls ever to win at Madison Square Garden. And she could ride as well as she looked. She won the National Horse Show Saddle Seat Event Final in 1960, and is most remembered for the showmanship with which she glamorized every move in the ring.

Instructor, Richard Lavery, Sr. *Rider photo by George Axt*

The third of many good Louisville, Ky., winners at Madison Square Garden was Sarah Nutting. Her victory came in the 1961 National Horse Show Final. Sarah was a rider of great appeal and seemed to dominate the ring with her presence. She and Storm Cloud were breathtakingly beautiful, and for this quality in her horsemanship she is best remembered. Instructor, Helen K. Crabtree. *Photo by Sargent*

Gloria Green, Harrison, N.Y., and Sample Card were one of the best-matched teams ever to represent the East in the AHSA Medal Final. Gloria won the class in 1961 with a flawless ride, and she is remembered for the smoothness of her work.

Instructor, Joe Vanorio. *Rider photo by Jay A. McClasky, Instructor photo by Hank Cohen*

Nancy Ripa, Newport, R.I., triumphed in the "Good Hands" Final in 1962. She survived the grueling test of everything in the book to best a top field and is remembered for her final, flawless ride. She was the second of Joe Vanorio's winners in the 1958–1968 years. Prior to this time, from 1941 to 1958, Joe coached eleven riders to Medal or "Good Hands" Championships. A remarkable record.

Instructor, Joe Vanorio. *Photo by Budd*

Lindy Patrick, Pasadena, Calif., was the AHSA Medal Final winner in 1962. One of the most versatile equitation riders ever to show, Lindy also held the Medal Final in Stock Seat, in Dressage, and was a formidable contender in the Hunt Seat Finals. It is easy to understand why she is remembered for her cool, competitive ability under stress.

Instructor, Helen K. Crabtree. *Photo by Freudy*

In 1963, Sue Ellen Marshall, Louisville, Ky., was the winner of the National Horse Show Equitation Final mounted on her attractive black mare, Anne Howe. A very dainty girl, she is best remembered for the beautiful combination of pretty rider and pretty horse.

Instructor, Jim B. Robertson. *Rider photo by Ralph Crane, Instructor photo by Frederic Beck*

Randi Stuart, Tulsa, Okla., gained her first Finals victory in 1963, winning the Medal. In 1964 she won the "Good Hands." She followed with seventeen world's titles with I've Decided (three-gaited), Legal Tender and Sensational Princess (five-gaited). In 1967, AHSA voted her Horsewoman of the Year. Now, almost fifteen years later, Randi Stuart Wightman is still winning, having shown two of horsedom's immortals, Yorktown and the incomparable Summer Melody. Her current World's Champion in 1979 and 1980 is the gaited mare, Cactus Flower. Randi is truly one of the great American horsewomen.

Instructor, Helen K. Crabtree. *Photo by Freudy*

Julianne Schmutz, Louisville, Ky., was the beautiful winner of the AHSA Medal Final in 1964. A complete horsewoman, she won with her World's Champions Stonewall Imperial and Commander's Countess (five-gaited), Top Hat (Harness pony), and then on to the immortal Forest Song and their many triumphs. In 1979, Julianne Schmutz Lynch drove her Harness mare, Diamond Minx, to be named AHSA Harness Horse of the Year.

Instructor, Jim B. Robertson. *Photo by Sargent*

Edward Lumia, Croton-on-Hudson, N.Y., is one of very few riders ever to win both the AHSA Medal Final and the "Good Hands" Final in the same year. This he did in 1965. A handsome, good all-round rider, he is best remembered for his brilliant mastery of riding without stirrups.

Instructor, Helen K. Crabtree. *Photo by Morris*

Andrea Walton, La Porte, Ind., is also a "Grand Slam" rider—in 1966 at fourteen, winning the AHSA Medal Final at its new home, the American Royal, and in 1967 winning the "Good Hands" at the final show held in the old Madison Square Garden. To date, Andrea is the winningest saddle-seat rider in AHSA history, including an undefeated season in 1967. Superior horsemastership and technical perfection led her to win the World's Championship in 1968 with her five-gaited pony, Right as Rain.

Instructor, Helen K. Crabtree. *Photo by Morris*

Judy Fisher, Muncie, Ind., won the "Good Hands" in 1966 and the AHSA Medal Final in 1967. Judy's smooth workouts were unsurpassed. For this polished dexterity she is best remembered in equitation. As Judy Fisher Hastert she is still showing and winning at the major shows in the beginning of the '80s.

Instructor, Mrs. Harold Lahr. *Rider photo by Ralph Crane, Instructor photo by Ruth Chin Studios.*

Redheaded Janet Henry, Tulsa, Okla., and her colorful mare, Powder and Paint, blitzed the American Royal to win age group, show championship, and the Big One—the AHSA Medal Final in 1968. Janet's outstanding trait was' her cool handling of the fiery mare to make faultless rides. Instructor, Helen K. Crabtree. *Photo by Morris*

Jennifer Miller, Bedford, Ind., was a very popular winner of the "Good Hands" Final in 1968, two weeks after having taken second in the Medal Final. She had magnetic style coupled with complete control. It was a triumphant year, as she also rode her three-gaited Jasper Wildcat to the Juvenile Gelding World's Championship.

Instructor, Helen K. Crabtree. *Photo by Ralph Crane*

In 1969, Janet Henry, Tulsa, Okla., again riding her brilliant mare, Powder and Paint, challenged the field all year. At New York, she triumphed over a top group to win the "Good Hands," having been declared World's Champion at Louisville two months before.

Instructor, Helen K. Crabtree. *Photo by Sargent*

In 1969, Barbara Hoffman, Highland, Ill., aboard Sugar and Spice, won the triple-workout AHSA Medal Final. Started riding by her mother, one of the author's first students, she went on to become a student of Marion Brown, who coached her to her national wins. This is a family story, as Barbara and her two sisters turned to Hunt Seat and all three became instructors—Kris at Lindenwood College, Debra at Stephens College, and Barbara at William Woods College.

Instructor, Marion Brown. *Rider photo by Morris, Instructor photo by Gravemann Studios*

Julee Lampkin, Oklahoma City, Okla., was the happy and very poised rider to win the 1970 AHSA Medal at the American Royal aboard the elegant Top Secret. Julee mixed precision, elegance, and ring brilliance, a tribute to her trainer-instructor.

Instructor Harold Adams. *Rider photo by Morris, Instructor photo by M. F. Koch*

In 1970, Susie Maccari, Fort Lauderdale, Fla., riding the well-known Georgia Denmark, was great to win the "Good Hands" and give the staid New York spectators a sight to be remembered. What they did not know was that they were seeing the first act of the serial known as "Those Super Maccari Sisters."

Instructor, Dick Gray. *Rider photo by Morris, Instructor photo by National Horseman*

In 1971, Susie Maccari starred again, taking the AHSA Medal aboard her new mare, Top Secret. This sharp rider proved that she was for real when she displayed her same elegant flair on a totally different type of mare—the mark of truly gifted riders.

Instructor, Dick Gray. *Rider photo by Sargent*

Now here came Judy Maccari! While sister Susie was taking the 1971 medal, Judy wowed everyone to win the 1971 "Good Hands," riding the bay gelding Bombay. Judy's ride without stirrups on an exchanged horse will always remain in experts' minds as one of the great moments in equitation.

Instructor, Dick Gray. *Rider photo by Morris*

Mary Lib De Nure, Albany, N.Y., and Pipe Major lit up the equitation scene more than it had ever been done before. Color, style, brilliance, perfection—they had them all. Mary Lib's first notice of greatness was her winning of the "Good Hands" in 1972. Then came 1974 and the American Royal, where they thrilled everyone to take the AHSA Medal and the UPHA—memorable performances.

Instructor, Jan Lukens. *Rider photo by Holvoet, Instructor photo by Mosedero*

Nineteen seventy-two saw Judy Maccari take over Top Secret to win the final two of the Triple Crown, the AHSA Medal and the first holding of the very conveted UPHA—the United Professional Horsemen's Challenge Cup Final, in which the showing of the horse is the predominant requisite. The first rider to win all three Finals, Judy exemplified the supreme horsemanship that rightfully characterized such an honor.

Instructor, Dick Gray. *Rider photo by Bob Foster*

Sherrie Phelps, O'Fallon, Mo., rode the great
equitation mare Tailored to Taste to win the
National Final of the UPHA Challenge Cup in
1973. Much credit for the excellent response
of the mount must be given to Sherrie, as she
herself primarily trained her. Sherrie was a
bold rider who seldom made an error—a goal
for all who ride. A fine rider in every sense.

Instructor, Ruth Palmer. *Rider photo by
Morris*

A more elegant pair never entered the ring than Dana Lyon, Houston, Tex., and Last Revenge. In 1973 she completely dominated the equitation scene, winning the Big Four—Lexington, Louisville, the AHSA Medal at the American Royal, and the "Good Hands" at the New York National. Dana's superb presence under fire attracted *Sports Illustrated* to cover our stables activities at New York, a first for Saddle Seat Equitation.

Instructor, Helen K. Crabtree. *Rider photo by Sargent*

Linda Lowary, Tulsa, Okla., and her sporty bay gelding, Hot Toddy, looked as if they were winning the walk-trot stake when Linda topped the field to win the "Good Hands" at the National in 1974. Always a clever rider, Linda went on to triumph with her World Champions, unforgettable Happy Hour, the elegant Mandala, and in 1979 the amateur three-gaited Springtime Santana. More proof that good equitation is good horse training.

Instructor, Helen K. Crabtree. *Rider photo by Gloria Axt*

Kate Williams of Tulsa, Okla., was one of the most poised riders seen in years. That her presence was mental as well as physical is proven by her two consecutive wins in 1975–"Good Hands" and the AHSA Medal. Riding Tailored to Taste, Kate made it look easy, but she totally proved her depth as a rider when she went on to win World's Championships with Barbados Exit (three-gaited) and Great Big Country (five-gaited). Her brilliant mentality and physical courage still made it look easy!

Instructor, Helen K. Crabtree. *Rider photo by Finton*

Elizabeth Finch, Houston, Tex., paired with her handsome Brandywine Fizz, became the fourth winner of the coveted UPHA National Final in 1975. Beauty, performance, artistic pairing of rider and horse were firmly established as the "winning touch" and no rider ever had those qualities in more abundance than Elizabeth Finch. Elizabeth was the first winner to appear as guest judge of the UPHA Finals the following year—an honor unique to this particular class.

Instructor, Dorothy Dukes. *Rider photo by Holvoet, Instructor photo by Sargent*

Ann Swisher, Oklahoma City, riding the great-fronted Rambler's Top Billing, was one of the most pictorial and popular Finals winners, taking the UPHA in 1976. Featured in the July Bicentennial issue of *National Geographic* magazine, Ann epitomized the ideal American teen-age athlete—great beauty and great ability—and went on to further glory with her nationally renowned five-gaited gelding, Popular Time. Humility, presence, real horsemanship—Ann had them all.

Instructor, Helen K. Crabtree. *Rider photo by Lois Rappaport*

In 1976 Virginia Cable, Lima, Ohio, rode her sharp gelding Stonewall's Highland Ace to win the "Good Hands" at Madison Square Garden. A smooth, consistent rider and very gracious young lady, Virginia left no doubt as to her ability when she went to Kansas City the following week to annex a convincing win of the AHSA Medal. Truly every equitation rider's dream.

Instructor, Jim B. Robertson, *Rider photo by Ken Inman*

Fourteen-year-old Shauna Schoonmaker, Denver, Colo., built a solid wall of victories in 1977 on her grand gelding The Deputy. Climaxing with the Equitation Championship at Louisville, Shauna was motivated for the "big one," to her, the UPHA Championship—and win it she did. Sheer horse-training ability gilded this aggressive rider and this victory was not just one brilliant accomplishment, but served notice of even greater things to come.

Instructor, Helen K. Crabtree. *Rider photo by Sargent*

In 1977, Carol Reams of Ashland, Ky., was the second Robertson-trained rider to take both the NHS "Good Hands" and the AHSA Medal, truly a remarkable feat. On Starheart Mac, Carol was near invincible riding without irons and was an excellent horse handler as well. Back-to-back double winners in 1976 and 1977 must be admired.

Instructors, Jim B. Robertson and Jimmy Robertson. *Photos by Jamie Donaldson*

Dabney Cubbage, Henderson, Ky., and her enchanting mount, Missy's Flying Genius, were one of the best-matched teams ever to appear on the equitation scene. When they were paired up in 1977 it became evident that Dabney would steadily rise to the top. Every show proved their potential and the following year it was no surprise when this excellent horsewoman won the 1978 AHSA Medal.

Instructor, Jane Bennett. *Rider photo by Sargent*

Todd Buchanan, North Liberty, Iowa, rode his handsome gelding, Society Selection, to win the UPHA Finals in 1978 in a most convincing manner. A great crowd favorite and first young man to win a Final since Edward Lumia in 1965, Todd was a very popular and deserving rider. A grand all-around horseman and a super young man—Todd Buchanan.

Instructor, Ann Judd. *Rider photo by Jamie Donaldson, Instructor photo by Ron Judd*

Mary Lou Gallagher, Tulsa, Okla., rode Fancy Stonewall to win the 1978 "Good Hands." Flawless workouts were her forte and the Garden was made for this cool-headed rider. She was always so composed and cheerful that her perfection was deceptive to some. But anyone who saw her World's Championship rides on her juvenile gaited gelding, Lad O'Shea, in 1977 and 1978 will agree that Mary Lou Gallagher was the complete horsewoman. She made it look easy.

Instructors, Helen K. Crabtree and Redd Crabtree. *Rider photo by Sargent*

Shauna Schoonmaker and Warlock! Any equitation enthusiast who ever saw this pair will never forget them. The victory in the "Good Hands" in 1979 was only a repeat of an entire season of brilliant exhibitions of equitation—"horse training in its most sophisticated form." The glorious horse and the ultimate rider who never quit trying attained a place apart—she dared to be great.

Instructor, Helen K. Crabtree. *Rider photo by Ken Inman*

Kendy Almeida, Hartland, Mich., riding Supreme Dugger, was the honored winner of the first UPHA Junior Final to be held. This combination was well on the way to greatness under the author's tutelage, but when Debbie Wathen left the Crabtree employ that spring and took over this talented pair, the ultimate reward was an unforgettable and well-deserved win of a historic class. The year was 1979, marking the first national recognition of our marvelous group of riders thirteen years and under.

Instructor, Debbie Wathen. *Rider photo by Sargent, Instructor photo by Todd Buchanan*

Diane Caldemeyer of Evansville, Ind., fulfilled every rider's dream when she won the UPHA Finals in 1979. Grand Time was a hot horse and he required 100% horsemanship and that is what Diane gave him. Always brilliant, Diane was at her best riding her bold-moving horse without stirrups—an unusual accomplishment for a tall rider.

Instructor, Lillian Shively. *Rider photo by Sargent, Instructor photo by Joe Hargis III*

Ashley Tway, Oklahoma City, Okla., was Harold Adams' second rider to win "The Medal." On her lovely mare, A Supreme Lady, Ashley had been improving for several seasons and made the good work pay off in executing an incredibly involved workout and then change of horse, to take it all at Kansas City in 1979. Ashley's mare was lost in a tragic fire several weeks later, making the thrilling win even more meaningful for this splendid rider.

Instructor, Harold Adams. *Rider photo by Ken Inman*

Nineteen-eighty was the first year that a rider ever won the "Good Hands," the AHSA Medal, and the Senior UPHA Challenge Cup—a remarkable feat that reflected a beautiful picture of Janice Christensen of Madison, Conn., and her lovely gelding, Vanity's Sparkling Coin. Jane Bennett deserves full credit for Janice's meteoric rise to success in her final year of competition. *Rider photo by Sargent*

In 1980, thirteen-year-old Jama Hedden of Marietta, Ga., won the Junior UPHA Challenge Cup Finals. A brilliant team with her high-going gelding, Cedar Creek's Mr. Go, they were most admired for their flashy rail work. Instructor, Lillian Shively. *Rider photo by Inman*

30

How to Become a Teacher

Almost every mail brings me letters from young girls who wish to get into the horse business. I find these letters more difficult to answer than any other problem. Perhaps the days of the horse business being strictly a man's game are gone, but the opportunities for girls to enter the field are certainly limited.

Of course, the obvious answer is for the rider to enroll in one of the good colleges offering riding courses, but there are some riders who for various reasons do not wish to attend college or are unable to do so. For the young man, stable apprenticeship is not too difficult. If he is truly interested and willing to work, most young men can begin with at least summer employment in a good stable. This work is generally on the end of a brush and fork, as stables just do not have riding jobs for every horse-crazy youngster in town. But, nonetheless, the first step in becoming a horseman is fairly available to a young man. "On the contrary, grooming is a profession that is just now opening up to girls, and generally holds little future."

The preceding quotation was written in 1969. How things have changed in thirteen short years! I am going to hazard a guess that by the mid-'80s 50% of all grooms will be females.

At first girls were not considered strong enough to do the hard physical labor. Some never will be, but the majority of young women who love horses and want to work with them have a certain athletic ability and are able to handle caretaking chores.

Some very fine girls pioneered the groom profession and gave it the moral and social status that made the work acceptable to heretofore skeptical parents who had been horrified at the idea a few years ago. Trainers frequently say that the girls are neater and more thorough than many men. And they will tell you that no one is better with a sick or lame horse than an animal-loving girl or lady.

If you are in a neighborhood where there is a public riding stable, go to the management and explain your problem and offer your services in any way that they can be used. You may help with the book-ing of lessons, assisting riders on the horses and adjusting the tack for them, observing the lessons and whatever training or teaching that occurs. The very first thing you must do, however, is to make a very definite and businesslike arrangement. You really should not expect pay for this first work, as you are more the learner than the teacher. Another definite step is to have specific hours when you are to be at the stable—and then stick to them. Any stable operator can become a raving maniac when even the best-meaning outsider is constantly underfoot, and I think this is one of the main obstacles in the way of management's agreeing to take on an aspiring trainer. If you will broach the subject first, pointing out that you are aware that no stable wants someone constantly underfoot, that you are intensely interested in learning while you are contributing to the efficiency of the stable, and that you wish to have definite hours when you will be expected to assist—and *stick to it*—then you may be seriously considered.

Another point in question—and one that should be brought out in the open—is that, should you help at the stable, under no circumstances must you ever repeat stable happenings to the customers, outsiders, or other stable-owners. There are certain training procedures of every trainer that are closely guarded secrets. There are times when the best of horses work poorly, or the finest riders have bad days, and nothing will separate you quicker from your opportunity than talebearing.

I think that it goes without saying that anyone who wants to become a trainer and teacher and is far enough into his teens to be certain that he is dedicated to this idea must have had considerable riding and showing experience. It may have happened that an absolute novice has made the grade, but it is well-nigh impossible. There are so many ramifications to this business that it takes not months but years to attain anything like professional status. I have found that girls must have acquired a wealth of riding experience and then work back down the ladder to the more basic fundamentals of horse care, stable-management, grooming, feeding, purchase of feed and bedding, and the thousand and one other things that make up the general knowledge of a competent horsewoman.

There are certain things that all serious students of horsemanship can do to further their own education, whether they have the advantage of outside help or not. It is extremely helpful to have a complete understanding of the divisions that appear in horse shows and the rules that govern these divisions. Without a doubt, one should be a member of the American Horse Shows Association, which entitles you to the current rule book. Join the United Professional Horsemen's Association in your area and work on the chapter projects. The AHSA rule book is the bible of the show-horse world, and while it is not perfect, it is the very best and most comprehensive work available and contains all rules governing the showing of horses. There are three monthly trade magazines *Horse World, Saddle and Bridle, National Horseman,* and the weekly *Saddle Horse Report* (which also publishes *Walking Horse Report*). The Morgans and Arabians have their own breed publications which may be subscribed to by the public. A lot can be learned from these periodicals, not the least of which is a familiarity with the current stables, riders, and horses. An awareness and assessment of what is going on in the sport is an important aspect of our business. I am afraid that you might have a difficult time in joining any stable rank if you did not know who the current champions are.

The American Saddle Horse Breeders Association put out a very good book several years ago and have currently revised it. The title is *The Horse America Made,* and it was written by Louis Taylor.

The most recent additions to a library of films and books on riding are the series of equitation films put out by the American Horse Shows Association. As a student of equitation you should make an effort to study all three films—*Stock Seat, Hunt Seat,* and *Saddle Seat.* Of course, the latter has more immediate information for your education, but you should be very familiar with all three seats, as the basic seats are all founded on rider and horse balance and vary only through the conformation of the horse and the use to which it is put. The *Saddle Seat* film was made here at our farm. For two days we shot movies, and then the entire film was developed from the material on hand. Ideally, retakes would make for more perfection, but this was financially impossible. You may rent this film from the American Horse Shows Association, 598 Madison Avenue, New York, N.Y. 10022.

One of the best books on riding I have ever read is by our renowned president of the United States Equestrian Team, William Steinkraus. Published by Doubleday, it is entitled *Riding and Jumping.* I know that this book is concerned with the forward seat, but Mr. Steinkraus is an excellent horse psychologist, and it is in this vein that I think you would particularly benefit. The entire book is worth while from every standpoint.

George Morris, top instructor of Hunter Seat Equitation, has written an excellent book of that name and it, too, can teach any aspiring horseman a great deal.

Equus magazine will teach you a lot about the physiology and psychology of the horse and it is well worth studying and enjoying.

While I have never been a student of dressage, I was excited to find on reading another Doubleday publication, *The Complete Training of*

Horse and Rider, by Alois Podhajsky, former director of the Spanish Riding School in Vienna, that—here again—I came across ideas and exact terminology that I had been employing in my own instruction. You cannot read too much, if you read worth-while material.

Ride, read, study, participate, attend shows—add all you can to your general horse knowledge. Riding is one of the fastest-growing industries in the United States today. At least a dozen times a year we receive calls for recommendations for teachers or teacher-trainers. The need for good equitation teachers far exceeds the supply. It is a most rewarding profession. It is hard work, but never dull. It is creative, stimulating, rewarding. Your work with children will keep you young —mentally and physically—and no job in the world will expose you to a greater range of fascinating friends—human or animal—than the wonderful world of equitation.

The goals in equitation are many: For some, the comradeship and achievement of training the back-yard pleasure horse; for others, the ultimate show-ring pinnacle—the five-gaited horse. Randi Stuart and her ten-times World's Champion mare, Sensational Princess, are the results of the orderly process of good equitation. *Photo by Sargent*

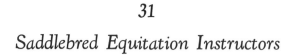

31
Saddlebred Equitation Instructors

Stephens College in Columbia, Mo., was where collegiate instruction in equitation began. Founding the department was Annie Lawson (Cowgill), who remained there many years. She was followed by Shirley Hardwicke, who also had a long tenure. Now in 1980 Cecile Hetzel takes over and the reappearance of Stephens College girls is again welcomed in the show ring. Always a leader, Stephens offers excellent opportunities to those who hope to continue their horse-oriented careers. *Photo courtesy Stephens College*

William Woods College, Fulton, Mo., is the first college to offer a degree in riding. Responsible for this growth is Gayle Lampe, pictured here with her staff. Frequent appearances of the William Woods students at major shows attest to the validity of the program. Left to right: Kathy Lowe, Jean Kraus, Lynn Burton, Jim Carey, Dot Backer, Deborah Booker, Bonnie Laasko. Seated, Gayle Lampe. *Photo by Avis Girdler*

Fern Palmer Bittner has been director of horsemanship at Lindenwood College since 1957. Under her excellent guidance there is offered the Bachelor's Degree with an emphasis on riding.

Kraft Vohsen is part-time Stock Seat instructor and Celia Baker is the part-time Hunt Seat teacher. Both the Palmer name and Lindenwood College are very important parts of the Missouri horse heritage. *Photo by Hammond*

Mary Lou (Mrs. Howard) Funderburgh has been a holding force for Saddle horses and equitation in the Kansas/Nebraska area for many years. At her Mary Lou Stables in Wichita, Kans., she has consistently developed winning horses and riders. Pam Coleman was one of her best, and now Pam's daughter, Cathy Coleman, is pictured here winning in the familiar way of two generations of well-taught riders. *Rider photo by Macklin, Instructor photo by Dixon*

Nancy Whipple is the very successful equitation instructor for the well-respected Bill Becker Stables of Concord, N.C. Taking over the entire equitation program as well as being an assistant trainer to Bill, since 1974 Nancy has turned out many excellent riders of national rating. *Rider photo by Lois Rappoport, Instructor photo by Charles E. Spencer*

240

Ruth Gimpel has operated the famous Tampa Yacht Club Stables in Florida for many years. Several noted trainees had been in this location, but Ruth has stayed and has been a vital factor in keeping horse interest thriving in her area. Her riders are consistently good and her combination of Susan Levine and her former World's Champion, Socyatee, is obvious proof of the expertise of Ruth Gimpel. *Rider photo by Sargent, Instructor photo by R. Warren*

Kay Cox and her husband, Billy, operate a highly respected stable in Montgomery, Ala. As Kay Singer, she was an outstanding equitation and juvenile rider in the South. She is a good teacher who gets better every year, and is producing sound, winning riders. Her future is boundless. This was written in 1969 and the prediction was sound. Many champions have followed. Currently their daughter, Kristy, is a fine example of the excellent teaching at Cox Stables. *Rider photo by Donaldson, Instructor photo by Robert Lyle Studio*

Anne Tracy Speck is a very dominant force on the west coast. She is an extremely talented and hard-working trainer/teacher and has revitalized equitation in her area. Increasingly, many of today's riders have started with her excellent training.

Tina Armstrong, pictured here, is one of the very best and a worthy representative of Rancho Del Mar, Anne's fine stable in Del Mar, Calif. *Rider photo by Fallaw, Instructor photo by Girdler*

Dick and Jeanette Durant operate their stable in Lockport, Ill., and have been extremely successful. They are a credit to their craft. Jeanette is one of the best instructors and trainers in the country and has been responsible for producing scores of good riders. Morgan Friedman, pictured here, was one of her best in the late '70s. *Rider photo by Donaldson, Instructor photo by Canon Studios*

The Keith Bartz family is most respected in the horse industry. At their Hollow Haven Farm in Chanhassen, Minn., they turn out excellent riders. Carol Bartz has had innumerable winners in both pleasure and open saddle seat equitation. Husband Keith had the honor of judging the 1980 Pleasure Horse Championships. Their daughter, shown here in Saddle Seat competition, was a top winner in recent years. *Both photos by Rick Bate*

Marilyn Fields operates Walnut Way Farm in Shelbyville, Ky., and turns out excellent riders. A summer program is responsible for many new juveniles in the show ring. A hard worker for UPHA, Marilyn gives freely of her time in promotional work for the American Saddlebred and can ride a show horse with the best. The author is proud of working with Marilyn in her education in earlier years.

Rachel Wolford, Equitation Champion at Louisville in 1976, is a fine representative of Marilyn's teaching. *Rider photo by Sargent, Instructor photo by Terri*

Marsha Henry Shepard is a complete professional horsewoman. Equitation instructor at the famous Bobbin Hollow Farm, Amherst, Mass., Marsha not only teaches Saddle Seat on Saddlebreds and Morgans but is a World's Champion herself in showing the grand lady's mare, Tiger Lil. A very responsible and bright woman, Marsha is always willing to give her time to the promotion of horse activities. She and the entire Henry family have done much for the industry.

Ellen Kilmer represents top instruction in every way. *Rider photo by Darkroom on Wheels, Instructor photo by Sargent*

Sally Lindabury of Misty Hills Stable in Troy, N.Y., is the capable trainer and equitation instructor. She has produced many top riders, both juvenile and adult, but no one has ever done a better job with an entire family. The William Shaefers—Mr. and Mrs. William Shaefer and the two children, Joy and Billy— are all good. Nationally rated Joy is pictured here. *Rider photo by Budd Studio, Instructor photo by Schaefer*

Bill Beckley is turning out excellent riders and
horses at Skylinvue Farm in Wallingford,
Conn. A successful competitor for Jan Lukens,
he apprenticed at her stables. Following a
year of working for Redd Crabtree, Bill was
ready to take over a public stable. His attainments
are proof that knowledge, hard work,
and excellent character make for success. The
entire Northeast is fortunate to have Bill Beckley
in their area.

Kate Harvey, a ten-and-under, was his first
World Champion—but certainly not his last.
*Kate Harvey photo by Donaldson, Beckley
photo by Alan Lisanto*

If Dick Wallen had done nothing but teach his own eleven children to ride, he would have added a great deal to the equitation picture. The Wallen Stables in Sioux City, Iowa, consistently turn out champion riders. Dana Davis won just about everything in the Midwest and shows here the "Wallen style." *Instructor photo by Tod Benson, Rider photo by Morris*

Rick Wallen operates his own stables in Neenah, Wis., where he trains the Siekman horses and offers public training and equitation. Very talented and hard-working, Rick has developed a variety of champions since 1971. Rick is not alone in carrying on the famous Wallen tradition. His sister, Linda Jo, operates her own stable in Kankakee, Ill., and brothers Monty and John both have training stables in Stillwater, Minn., and Springfield, Mo., respectively.

Rick has made champions in Saddlebred, Arabian, Hackney, English Pleasure, and Equitation. Doug Eberhard, pictured here, is one of his best. *Rider photo by Holvoet, Wallen photo by Zernicke*

Ruth and R. S. Palmer have been turning out well-mounted equitation riders for several years. At their Palmer Stables in Weldon Springs they produce results that add greatly to the success of the St. Louis area riders and future adult owners. Ruth is a former pupil of the author, one she is most happy to claim and a woman who represents the best in sports. Pictured here is the Palmers' daughter, Rhonda, who was almost without defeat in Missouri for several years. *Rider photo by Holvoet*

252

Annie (Mrs. John) Cowgill has been identified with equitation for many years. As former Head of Riding at Stephens College, Annie has instructed thousands of riders. She was a member of the AHSA Equitation Committee and its chairman several years. Now operating Jo-Ann Stables near Springfield, Mo., with her daughter, she is a neighbor of the pictured rider, Janet Green, who has become one of the top trainers of the present day. *Instructor photo by Spencer Studios, Rider photo by Sargent*

In true pioneering spirit, Had-Wel Stables was probably the first important academy operation in Oklahoma. Dick Hadley and sister Patty followed in their mother's footsteps by developing hundreds of good riders. Now, Dick Hadley, one of our busiest and best show judges, has relocated on the outskirts of Oklahoma City with the new Had-Wel Stables, which is one of the finest facilities in the country.

His student, Mary Lynn Duncan, was an outstanding rider and exhibitor in the '50s. *Instructor photo by Shiflet, Rider photo by Horst*

Bob Mannix was one of the mainstays of equitation for many years. He was a member of the AHSA Saddle Seat Committee and judged both the Medal and "Good Hands" Finals on many occasions. His students were thorough riders and always displayed a certain "Mannix elegance." Bob turned out several good side-saddle riders, the most noted being Janet Sage, who won the "Good Hands" in 1949. The M. Robert Mannix Stables in South Miami, Fla., was his last location. Bob Mannix was a profound influence in equitation from the 1940s until his death in 1978. *Instructor photo by Schuessler, Rider photo by John R. Horst*

Charlotte Stubblefield operated one of the best equitation schools in the Middle West at Atlanta, Ill. One of her top riders, Laurie Anderson, was highly regarded in equitation and juvenile ranks. Mrs. Stubblefield's untimely death robbed us all of a good friend and talented peer. Her presence is still reflected by riders now showing and her place in equitation history is an established fact. *Instructor photo by Hardin, Rider photo by Hardin*

Nona Rutland operated the Audubon Park Stables in New Orleans and Camp Riva Lake in Tennessee for many years with her partner, Kit Pillow. Nona produced many good riders, notably the superstar, Joan Robinson, pictured here on her forever remembered mare, Beloved Belinda. Zelpha Corkern is another student of note. She is a successful trainer and teacher. Nona Rutland was definitely a cornerstone of modern equitation. *Instructor photo by Grace Moore, Rider photo by John R. Horst*

32

The Psychology of Teaching

Instructors have many things to think about. First of all, you must know what you are going to do before you do it. Now, I know this sounds like oversimplification but in teaching situations when one is confronted with student after student it becomes very difficult to maintain enthusiasm and imagination—the two most important attributes a teacher should have. Of course, we have to assume that the professional teacher is well qualified and we hope that the parent-teacher will be well versed and have studied everything that will prepare him to help a rider. Let us confine ourselves to the professional teacher because his or her problems are universal and would encompass the amateur helper.

First of all, in teaching, try not to have the parent at every lesson. To the onlooker, and particularly to the parent who always expects the most from a child, repeated corrections become very difficult. You, as teacher, know that learning a skill involves repeating instructions many times. Parents, to whom everything looks so easy because it is logical, will twist and turn in the chair in a paroxysm of agitation and annoyance when a child does not respond instantly to a command or repeats a mistake. Now, that is the process of learning. It is a very good idea to inform the relative and student too that learning is not a gradual, consistent upward climb. There are plateaus and there are depressions, but the overall picture should be a jagged ascending line.

The rider loses his concentration because one glance at an annoyed parent will blow the mind of the learner, for whom concentration is an absolute must. I like to keep parents away from lessons until the student is well along and then invite them in to see a particular lesson in which I call for the rider to do all of the things that have been learned so well, avoiding the difficult points that the child has not yet mastered. It does not take very long for a child to appear to be riding very well and that should satisfy the parent and keep Mom or Dad from giving every lesson over again on the way home in the car.

After the riders have learned their lessons and are well into the shows, then we have another problem. The parent-turned-judge! This is a common phenomenon and is a malady which results from two exposures . . . a blue ribbon or a prolonged period of low placings! Everyone who has ever taught will recognize the universal wail, "But, Mrs. Crabtree, I just don't understand why Jennie Sue didn't win. Why, she never made a single mistake." A teacher can shrug off a remark like this just so long and then you are forced to tell the parent that, in spite of the fact that the rider did not commit any obvious errors, he or she really did not do anything exactly right.

It is a rare parent who does not come apart at least once in a rider's lifetime. This is a time for a quiet, private explanatory talk. Be sympathetic and try to take the parent's side if it does not involve criticism of other riders. That must be avoided like the plague. You must explain that judging is based on a combination of points for positive performance and deductions for mistakes. The obvious mistakes are easy to spot. Even someone who has never seen a horse show will know something is wrong when everyone but little Jennie Sue is trotting around the ring and she is stalled at the gate. What is not easy to see is the middle learning stage when the rider is "going through the motions" and does present a comparatively "faultless" picture but is getting no results from the horse. I have selected two pictures of Suzanne Fisher that illustrate this point.

I have never had a rider make a more rewarding climb to the top, and I must say that her parents were never guilty of confronting me with the parent problem we are discussing. These pictures perfectly illustrate the world of difference between "no mistakes" and a superior ride. Many who read this book will recognize Warlock and say, "Oh, sure . . . anyone would look better on him," but this is just not so. The mare in the first picture is a champion performance mare, Starheart Love, and is capable of looking just as exciting as the gelding. This picture was made in July at Cincinnati and the victory pass is one year later at Dayton. In between these times, Suzie, having "jelled" as far as seat and hands were concerned, went on to take what personal skills she had mastered and use them to ride a really good performance out of her mount. One of the most exciting moments of my teaching career came at the American Royal in 1979 when Suzie finally put it all together and won the fourteen-to-seventeen age group in a spine-tingling ride. I could see her first blue ribbon coming, and she rose to the occasion at the right moment and made as sharp a ride as any student I have ever had. That was just four months after the picture was taken at Cincinnati. After that it was "Katy bar the door" because she had reached that exciting point

where all of her learning had made her capable of putting up a superior ride and she finally realized that she could do it.

Now compare the two pictures. In the second illustration, the rider
is very obviously concentrating on getting results from the horse.
Even though it is a victory pass and the competition is over, the rider
is asking for and getting superior performance. Many blue ribbons
and championships followed in 1980, climaxed by a very close reserve
in the AHSA Medal Final at the American Royal—almost a year to
the day of Suzie's first blue ribbon. That is what talent, patience, and
understanding parents can make possible.

Again, we come to the word "patience." The teacher must have it,
the poor horse needs it, and the parents should strive for it. The entire
family must learn to assess the rider, give credit for the good, and
overlook the bad.

All things come in due time if we accept the natural progression
that comes with a talented rider, good horse, and a smart instructor.
Too much too soon is never good, particularly in riding competition.
Early wins spoil all but the most astute parents.

At this writing, I am buying a horse for one of my second-year
riders to keep at home to ride in the small local shows. I found a
great-dispositioned horse that is just right for the job as the horse will
be stalled at a local stable that does not have a show-horse training
department. Everything about the horse was suitable—a real find.
The father had a reservation, wishing that the horse had more motion.
The answer was obvious: with his looks and conformation plus extreme motion the horse would have been stake-horse material and
price, neither of which was what was needed. The second thought
was that the father was willing to buy more horse if his daughter
could perhaps tie over a couple of riders in that arena who were not
only several years older but were rightfully established as tops in their
area. There is always a temptation for an agent to grab the bait and
run when the prospects of more quality are mentioned, but there
comes a time when you take a deep breath and explain that the pur-
chasing rider is just not ready to win over the more experienced riders
and, no matter how much money is spent, it is not a sound approach
to maximum learning. I was so relieved when the father could see the
logic of this explanation.

How important it is that the parents really understand equitation
and what it can do, not only for the rider but for the entire family. In
1979 I gave an address to the membership of the UPHA at our annual
convention. It was about the relationship between the trainer and the
owner. The salient points are listed here. The teacher is responsible

Suzanne Fisher was doing everything right in this ride except getting a top performance. A great example of how to be perfect and lose a class. *Photo by Donaldson*

The same Suzanne Fisher a year later after she had learned that you ride the horse, not the tack. *Photo by Inman*

for educating the parents as well as the rider and only complete candor and a careful evaluation of what is really important must dictate what you say.

1. Establish a mutual trust by explaining what services you have to offer and just what the parents and the child will need to do to get the maximum worth from the money they spend with you.

2. Frankly state the difficulties to be encountered along the way. Everyone can understand the truism that we don't get big thrills and little disappointments, and it needs saying.

3. The well-being of the child, firstly as a developing human being, and secondly as a rider, must be the deciding factor in every decision that the teacher has to make. This should be made perfectly clear, as sometimes what you know is best for an individual is not apparent to the child or his family.

4. Avoid any derogatory remarks about a previous trainer. Loyalty is one of the finest principles that any child can develop and it must be practiced. If you are good enough to merit someone's coming to you from another stable, the wisdom of the move will be apparent soon enough. And the child who is encouraged to gossip and complain about the previous trainer is only practicing to talk about you at some future date. If you respect the loyalty that the new rider has for the former teacher, you can expect the child to be loyal to you if you deserve it.

5. Never jump right in and criticize the horse that the new rider brings with him. Pride of ownership is a very strong emotion, particularly in young children, and any criticism can be devastating. When the youngster observes better horses and begins to realize that the old horse is holding him or her back, then you will know how to handle the problem of getting the youngster to give up the prized possession, dog that he may be, and go on to a horse on which he or she can improve.

6. Warn the parents of friends bearing sympathy! Misguided people will so often rush up to a young rider after a class and—totally unaware that the child is satisfied and thrilled to have won a yellow ribbon—tell the child that she should have won. Perhaps she should have, but do not let anyone spoil the child's delight in the class. And if the child is disappointed, the crime is even more destructive.

I had a fine owner absolutely spoiled at a big show several years ago by a magazine correspondent who told the rider she should have won a class that she clearly did not. By the end of the evening she was in tears—and this was an adult who knew that, through no one's fault, her horse had just made a bad show, because I had already told

Whenever anyone speaks about riding and showing horses being a family sport, I have to think of a gallant little horse named Duke of Crebilly. He has been a winner and valued member of every family that owned him. This picture was taken in 1980 when he had been owned only a short time by the Gilbert Nutt family of Louisville, Ky. If Duke were a person, he could be president of this country. He has no enemies and· he specializes not only in winning but in making everyone around him happy. He was fourteen years old when this picture was taken and just two weeks away from being reserve World's 3-Gaited Juvenile Champion. Debbie, his owner, and her entire family of father, mother, sister, and brothers adore this horse. He has changed the entire family's life style and they all go to the shows together to cheer on this universal favorite. *Photo by Sidway*

her so and she was a smart rider who knew that she had gotten a bad ride.

7. Do not overpraise a rider. Winning is pretty heady stuff (remember how many pro athletes have succumbed to their own feelings of importance) and we may be setting ribbons, not improvement, as the goal.

Teachers have a great moral obligation when they take on the instruction of young people. Whether they are aware of it or not, the young riders are at a very impressionable age. When I write of morals, I am not referring to sex, drugs, or serious anti-social behavior . . . that is the parent's responsibility. I am referring to the development of the desire for excellence—to be the best person by practicing perseverance, consideration, and appreciation; to consider others' feelings and fight the natural tendency to jealousy by learning to take joy from another's success.

Really caring what happens to the riders and the horses is the most important function a trainer performs. Training and teaching are as creative as painting a picture or writing a beautiful poem. Part of you, as the trainer and teacher, is in every horse and rider you train. If and when they leave you it HURTS. Keep this in mind when someone new comes into your stable—someone is hurting. Be kind. It will help the supplanted teacher and it will make you a better person.

In many instances, riders develop a feeling of closeness for an instructor that they do not have at that moment for their parents. This is easily explained. We are the focal point of the most interesting part of a horse-crazy child's life. We do not have the onerous task that parents have of so often having to say "no" to the child. Ours is an idyllic relationship but not one to be misunderstood.

We are not only influencing a young mind at a very formative time, but we go much beyond that. Entire family life styles and futures very often result from an equitation rider in a family.

As a professional, search your heart and decide whether you are honestly interested in the welfare of the young people with whom you will be associated. If you are just going along because that is where the money is, then don't do it. The responsibility is tremendous but it is very worth while.

33

Teaching the Adult Rider

The approach to teaching adults to ride and show is entirely different from that employed in dealing with children.

First of all, we face the fact that an adult has been giving, not receiving, instructions for years. The role of student is very foreign to a grandmother. Another factor is the physical one. Older persons are not as agile as they once were and from the very first a mounting block should be used . . . not as something special, but represented as an everyday convenience for many riders. Nothing is more frustrating and embarrassing than straining to get one's foot in a stirrup while everyone stands around grunting for you. To ask a groom to give you a leg up has two disadvantages. First of all, you may lose a groom, second—if my experience as a professional is any criterion—I think that getting a leg up is one of the most difficult things that was ever thought up.

One year we were bringing out a huge ex-harness horse that we had trimmed that winter and he was going to make his three-gaited debut at the River Ridge show. I have always been a very slender person but, like almost everyone, I do tend to "eat my bedding" in the winter. When I walked up to this big horse, I could not even see over his withers. Trying to reach the stirrup was futile as the riding habit had shrunk at Christmastime, so there was nothing to do but accept the groom's offer to give me a leg up. After three abortive attempts to co-ordinate our efforts I finally made it . . . really made it big. I went so high in the air that when I descended the horse had moved forward and I lit on his rump with the crotch of those tight jods firmly lodged under the cantle of the saddle. I could not get the horse stopped, I couldn't hang on with my legs because they were right above his flanks. My bouncing the trot was perilous, and the hallway seemed twenty feet down to the concrete. I did the only thing I could do—clucked the horse into an easier-riding canter and tried to reel in the reins to stop him. By this time he had gone into an inexpert crow-hop buck and I was doing a total balancing act. Fortunately, the end of the hall stopped the horse before he lost me. It had to be too funny to be humiliating. In fact, it was so hilarious that a dour trainer whom I had never seen even smile before was convulsed with laughter. So much for my enthusiasm for a leg up.

There are certain things that we can give up in dealing with open riders as opposed to equitation riders. We have to be interested in the results and we must have balance to have control, so balance is indispensable. Where we can allow variances is in the sophistication of the foot position. Most riders are female, so I am going to deal with women's problems. For years, the woman has been wearing shoes with varying heights of heels. In the process, her Achilles tendons will have shortened somewhat—just enough that getting the heels down is going to be extremely difficult. I find that if I explain this fact to the rider and ask her to show me just how far the heels can be lowered in comfort, then I will have an idea of how much foot position I can get from that particular rider. It helps to ask the rider to raise her toes as she depresses the heels. Much stiffness will be avoided and the learning rider's natural tendency to tense the muscles may be moderated. If you keep asking for lower heels, then you are going to trade this problem for one much worse because your rider will tie up every muscle in her body in an effort to do something which she is physically incapable of doing. The same goes for the tendency to clutch with the calf, with resulting toeing-out. If the rider can refrain from committing an extreme fault that would nullify any effort to keep good thigh and knee contact, I let the rider alone. There are just some things that are beyond the restricted joint movements of an adult.

Now a word about pre-lesson discussion. I find it very worth while to sit down and tell the rider exactly what her reactions will be. She will be aware of height. This will go very quickly, probably by the third lesson, hopefully before. When a child gets on a horse, the ground is just as far away, but an adult adds other extenuations to the high position. She immediately considers the real possibility that a fall could result in a broken bone plus all of the ramifications that go with being incapacitated. Children do not need to feel this peripheral sense of responsibility. If you will tell your rider to expect to feel this way, then she won't.

Another very important psychological problem is the tendency of the adult riders to have very little patience with themselves. Children may be bored or resentful after being repeatedly corrected for the same fault, but adults become mortified and tend to wallow in self-recrimination and pity. If you will explain this to the tyros and tell them that they will feel this way—that all adults do, that they are not dumb and untalented because they cannot do everything instantly

Joan Schlemmer had only a year here at the farm, but in that brief time she and her beautiful gelding, Hot Pilot, had a lot of fun and a lot of success. This picture illustrates so well the practicality of applying sound equitation principles to the adult rider. I could have made life miserable for Joan by harping on keeping her head up and not toeing out, but neither fault, both of which are very common in adult riders, kept her from presenting a beautiful overall picture. Joan had wonderful concentration and horse sense and this picture of a good horse doing all he could do reflects his expert rider. *Photo by Inman*

Hot Fudge—few horses were ever better named or more popular than this personality mare wonderfully matched with her aggressive owner, Jean Fetner. Winners everywhere, this pair were made for each other. I got them to train when the mare was just a four-year-old, so actually all of her training life was aimed at becoming a suitable ladies' horse. This mare had a Puckish sense of humor, and Jean learned to let the mare be herself in the make-up ring, because when the class started it was all business—the blue ribbon business. *Photo by Holvoet*

When Ruth Pfeffer started to ride her mare, Sea Beauty was already a World's Champion stake mare. There was a reasonable doubt that she was too much horse for an amateur. But many hours later made success a reality—my hours getting the mare to accept both diagonals and to develop a responsive mouth, and Ruth's hours of practice with the determination to succeed. And succeed she did. This picture taken at the famous Lexington Junior League Horse Show tells it all. *Photo by Sargent*

simply because they realize the logic of the instruction—then the rider will be able to continue on with the flow of the lesson and deal with the oncoming situations instead of interrupting their concentration to worry about the past mistakes. Stress the fact that corrections are not necessarily mistakes but simply suggestions for a better and easier way to improve.

All of my adult show riders have been very interesting. One rider was attempting to get up her nerve to re-enter the show ring after a horrendous horse accident that seriously injured her and incapacitated her physically for three years. She had bred and owned the little mare that she wanted to send to us and, hopefully, learn to show. I have never seen a more gallant accomplishment. One knee was permanently restricted in movement, but Ilona wanted to ride again more than anything in this world and she really worked. We took our time, working for relaxation that would bring back the balance necessary for confidence. It did work, and at the end of the summer Ilona Michniewich rode out of the ring at Louisville awash in tears of joy. She had gotten a ribbon at Louisville! She went on to much glory with her lovely mare, Venus in Grey, for Sally Lindabury at Misty Hills Stables in the East. She even got her husband interested in riding and he shows pleasure horses with good success.

It takes a lot of nerve for an adult to enter competition against a group of ex-equitation riders who have had years of instruction and experience. No grown person enjoys getting clobbered by a seventeen-year-old kid, but the chances are very great that this will happen at first. The wise instructor will find as small a show as possible where the ring conditions are good and the entries are not too numerous. The first show ride is going to be difficult enough without having to contend with heavy traffic. The rider should concentrate on just getting around the ring in the best fashion at the three gaits and let that be enough for the first trip. Don't offer any criticism at the gate, constructive though it may be. Praise something, if it is only one thing that went right. The rider is on his way and enjoyment has to come first. There is plenty of time to work on corrections. Most grown riders will connect suggestions in succeeding lessons with prior ring situations, so you do not have to be obtuse about your instruction. Now that is where the children would have to have the corollary pointed out to them—not so with the adult.

Two of the most interesting riders I have ever had were with me at the same time. Both past middle age, both petite, and both having the best times of their lives. They had owned and shown horses as young girls but they were not accustomed to the "big time" that their new horses merited. I refer to Jean Fetner with Hot Fudge and Ruth

Pfeffer with Sea Beauty. But how lucky can a trainer be? Those horses were two of the very best, and the rewards of the ladies' efforts were wonderful. We called them "The Bobbsey Twins" and they contributed to some of my most precious horse-show memories.

Joan Schlemmer and Hot Pilot were another enchanting team to work with. These three ladies were very petite and gave the lie to the common fallacy that only the tall, willowy figure looks good on a horse. They not only rode well, they looked good.

You must expect to spend more time in conversation with the adults, but I certainly think that discussion is very important. Besides, that is a service that should be included in the training fees. You must remember when you have an avid grown horsewoman in your care that she is somewhat of a rarity. Almost all little girls go through a horse-crazy stage—that is to be expected and the rate of dropouts proves that "once a horse lover" does not always mean "always a horse lover." The adult who wants to ride and show horses for many years is a rare jewel and should be treated as such.

34

How Trainers Influence Young Riders

The impact of trainers upon equitation and equitation riders on our top showmen increases every year. Gone are the days when almost everyone left the arena when the "equitators" rode in. The majority of the top trainers have more than a casual interest in horsemanship. Many have riders from their own stables in competition even though they hire instructors to do the teaching. Most of them have sold a horse to some competitor, or are hoping to do so. Many are judges or they are just there because the equitation classes, especially at the large shows, are some of the best classes of the entire week and there is much to enjoy and much to learn by watching.

Whether the trainer is aware of the fact or not, every professional has an influence upon those young riders who watch him show. One day I was discussing the influence, good or bad, that the rider can have on his horse's performance. The case in point was a horse who had been recently crowned a World's Champion at Louisville. He was a powerful, exciting horse but he won his honors ridden by a trainer whose style was quite exaggerated—never posting, flying loose from the horse at some strides, beating out the trot at others, and using his hands very erratically. Since your rider may ride in a small group, all students are either riding or observing the lessons, so ten very eager youngsters entered the discussion. Everyone agreed that the horse showed well, that the win was deserved, that the rider had gotten a good show out of his horse. Then came my question: "If this is all so, how can we justify equitation lessons in form and balance when a win like this is possible?" One of the most worth-while lessons a young rider ever learned was learned that day. It was simply this: Yes, the horse was a deserving winner but was he the BEST he could be? Ridden without interference, could this good-enough horse have been a GREAT horse?

The lesson is loud and clear; to be the best of riders you must never put a ceiling on how good your horse can be, but in reaching for perfection you must know the point at every moment beyond which your horse cannot perform. You must employ all of the aids to get the collected brilliance of performance that comes from a graceful seat in the saddle and comfortably demanding hands on the reins.

One rider who rose to the imposing height of 4′ 10″ asked me why Tom Moore rode his reins so long when instructors all train their riders to have a workably short rein. I said, "Honey, when you know as much as Tom Moore and can ride with your head, your hands can go anywhere as long as they are helping, not hindering the horse. But the main reason is that if he puts his elbows forward to his hip bones, his fingers would be in the horse's mouth!"

We must learn what good performance is, and this we can do by watching. We must learn how to get this performance. This we can do by watching and analyzing how the rider is controlling the performance and, lastly, we can take all we have learned and modify it to fit our own build and ability and the conformation and potential of our own horse.

I have selected four outstanding showmen to illustrate this point. Each has his own style, no two look alike, all are successful, but each has his own way of getting there. You may be assured that the one point they have in common is that they get the most each horse has to offer and in doing this they know each horse they ride, they know the outer reaches of that horse's capabilities, and they know that only a horse aided by his rider, not interfered with, can attain the balance and willingness that result in a superior performance.

One rider in particular has a physical build that he has made into an asset. Tom Moore is exceptionally tall for a show rider, but instead of trying to minimize his own height, he has succeeded in training his horses to have such extreme elevation that the onlooker's eye is drawn to the animal, and the team of Tom and his horse are both so exciting and so compatible in style that we remember only the pure perfection of the pair when we recall the 14.3-hand Bellissima or the 16.2-hand Yorktown—Tom Moore, inimitable, inventive—a superb horseman. One of the all-time greats.

It is difficult to write about someone in one's family. There is the attempt to be brief (which you never are) in order to be fair, and then there is the problem of pride in your own, and the equally personal tendency to be critical. I shall try to avoid all pitfalls, because I want to talk about Redd Crabtree and the lessons the equitation riders can learn from him.

The first point is patience. I think this theme runs all the way through these four trainers, but I believe that Redd's record with five-gaited two-year-olds has a lesson for everybody.

With three home-grown colts, he won the Two-Year-Old Gaited

This picture of Tom Moore riding Danish Doll perfectly illustrates his great ability to produce the absolute maximum performance from his mare, as he has done for an incredible number of World's Champions in all divisions. *Photo by Donaldson*

Stake at Louisville within four years. Our lesson is this: the training time with two-year-olds is obviously brief and every second counts. Redd saw this at an early age when I always had riders from out of state. It is not the quantity of the work but the quality that gets results.

However, with the young horses having less than a year of riding, time obviously is also a factor. The most important aspect of these wins was not only that three colts won as babies, but that they had been so conditioned that they lasted and went on to be World's

Chat Nichols, St. Charles, Ill., will probably be best remembered for his magnificent victory in the World's Championship Gaited Stake with Mountain Highland Encore in 1979. What many may not know is that Chat Nichols had been studying and applying the best of equitation principles to produce one great horse after another for over twenty years. During the early morning workouts at the shows, Chat would watch the young riders' lessons with great intensity. He never taught equitation in the formal sense of the word but Bonnie Byrne, who assisted him for several years, would not be the outstanding trainer she is today without having learned the practical application of all that good equitation means.

Shown here on the former World's Champion fine Harness horse, Duke of Daylight, Chat is at his best in this display of balance interplay between horse and rider. Form—always form—and it came from the understanding of collection through the aids. *Photo by Morris*

Don Harris, a fine trainer of American Saddlebreds, exemplifies the wonderful results that come from his methods.

From the beginning, Don would select a pretty horse to work with. That was half of the battle. Don was a basketball player and he learned poise and balance on the court. I believe Don learned aids and diagonals from his exposure to top equitation when he moved to Kentucky and he learned to show a champion when he got Giddy-Up-Go. That is where he learned that good horses are worth waiting on and that no horse is any better than his own attitude, which can be molded by the trainer's patience and understanding.

Without Giddy-Up-Go there would have been no Imperator, the great gelding who won Don his first World's 5-Gaited Championship in 1980.

When we think of Don Harris, we think of precision and coolness. The lesson here is to let the other riders beat themselves while you keep your own horse doing his special thing. No one has ever done this better than Don Harris. *Photo by Donaldson*

Champions as three- and four-year-olds and one is still winning, being a World's Champion Juvenile horse in 1980.

As teachers and trainers of equitation riders and horses, there is a lot to be learned here. We are dealing with avid young learners and we must be careful that we do not burn them out. This is a real temptation when we are faced with exceptional talent. How many times we have seen tiny five-year-old children who amaze us in the ring, only to be gone from riding by the time they are eight years old. We have to keep our early riders "sound" just the same way that we have to remind ourselves that two-year-old colts cannot take the work of aged horses. Redd has always had the foresight and the self-control to resist the temptation to overdo the young horses and to bring them along gradually so that they would peak during the world's championships. I think that so much of this he learned from Garland and Frank Bradshaw, who would sit back all year and then "gotcha" at Louisville! It all comes back to the word "patience."

I had a very good lesson in patience one summer when I was privileged to show the lovely big three-year-old mare, Silver Shadow for Redd because he also had Big Country that year. I was all set and anxious to win the class at Lexington, but several days before the show a tragic accident befell the highly developed race filly Ruffian, who crashed to the track with a broken front leg during a match race. None of us will ever forget the horror of that moment and it has had a great bearing on the things we ask of our young horses here at the farm.

I knew that Silver Shadow had a lot more than I asked her for at Lexington, but I could not get the Ruffian accident out of my mind. So I waited, hard as it was, and we were finally rewarded with the three-year-old class two months later at the Indiana State Fair. If our horses and riders are young and immature we must be patient. "Make haste slowly" was never more apropos than in this situation.

Everyone wants to win and the most genuine and devastating tendency in any individual competition is the insidious feeling that one has to prove oneself every time the gate opens. No rider who is without a desire to be the best is a good competitor but ambition can eat you up. If you are good and doing the best you can, then that is all you can do and you will improve every day that you live. Trying too hard will destroy you, no matter how pure your motives may be. Redd had this problem for a time but, thank heavens, it is all over and we can all enjoy the shows. I have this to fight constantly as an instructor, as most of us do, and we have all seen it happen time and time again with our riders. They will be going their very best when each one thinks he is one of many good riders but just let one win an

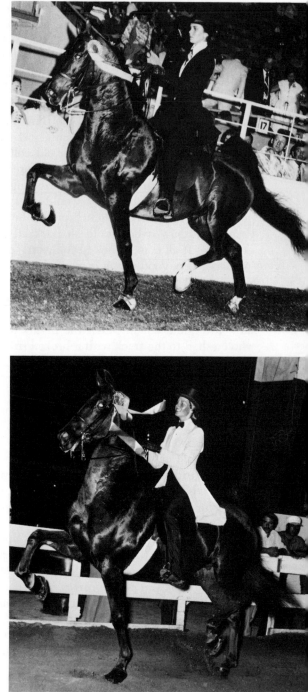

These two pictures are graphic
proof of the harvest to be reaped
from equitation training and experience. Ann Swisher went directly
from winning the UPHA Final to
showing and winning with her
well-known five-year-old stake
gelding, Popular Time, a beautiful
bundle of dynamite trained by
Redd Crabtree.

Lisa Rosenberger was a very close
reserve in the 1974 AHSA Medal
Final. Following that, she worked
as training assistant to the author,
and as Lisa Green she became one
of the most expert women in the
professional ranks. Cynthia Wood
and I combined forces to educate
this promising young rider and the
horse industry has profited from
our endeavors. *Swisher photo by
Holvoet, Rosenberger picture by
Donaldson*

Redd Crabtree showing Cora's Time. *Photo by Inman*

Anyone who ever saw the five-gaited pony Ric Rac show in the late '70s will never forget this exciting equine time bomb and the super rider who kept him one inch from disaster—Kerry Lowary. Time after time Kerry held this pony in control and they were often the talk of the show. Ric Rac was tough and many trainers marveled that a young girl could control him. Her formula? Perfect equitation = perfect performance. And she watched the trainers! *Photo by Donaldson*

important class and all perdition breaks loose! I always caution my riders to watch out for this phenomenon—and I caution the parents as well. The terrible trap here is that the riders feel compelled to be good because they fancy that it is expected of them—but they commit an even more stifling error; they try to remember just how they "did it" and make an attempt to duplicate a ride. This is sheer disaster, first of all because it is impossible and, secondly, it leaves no margin for improvement—and that is what we are all in the ring for.

What does it take to win? It takes determination and talent. Fifteen-year-old Gretchen Keller won the 1980 AHSA Medal at Lexington in a 53-rider class. It was her first year in equitation and also the first for her horse. The odds were awesome, but when you do your best and you are willing to work to get there, it is possible. Gretchen learned from every class she watched. *Photo by Jamie Donaldson*

Except for the very first two years of riding, Redd learned his lessons everywhere he could. As a teen-ager, he would always be at the track before anyone so he could observe the trainer's methods. Our family owes an unpayable debt of gratitude to so many wonderful trainers who took the time to discuss their methods with Redd and permitted him to see them work out problems that generally only the trainers themselves are privy to. As mentioned before; the Bradshaws, plus Earl Teater, Lloyd Teater, Fritz Jordan, and most certainly Lee

Roby, for whom he worked one summer, were wonderful to this aspiring young trainer. Don Harris mentions with great affection the tremendous help that Eddie Gutridge always gave him, Chat Nichols had John Hook, Tom Moore had Chester Caldwell, and all trainers and riders can name you kind and unselfish professionals who were glad to give a hand up the ladder. You, as instructors, can do your part by helping with clinics and any other public service that will advance the cause of riding, and the top riders can be kind and helpful to the little tots who have already made them their heroes. We all have a responsibility at the shows—teachers, trainers, parents, even the grooms—to set a good example because, believe it or not, we are all being watched while we are watching!

There is one last thing I want to mention about Redd Crabtree and that is his lightness and grace in the saddle. I have chosen this picture of him on the World's Grand Champion Five-Gaited Mare Cora's Time—not that it is her best picture, but because it so beautifully shows the light control and airy balance that characterize this rider. A terrible accident a few months before this show at the American Royal had gravely injured Redd's left arm and he had lost the feeling in his hand, so that he was unable to wear gloves or to have full use of his hand. I certainly do not advocate one-handed riding, especially in any juvenile rider, but Cora's Time was a very gifted and hot mare and she could wind right off of her feet without the most delicate sort of control. Don Harris had this problem with Giddy-Up-Go and he had to take a firm, sympathetic, but definitive hold to maintain his control. With Cora, she had to be free—and no picture could better illustrate the lightness of touch or a rider's thinking ahead of a horse better than this one.

I think Redd and the other three trainers have learned from every horse they have ever trained, as we all should. Instructors are learners just as much as their students and the students should learn something from their horses at every ride. And let us put in a word for perseverance. Not one of these four trainers whom I have given as inspirational examples would have risen from the heap if they had not been willing to WORK. Wishing just will not make it so!

35

What We Learn from the
Fine Harness Division

There is much to be learned about balance and collection from observing the fine harness classes. Many will ask, What has this to do with equitation? Why look at an event where there is no rider? I do not believe that there is a better place to learn how to handle a horse's mouth than in harness. Granted, there is the artificial help from the martingale and the overcheck, but observe the subtlety of the rein work, which not only is the element that sets the horse's head, but also has the awesome task of urging the horse forward to make this collection possible. As students so often hear, you must use all of the aids in conjunction to get balance and collection. Pity the driver who sits behind the horse, not on his back. Lost to him are the leg and body aids. The whip and the voice are all of the forcing aids he has, so the restraint of the bit in the horse's mouth must be exactly right for that moment and that step, to keep from overcontrolling the horse and discouraging him from moving forward into a high, collected trot.

It is true that only a few horses are born to wear an overcheck and not all horses can be fine harness horses just because they have extreme motion. But the same thing holds true of the equitation horse. How can we teachers expect a student to set a horse's head when he has a neck like a Hereford steer? We have to have the material to work with, whatever the division we show in.

But simply having the conformation and motion for the fine harness class still does not guarantee results. The driver must inspire and animate his horse to such an extent that the horse will move into the bit, set his head as a result of the bit and martingale influence, and then "go marching." As young riders, we can see control demonstrated by the use of varying degrees of taking hold of the horse's mouth and releasing it. It does help if a horse is ambitious, as you certainly know as well as anyone that there is nothing harder in the world to ride than a lazy horse. With no body aids to help him, observe how the driver uses his other aids to get set up for the passes in front of the judge. If the horse has been trained with the whip in conjunction with the voice, then a conditioned response has been set up and a cluck or a snap of the whip will urge the horse on. How often have you heard your instructor ask you to do the same thing? It is very risky to hit a horse to increase his performance or speed in front of the judge, either under saddle or in harness. That is where training is so very important. We set up responses that we can count on before we get in trouble.

Now we come to the opposite type of horse—the one who lugs and wants to go a road gait instead of a park trot. Watch these drivers carefully. They know that if they keep a death grip on a horse's mouth for any extended time the mouth will deaden, just as surely as you know you will put your horse's mouth to sleep with unremitting curb pressure. So the driver does what you do. He takes every opportunity to ease the pull on the reins to restore blocked circulation and to regain the horse's attention. When there is no feeling, there is no response. You know that from riding . . . now observe it in driving.

Another good lesson that the equitation rider can learn—perhaps the most valuable lesson of all—is just what the results should be when the command "Show your horse" is asked for in the open and stake classes. You may hear the same command in an equitation class. What does it really mean? So many misguided riders, and drivers too, take this for a license to race. Watch the top drivers. Some will speed up slightly because their horses will work better. Others will keep the same speed because the trainer will know the exact speed at which his horse goes best and if he has that dreamed-for animal that is always at his best, then there is no need for speed. Showing the horse on command was never intended to indicate speed—only to permit it within limits of control. As a judge, I like to call for showing of the horse in equitation because the rider who has been riding as he should have during the entire class will already be at his best speed and performance and those contestants who take off in a cloud of tanbark have either been loafing or they just do not know what showing is. They are the prime candidates to have someone explain a fine harness stake to them.

I have made an odd choice of pictures to illustrate these points, as the picture of the 1979 and 1980 World Grand Champion Horse, La La Success, is pictured being shown by her owner, Mrs. F. D. Sinclair, as a four-year-old in an amateur class. The driver's obvious enjoyment and poise complement the young mare's balanced trot and freedom. This show experience did nothing but enhance the mare's

Mrs. F. D. Sinclair driving La La Success. *Photo by Inman*

Charles Crabtree showing Glenview Radiance. *Photo by Morris*

showing when she made the transition to the open competition for her trainer, Charles Crabtree. In the next picture we see Charlie making one of the all-time memorable harness shows to win the Junior Fine Harness Stake at the American Royal with Glenview Radiance, who earned ten World's Champion titles as a ladies' or amateur horse for Mrs. Sinclair. I chose this "switch" because the wild-going junior mare, who was immediately to be turned over to her amateur driver, could have been spoiled right in this class if she had been permitted to race around the ring when "Show your horse" was called for. Horses are very impressionable at an early age, and particularly when they are so very "on" for a class as this "bursting out of the harness" picture illustrates.

The next time that the announcer calls for showing the horse in an equitation class, keep these two illustrations in mind. Overriding and overdriving are the same. They do not happen just one time. You pay a long time for this mistake.

36

American Saddlebred Pleasure Equitation

American Saddlebred Pleasure Horse Association Equitation (left photo). The ASPHA International Equitation Medallion Championship Trophy (right photo).

According to the latest information from the American Horse Shows Association, the American Saddlebred Pleasure Horse classes are the fastest-growing divisions of any breed. *Photo by Ken Inman*

AMERICAN SADDLEBRED PLEASURE HORSE ASSOCIA-TION PLEASURE EQUITATION MEDALLION CLASS

Sponsored by Saddle and Bridle Magazine

The intent of this class is to foster interest in the American Saddlebred Pleasure Horse; to promote excellence in Saddle Seat Equitation; to encourage sportsmanship; and to create wholesome competition among pleasure horse exhibitors.

It is also intended to give further incentive to those who show and love American Saddlebred horses and who might not be able to compete on a par with equitation riders showing in open saddle seat classes, due to financial circumstance or location.

RULES AND REGULATIONS

ELIGIBILITY

1. Eligibility to compete in the *Saddle and Bridle* Medallion Class is limited to those riders who show ONLY American Saddlebred Pleasure Horses in equitation during a given show season. Country Pleasure Horses and Show Pleasure Horses may both compete.
2. A minimum number of three entries is required.
3. The rider need not be a resident of the zone in which the show is held.
4. One Medallion Class win eliminates that rider from further competition in qualifying classes that season.
5. The winner of a Medallion Class must return the card, attached to the ribbon, properly filled out, to *Saddle and Bridle*, 375 N. Jackson Ave., St. Louis, Mo. 63130, to be eligible to compete in the International Finals.
6. All Medallion Class winners eligible are for the International Finals to be held in conjunction with the American Saddlebred Pleasure Horse International Championship Horse Show, in Springfield, Ill., in the fall.
7. The qualifying season begins immediately following the International Finals. The International Medallion Champion is ineligible for further competition in Medallion Classes.

HORSE SHOW INFORMATION

1. The medallion suspended on a neck ribbon and five ribbons are to be furnished by the horse show, the money to come from entry fees, a sponsor, or sponsors. They may be ordered by sending $30.00 to: *Saddle and Bridle*, 375 N. Jackson Ave., St. Louis, Mo. 63130. Phone (314) 725-9115.
2. Suggested prize list wording;

PLEASURE EQUITATION MEDALLION CLASS

Open to all saddle seat pleasure equitation riders, 17 years of age and under, at the time of the finals, riding an American Saddlebred Pleasure Horse or Country Pleasure Horse. The winner is eligible to compete in the International Finals to be held at the American Saddlebred Pleasure Horse International Championship Horse Show. The winner is eliminated from further competition in qualifying classes this season once he has qualified. Medallion and five ribbons.

3. The judging specifications should be read by the announcer as the riders enter the show ring.
4. When entering the International Finals, the rider must indicate the horse show and location at which he/she qualified. The medallion and neck ribbon will be worn in the Finals.

JUDGING SPECIFICATIONS

1. The current AHSA Rules for Saddlebred Pleasure Equitation should be used as guidelines for the judging. In addition, it is recommended, that the judge upon his discretion, ask for a stop on the rail, the horse to stand quietly, demonstrate a brisk trot, and a hand gallop.
2. An appropriate workout is to be selected by the judge and the top four riders are required to work. It is recommended, that in the case of a relatively small class, all riders be given the opportunity to work, rather than leaving a few out of the workout.

WINNERS

1. It is recommended that the winner of a qualifying class dismount to have the Medallion ribbon placed around his or her neck, and remount to leave the ring.
2. The International Champion will receive a bronze sculpture, donated by *Saddle and Bridle* Magazine, for permanent possession. This trophy, created by Sally McClure Jackson, is a replica of the American Saddlebred Pleasure Horse Association logo, and will be presented exclusively to the Pleasure Equitation Medallion International Champions.

THE PLEASURE EQUITATION MEDALLION FINALS, 1979

1. Sandy Bernd, Neenah, Wis., self-trained
2. Lisa Haywood
3. Nancy Anderson
4. Ann Mero
5. Denise Lullo
6. Gretchen Keller
7. Janet Crampton
8. Jill Baahlman
9. Debbie Dowd
10. Lois Poggemeier

ASPHA NATIONAL PLEASURE EQUITATION CHAMPIONSHIP, 1979

1. Sandy Bernd
2. Lisa Haywood
3. Nancy Anderson
4. Jean Phelps
5. Jennifer Sterne
6. Janet Crampton

THE PLEASURE EQUITATION MEDALLION FINALS, 1980

1. Peg Paulus, Cedarburg, Wis., Trainer—Dave Patton
2. Liso Petro
3. Carol Jones
4. Jackie Erdmann
5. Diana Dixon
6. Janet Crampton

ASPHA NATIONAL PLEASURE EQUITATION CHAMPIONSHIP, 1980

1. Liso Petro, Racine, Wis., Trainer—Fran Nix
2. Doug Eberhard
3. Carol Jones
4. Michelle Sprengelmeyer
5. Lisa Jensen
6. Janet Crampton

A historic picture in which Bill Thompson, editor of *Saddle and Bridle* magazine, presents the first Medallion Championship trophy to Sandy Bernd. Springfield, Ill., 1979. *Photo by Inman*

Sandy Bernd shows all the style and happiness that are truly Pleasure Equitation. *Photo by Inman*

Peg Paulus displays the perfect combination of control and happy aggression of both horse and rider that exemplifies beautiful Pleasure Equitation. *Photo by Schatzberg*

The Medallion Class Finals were first held in 1979 at the ASPHA International Championship at the Illinois State Fairgrounds in Springfield, Illinois. Created and sponsored by *Saddle and Bridle* magazine, the Medallion is a qualifying event and, in order to qualify, a seventeen-and-under rider must win a Medallion in his home zone. Forty-one qualifying classes were held throughout the country. Seventeen riders came to compete and battled it out to see who would have the honor of being the first winner of the American Saddlebred Pleasure Horse Association Pleasure Equitation Medallion Championship.

No better example of form, ability, understanding, and pure horsemanship could have been selected than Sandy Bernd, Neenah, Wisconsin, riding her elegant home-trained mare, Valley View's Highland Heather. As a youngster, Sandy received beginning instruction from Don Brockman, but had done the majority of her own and her mare's training, assisted by her parents, Mr. and Mrs. James Bernd.

Sandy had won the 14-to-17 Pleasure Equitation Qualifying class and the National Pleasure Equitation Championship prior to the Medallion Championship to make a clean sweep. Further attesting to her thorough horsemanship is the fact that Sandy and her mare compete not only in Pleasure Equitation but also in the regular Pleasure classes as well as the ASB Western Equipment classes.

As Sandy and so many other riders have proven, good riding is simply intellectual and athletic versatility channeled to the type of horses they are riding. The ability to balance and control every horse according to his specific conformation, motion, temperament, and the task to be done knows no specific seat. Good equitation is founded on the one constant factor—balance of both horse and rider, combined with the ability of the rider to understand and control the motivation of his mount at all times.

This is one of the wonderful attributes of Pleasure Equitation—the wide variety of classes and activities that the rider can enter with his horse. But this is not merely accomplished by changing attire and tack. The challenge is to settle the horse into the physical relaxation combined with mental alertness that typifies the Western mount. Then to use the increased forcing aids to animate the horse to produce the commanding "stake horse with manners and perfect mouth" that transforms this same horse into a brilliantly collected open pleasure horse. Finally—or should we say initially?—the rider puts everything together to make the perfect equitation ride. This comes from the confident relaxed horse of the Western division who can accept the precise control called for in individual workouts with the versatility of both horse and rider to give that exciting performance on the rail. This is total control and is not gained by wishful thinking or even a complete academic understanding of all facets of the classes. It comes from the close harmony of good rider and good horse who have spent many productive hours of learning together.

It is very easy in Pleasure Equitation to fall into the trap of working for "error-free" rides, practically holding one's breath at the walk and creeping one's way into a passable trot and canter. Manners are based on positive control and if the rider can keep his horse comfortable in mouth and body while demanding maximum performance, then they will have the stuff of which blue ribbons are made. The horse must rely on the rider at all times and only total concentration and aggression of the rider can accomplish this. If there is ever a time to think ahead of one's horse, this is it. The rider who will not take control and keep his horse's attention from the first step of the warm-up to the exit from the ring at the end of the class will never be able to trust that horse to make a consistent show.

If there is any difference in Saddlebred Pleasure Equitation from any of the other equitation classes, it must be in the strictest adherence to the qualifications of the horse as a pleasure horse.

Ideally, all horses should have good mouths with the consequent quiet and ready response to the rider's hands. However, in Pleasure Equitation any head tossing, lugging, or arguing with the bits is absolutely guaranteed to lose a class. Now, when we say that the lugger who pulls the rider out of the saddle is wrong, we do not mean to imply that the good rider-horse combination is one in which there is practically no mouth contact.

Several years ago, when the drug rules were instituted at recognized shows, I suggested to a hunter trainer that perhaps the temptation to tranquilize the hunters under saddle might not exist if the judges did not favor those horses who worked on a completely loose rein with no contact whatsoever. His answer—"Helen, our classes are so large we have to eliminate as many horses as possible." I still feel the answer to that one is a good judge who can spot outstanding quality no matter how large the class.

The point I wish to bring out here is that it is unnatural for a horse to work with no mouth contact. So do not assume that negligible contact with a horse's mouth is proof of good riding or of a good pleasure horse. Your reins are your most immediate control and, as in the army, it only makes sense to maintain a short supply line. Sensitivity of the rider's hands is the key . . . keeping a firm, comfortable contact with the horse's mouth. Proper fit and interaction of the bits has never been of more importance than in the Pleasure division because only through the complete concentration of the rider and the horse's resultant response can perfect control be accomplished. I tell each of my riders that concentration is a purple thread direct from his mind to the horse's mind, and if either party breaks that thread, then we no longer have total control, of ourselves or of the horse.

Be sure to check the relation of the snaffle to the caveson. A low caveson can cause pinching when the snaffle is pulled upon. The real factor, however, is the curb and the frequent pinching of the lip between curb bit and curb chain.

Do not forget that things can go wrong inside the horse's mouth, and study how the snaffle and curb lie in relation to each other at various tensions. Taping the bits together after an intelligent evaluation of the bit action can often correct a head-tossing problem.

The following has been referred to previously in this book but needs repeating. Since so many pleasure horses are home-trained, the owner must be very introspective and make careful analyses of the work schedule. There are certain constants, and the first is that only steady work and conditioning can get your horse at his peak performance, and this you must have to demonstrate your best ride.

We have had two Pleasure horses. The first was Peacock Peavine, an "extra" when Kathie Gallagher bought The Tempest as her new amateur stake horse. The Five-Gaited Pleasure National Championship was initiated that year at the Kentucky State Fair, so we immediately removed Cocky's tail set when the prize list arrived and rode the horse with the Pleasure division in mind. We changed nothing at all. We had a winning stake horse with perfect manners, so there was nothing to change. Someone remarked that we would have to spend hours in the saddle "working him down" to pleasure level. That is just not true, as many trainers will tell you.

Manners are in the head, not the muscles. A bad horse will only get worse as you increase his stamina because you will get to the point where you cannot wear him down or you will have an unsound horse to deal with. A good-mannered horse will lose his enthusiasm and become a resentful, recalcitrant mount who is looking for the way out when he is overworked.

The horse that has been ignored all week and ridden for two hours Friday night to "get him settled" is not going to be a good ride at Saturday's horse show. Good manners, like good physical condition, come from consistent, intelligently planned training. This applies equally to the rider. You are an athlete, not a passenger, and your muscles must be in tone and your mind sharp. This does not happen at the movies or in front of the TV. If you want to be good, you have to work at it . . . not when convenience beckons, but when your own honest horse sense tells you.

To make the story complete, Kathie rode Peacock Peavine to the first World's Championship for five-gaited pleasure horses.

Our second pleasure entry was a nice well-bred young mare, good-moving, sharp-eared, but lacking the elegance of the head and neck that is so coveted in all saddle horses. The mare had been successful in far western shows but she was moving to the heart of top Pleasure competition. This mare had never had a set tail, was not an old ex-show horse, and was somewhat lethargic and unprepossessing.

What seemed called for was to keep the good natural motion and alert expression but add the brilliance and aggression that win.

Now you may be wondering why I am discussing training procedures when our main concern is equitation. Surely by now you must be aware that equitation and training are one and the same. The initial part of this book deals with how a rider attains perfection of form and control, but we must add more and more sophisticated training help to get maximum results.

To return to the pleasure mare: our climate was more conducive to well-being in the mare. Jogging for the first sixty days until we were at about four miles per day put her into excellent physical condition. She was ready for a long, hard class . . . and most pleasure classes are just that—hard, long, and exacting, as are the equitation classes. We taught the mare to trot on. Her natural temperament was such that she needed to be forced and would accept the hustling without spoiling her pleasant attitude.

One of the most difficult assignments in training the Pleasure Equitation horse is this very problem of attaining show-horse ways compatible with pleasure-horse manners. They must work together . . . two factors that seem to be diametrically opposed. We certainly found that jogging plays a very important role. The change to the snaffle driving bit is welcome. Sidecheck or overcheck will encourage the front elevation of head, neck, and forequarters without the possible resentment of the rider's lifting action with the full bridle that can develop when the animal has been ridden too much. Whenever you can, correct a bad habit with something that will not be associated with the rider. You will get much better results. Horses have the truly animalistic reaction of association; that is how they learn. So we must use all of our ingenuity to disassociate the major and temperamentally difficult corrections from the rider whenever possible.

I am gratified to report that all of our hard work paid off and the mare won her final class at the American Royal, defeating, among others, the 1980 Adult World's Grand Champion mare.

One of the most difficult assignments the home trainer has with the pleasure horse is to acquaint the horse with the crowded conditions of the ring, particularly to deal calmly with being passed or having to work in and out of traffic.

Your greatest constant help is your repertoire of aids . . . just what the term implies. Use your voice, always. This will develop the added dimension to the horse's reliance on the rider and be a real settling influence when needed. Too many riders take the physical approach to a problem that is essentially temperamental. Stops and starts must be taught. Certainly they are skills that the equitation horse must be trained in every day. Serpentine practice is invaluable as it is an expected workout in the major equitation class, and there is no better way to teach a horse agility. All horses need practice in working in and out from the rail. One cannot take it for granted that horses will naturally handle traffic without breaking a gait. Just turn your horse loose in the paddock to learn this. He will trot down the rail, but when he decides to dodge or make a turn he will invariably change to a canter or run. And if he is already at the gallop, he will generally change leads or cross-lead when he leaves the straight line. Therefore, we must teach the horse how to handle the weaving patterns that traffic demands by simulating the situations at home whenever possible. If you are fortunate enough to have someone to ride with, practice passing and being passed . . . it is going to happen to you in the ring and the intelligent trainer will have taught the horse how to handle the situation well before he enters his first class. With this particular aim in mind, a good exercise is to have the leading horse halt and have the following horse pass and go on for a suitable distance and halt. Then the "obstacle" starts again and this time is the passing horse. We call this "leapfrog" and it really does work. Using the leg aids to complement the rein handling is the practical application of formal equitation to informal situations. This is excellent practice for the rider in sharpening reaction time and a chance to learn to handle the "unexpected" with smooth moves that will maintain the maximum performance. Remember—your horse is only responding naturally when he breaks gait at a sudden direction deviation and he must be trained to handle the situations. Now do you begin to see the real value of individual workouts? They are formalized lessons in the handling of various everyday control problems, and that is why the equitation rider must realize that the manner in which he controls his horse's movements is of equal or superior importance to the actual figure itself.

Training the experienced three-gaited horse to become a Pleasure Equitation horse is challenging and a lot of fun. But it is not the most difficult of tasks. Experience in the ring has prepared most horses for the crowd and passing situations we have just discussed. Here your major problems will probably be the development of agility off the straight line (the rail) since most show horses have been ridden on the rail, except to pass, all of their lives. In fact, most well-trained show horses are actually fearful of correction or punishment when they are asked to pull away from the rail. This factor must be realized by the rider and dealt with gradually and with tangible praise and re-assurance. It is just not fair to expect a horse's mentality to expand that far. Changing of habits in a horse comes by doing, not by "under-standing." Again, the absence of punishment is not enough . . . the horse must have a more positive show of approbation.

Teach your horse to walk. Almost without exception, no horse that we get in for training knows how to walk. There are two obvious reasons for this; most professional trainers are very busy people and just do not take the time to develop the walk. Most judges will observe the first walk the first way of the ring, but almost invariably in the open three-gaited (even in pleasure classes) the command will be to "reverse and trot." Few show horses will settle to the walk on the second way of the ring. If you experience real difficulty with the walk on the reverse, then work your horse only circling right for several days, or even weeks, until the horse has forgotten the original sequence of reverse and trot with no intermediate walk. After you have the horse walking on command, then strive for a speedy, elastic walk that is really going somewhere. I do not subscribe to the flip statement that the walk and the canter only beat you, they cannot win for you. Ridiculous! If you have a good judge who knows what a good walk is, then it should be rewarded. I know that the walk of our previously mentioned pleasure mare had to contribute to her wins. Work into the ground-covering walk gradually. Chances are that your ex-show horse has been taught to perform a prance walk that is absolutely prohibited in pleasure. Your progress may be tedious, but it is the only way. To urge the horse too much and then jab his mouth will not only fail to produce a good walk but may very well teach a horse to fight the bits.

Correct and trouble-free passing at the trot or canter is not difficult at all. One only needs to pull off the rail in adequate time to pass the obstructing horses on the parallel, not the diagonal cutout, cutback. That is where you have erred badly—merely failure to plan ahead.

If you are preparing a green horse for the Pleasure Equitation and other divisions you will be dealing with different problems. Your horse's predictable responses will not be predicated on his prior ring experience because he will have had none. This is virgin territory and, aside from his very strong primary instincts, what the horse learns will be only what you teach him, intended or not.

Do not try to teach the horse everything at once. Develop three consistent gaits around the ring. Then, when he has learned an affinity for the rail, that will be the time to start the foundation movements of serpentine, circling, stopping, and starting. Every situation and locality is different, but you should try to get your horse into "group therapy" as soon as he is ready. Perhaps you can cajole your friends and neighbors into riding with you. This is an advantage we have here at Crabtree Farms, because we have an arena and enough trainers and horses so that we can work a colt into a group experience very easily.

If you do not have anyone to ride with, try to get something going

There was very little Mrs. Rudy Lewis had to learn after listening to her children's equitation lessons. She applied every good technique to her own practices and was rewarded by winning the Saddlebred Pleasure Mare class at the American Royal in 1980. One look at this mare's lovely collection and we see what concentration and horse sense can do. That's equitation! *Photo by Inman*

around the ring with you if it is nothing more than your little brother on a bicycle. But be careful! This is serious and not a lark. First of all, never work close enough for anyone to collide or be kicked. Bales of straw, a pile of stable sheets, a wheelbarrow—any of a myriad of fairly large objects found around the stable can be placed at intervals around the ring. Tape recorders can add the soon-to-be-encountered noise. Calm the horse, caress him when he works around the obstacles

Beulah Cates has been an outstanding saddle seat instructor for many years. With her husband, trainer Elton Cates, she operates a show and equitation stable in San Antonio, Tex. Recently they have been outstanding in their promotion and development of high-quality pleasure riders and horses. Carol Jones, Academy High Point Southwest Circuit Champion in 1979 and 1980. *Instructor photo by Cates, Rider photo by Sargent*

quietly. You must be very supportive at first and may even need to use strong aids to get the horse on a steady course, but that is the only way you can get it done. Severe whipping or jerking is not within the ken of the amateur rider at any time, and very definitely not here. The horse will only learn fear under these circumstances. He must learn to be brave, reinforced by his rider's ability and understanding. Then you will get your performance.

Blue ribbons do not come easily. If they did, they would mean nothing. The utter joy of setting a goal, working hard, and enjoying your work . . . that is your reward. The ribbons are just frosting on the cake.

37

Morgan Equitation

Morgan Equitation is so nearly identical to the equitation on the American Saddlebred that there remains little to say in discussions of this particular breed. Like the Arabians, with their definite designated divisions for both park and pleasure (plus the Half-Arab), there are greater degrees of style variations that may occur because of the differing performances of the horses but the basic seat and the demand for clarity of control called for in any championship or medal class remain constant factors.

Perhaps the greatest discrepancy that characterizes Morgan Equitation may be broken into two factors: conformation of the horse—essentially the same in both park and pleasure—and the horse's way of moving, particularly at the trot. With the pleasure and park horse participating in the same class, we must look at the two and discuss what differences there are and how we alter our riding to suit the choice of division.

Let us discuss the park equitation horse. First of all, what makes a park horse a park horse?

In motion, the park horse should perform all three gaits with brilliant action and animation. The definition of the park walk has long been a subject of great debate, but common usage and acceptance have permitted more and more of the prance to be accepted for the walk. Ideally, the "show walk" is one of high front action with a flat motion in the rear, but about one in five hundred horses can do this. The prance walk has split seconds of complete levitation and this is definitely not a "flat walk."

If you choose the park horse you face the immediate problem of teaching this horse to flat walk. This is a problem common to many breeds and is discussed at length in Chapter 36, "American Saddlebred Pleasure Equitation." I refer you to this chapter.

Now let us consider the trot. Because of the longer body and shorter leg of the Morgan, extreme action may tend to be choppy and

I have selected Jamie Lenore's pictures for a variety of reasons. He represented the best attributes of hard work, talent, good sportsmanship, and excellent instruction. Bob and Louise Rice can be proud of their efforts.

Equally at home on his undefeated roadster, Funquest Stello, or winning an equitation medal, Jamie showed an unusual body and leg contact for a tall rider. He proved that good equitation involves the entire body as well as the mind. *Photos by Bob Moseder*

somewhat difficult to post. Notice that I said longer body, not longer back. The extreme muscularity of both fore and hind quarters takes up back length and the length is measured more in the distance from the elbow back to the stifle than from the withers to the croup. What the equitation rider hopes to find here is a horse that has the attractive motion and carriage to enhance a rider's total picture without getting into rough gaits.

Some horses are rough-moving because they will not relax sufficiently to permit a smooth ride. If this is the case, letting the horse down temperamentally may smooth out the rough trot. It will certainly prepare the horse mentally for the stopping, holding of gait and pattern, and the complete discipline that are called for in work-outs.

Can you smooth out the trot by altering the horse's shoeing? Since Morgan Horse Equitation has not reached the magnitude of Saddle Horse Equitation, one must realize that there are rarely, if ever, Morgan horses who are exclusively equitation horses. The Morgan doubles in brass and so we must keep in mind the class requirements that must be met when the rider enters open competition. This is not the problem here that it becomes when we use the pleasure horse for equitation, but it does have certain ramifications.

Try different shoeing angles. Length of foot and weight of shoe can make some difference in certain horses, not all. What works for one horse may be disaster with another. Your best bet here is to get the advice and co-operation of a very good blacksmith. Begin your experimenting in the winter and give the horse at least a month to accommodate to the change. Shoeing is too expensive to try everything in the books. Give your idea time to work. Remember, too, that the adaptation of the park horse to the agility of the equitation work must be considered, and just plain equitation basics such as circles and serpentines may smooth out your ride.

I can think of no better place in this book to state unequivocally that equitation training will enhance your horse as a performance horse. We do not "take away" from an animal to create an equitation mount, we add to and refine the horse's natural and practiced attributes. Sure, we let a horse down a lot when we begin his equitation training but this is, hopefully, for only a brief period of adjustment. When we have polished and finished our conversion, the only thing we have changed is that we have a nice performance horse who has learned to be a better and more consistent performer.

Because of the aggressive trot of the park horse and a possible tendency for him to take a stronger hold of the bits, the rider must make every effort to relax his controlling muscles and the seat muscles. A sharp tap from the saddle on relaxed buttock muscles will not jerk a rider, but let that saddle rise into a rigid seat and the rider will bounce like a golf ball with the distinct probability that the hands will bump the horse's mouth, further compounding the problem. If you choose the park horse for equitation, then grace must be your middle name.

With the choice of the pleasure horse, the equitation rider must

Heather Bostrom, Detroit, Mich., was one of the youngsters who came to Crabtrees' during two periods of public teaching and I have never enjoyed a rider more. She could have been tops in any breed competition but it was the Morgan trainers who gave her the opportunity to show good horses and win. Only a ten-year-old, Heather learned and retained more than any transient rider I ever had. Her biggest wins of many were reserve in 13 and Under and sixth in the AMHA National Equitation Finals at Oklahoma City in 1980. *Photo by Ray Randall*

face shoeing restrictions that may not be tampered with. This is a fact of which all Morgan exhibitors are aware. What you can deal with is the comparison of yourself on a horse moving at a pleasure trot in competition with the bigger-moving park mount. We all know that only the rider is judged in equitation, and if you can keep this precept firmly in mind, then you will be able to ride your horse up to his limitations and not spoil the ride by trying to make your horse something that he is not. Neither do you want to fall into the fatal mistake of thinking that the quietude of a pleasure horse implies that you should turn into a do-nothing statue. As always, proper equitation is the riding that produces the best performance from each individual horse.

In readying yourself for equitation competition, adhere to the principles of body placement and general equitation practices that appear in the earlier chapters of this book. In this Morgan situation, I wish to deal with specifics that apply to equitation with the Morgan horse.

There is a conformation factor that goes with the Morgan and that is the full crest of the neck. This has a direct bearing on the distance from the rider's hands to the horse's mane (which may be drifting back, seeming to further shorten the separation of horse and rider). The fit of the saddle is extremely important and the new saddle described in the first part of this book can help the problem greatly. With the adjustable stirrups, the rider can stay back on his horse where he needs to be and the legs and stirrups will be back with him. The full rounded body of most Morgans makes it difficult to keep a saddle back. Many riders have bought long-treed saddles but, with the usual forward mounting of the stirrups, the rider's seat may go back, but the feet will either remain forward or they will slip back and forth as the rider posts. Especially on the pleasure horse where we apply considerable forcing, the leg position at the horse's ribs is a must. Legs should not have to move very far to be effective. Legs in constant position need only a squeezing and strengthening to accomplish their task.

To return to the hand-crest relationship; keeping back on the saddle will enhance the total picture and get away from the illusion that the rider is almost grasping the mane. One can only do this by moving the entire body back. One cannot do it by leaning back from the hips or waist. This will destroy body balance of both rider and horse and the beautiful picture of unity of the combination will be destroyed.

You will be able to elevate the horse's front only as much as his conformation allows. Trying more will only reap resistance and tension. Too much "riding" will often result in a stilted trot with a jerking hesitation that is anathema to any hope of a smooth rider or a comfortable responsive horse.

Quite often we see spurs in equitation and very seldom do we see them used wisely or with predictable results. A nagging tap will only annoy a horse and seldom sharpen his attention. Too much use can result in extreme resentment and defiance. So many of the kickers have learned this vice as protest to the injudicious use of spurs. Daily work at improving your horse's response is still the only way to develop a

When Ann Anderson and Topfield's Janet literally burst on the Morgan scene in 1979 they created a picture of such complete collection and brilliance that I felt it deserved a place in this book. First of all, note the combination of hand control coupled with the forcing action of the thighs and calves. Ann is somewhat tilted at the waist and has gone to her toes to get her legs where they belong. But these two actions are interrelated and are plainly caused by a saddle on which the stirrups are mounted too far forward. Ann's grace and expertise have overcome her saddle handicap and the perfection of the mare attests to the fact she is getting nothing but good directives from her rider. *Photo by Darkroom on Wheels, Paula Siste*

Anyone who has ever attended a Morgan Horse Show will carry the picture of Judy Whitney in their minds. She is always correct, brilliant, and in control of a superbly balanced horse. Whit Haven Valor shows the balance obtained by the total concentration of the rider. God endows an animal with talent, but only complete horsemanship can get results like this. Bob and Judy Whitney do not teach equitation at their stable in Cox's Creek, Ky., but by the remarkable demonstration of excellence in their training and showing they exert a great effect on young riders all over the country. Again, we see proof that trainers and equitation riders have reached a point of mutual influence. *Photo by Moseder*

Phil Price of Carrousel Stables in Bellevue, Ohio, is a trainer who reflects the influence of proper equitation. His many Morgan stake winners attest to the truism, Good riding, good horses. His mother, father, wife Conky, and sister Penny are all great credits to the horse industry and give very unselfishly of themselves to promote the Morgan horse and to help all breed owners. A splendid family. The perfect collection of this horse, Royal Oak's Annton, could never happen under a careless rider. Perfection does breed perfection. *Photo by Schatzberg*

consistent good performance. Last-ditch efforts with newly purchased spurs can land the rider in the ditch!

An advantage that the trappy-moving mount can offer his rider is his agility in tight figure work. I always admonish my riders to "squeeze the accordion" to literally shorten their horse's length from the tip of his nose to the hocks so that the shorter length will accommodate to a small turn or circle. Certainly we do not want to stand a horse on his head to make a ridiculously small circle, but if there is ever a combination to execute neat, tight figures that are completely free from the influence of the confines of the ring, then this rider mounted on the Morgan pleasure horse has a real advantage. Advantages do not just happen. The potential is always there, and the advantage comes when you as a rider or instructor think deeply enough to utilize your fortuitous position. Your advantages here should be obvious. You have the space-saving trot and canter coupled with the temperament that will accept the stringent control that precision demands. Your disadvantage is that you may fall into the trap of waiting for the workouts to show the judge your best riding. Just remember, you must be good on the rail to earn the privilege of riding the individual workouts.

I always remember a new owner who had come into our stable with nothing right but attitude and desire. We all worked hard and the child made excellent progress. We bought her a nice horse and had Nicholas make her an elegant habit.

The morning of the first show's age group the family arrived in a high state of expectation and I was horrified to see the child attired in the old original suit that looked to me more like pajamas than a riding habit. When I inquired where the new duds were, the mother said, "Oh, Mrs. Crabtree, we're saving that for the championship"! It was several weeks before the child ever qualified for a championship but, needless to say, the well-fitting habit made it possible to finally get there.

The pictures of the adults that I am including in this section should help every rider realize just what the end results of equitation are. The balance, control, and concentration are evident to the educated eye. Study these pictures. These riders are aware that only GOOD RIDING can make good horses and the proof is here for all to see. Equitation is not to be abandoned at age eighteen . . . that is only the beginning of even greater things to come. But come they will, if you establish a good logical formal equitation base as a young and learning rider.

38

American Morgan Horse Association Medal Class

AMHA medal classes are offered to any Morgan, AHSA regular member, or CHSA show or any show approved by the AMHA Youth Committee for riders who have not reached their eighteenth birthday. All riders must be current AMHA members and must be mounted on registered Morgan mares or geldings.

Shows offering medal classes are encouraged but not required to offer two additional classes in equitation.

Two or more individual tests of the top four contestants are required. Five properly appointed riders are sufficient to fill a class.

First- or second-place winners will automatically qualify for the Medal Finals at the yearly Grand National Morgan Horse Show. Qualifying winners will receive a silver medal; second, who will also be eligible to ride in the Finals, will receive a certificate. (This is the rule in 1980, but may be changed to winner only if increasing medal classes make the restriction more fitting.)

All who qualify are eligible to compete in the AMHA Medal Final held each fall at the Grand National Morgan Horse Show.

Since all classes designated as AMHA medal classes are conducted under AHSA Equitation Rules and Standards, with the exception of two qualifiers per class, listing of the class procedure and tests from which judges may choose should be referred to in this book.

The name of the winning contestant of the final competition will be engraved on a perpetual trophy, property of the AMHA and so display in the head office. A gold medal will be presented to the winner.

In the Final, groups of twenty or less will work on the rail and perform an individual workout. Finalists will be chosen if number of entries necessitate preliminaries and they will compete in the final ride-off.

Since 1973 and the establishment of the Morgan Grand National, the AMHA Gold Medal Final has been held.

Following is a list of winners and their instructors:

1973	Ann Hutcheson, Oakland, N.J.	Barbara Irvine, Instructor
1974	Alison Mauthe, Stone Mountain, Ga.	Jimmy Glidewell, Instructor
1975	Linda Brown, Brighton, Mich.	Penny Price, Instructor
1976	Jamie Lenore, El Cajon, Calif.	Bob Rice, Instructor
1977	Darlene Kay, Dover, N.H.	Judy Nason, Instructor
1978	Ling Fu, Albuquerque, N.M.	Tim O'Gorman, Instructor
1979	Michelle Raduano, Dover, Mass.	Abbott Wilson, Instructor
1980	Laura Ashmore, Tulsa, Okla.	John C. Sowle, Instructor

Ann Hutcheson, first winner AMHA Saddle Seat Medal Finals 1973. *Photo by Moseder for Tarrance Studios*

Jamie Lenore, AMHA Saddle Seat Medal Champion 1976. *Photo by Moseder*

Darlene Kay, AMHA Saddle Seat Medal Champion 1977. *Photo by Sparagowski*

Ling Fu, AMHA Saddle Seat Medal Champion 1978. *Photo by Schatzberg*

Michelle Raduano, AMHA Saddle Seat Medal Champion 1979. *Photo by Moseder*

Laura Ashmore, AMHA Saddle Seat Medal Champion 1980. *Photo by Inman*

39

Morgan Equitation Instructors

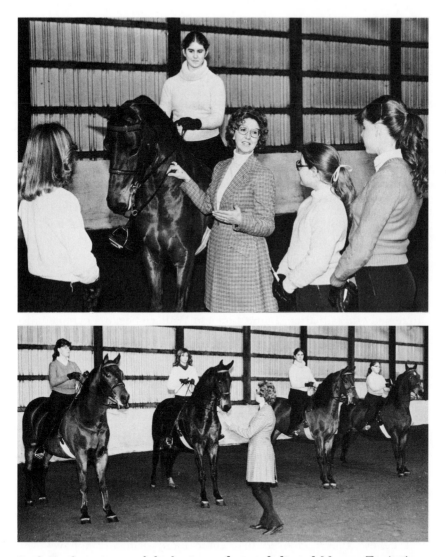

Leah Kaufman is one of the busiest and most dedicated Morgan Equitation teachers to be found anywhere. In Westfield, Ind., where she and her husband, Al, operate a first-class stable, Leah teaches all week and finds time to give clinics both at home and out of the state. Certainly a noteworthy contribution has been Leah's working with the mentally and physically handicapped children to teach them the joys of riding. She has been of invaluable aid to me in securing information and pictures of other Morgan instructors. *Photos by Patty Allen*

40

Tennessee Walking Horse Equitation

Walking Horse Equitation has had a yo-yo existence since the early 1960s, when Faye and Richard Mary of Baton Rouge, Louisiana, developed some superior riders who almost completely dominated Walking Equitation for several years. They set a standard of excellence that remains extremely high.

After the Marys, there was a low period in which equitation was negligible to say the least. Several of the trainers and their wives were aware of the slipping standards in the young people's riding and determined to do something about this unfortunate situation in which good young riders were willing and often able and ready for horsemanship classes that just did not exist.

If there was ever a dedicated, one-woman committee, then it was Laura Lou Brandon, who with her husband's encouragement set out to remedy this situation. Laura Lou and Wallace began a campaign to get equitation its rightful place in their shows. With the help and encouragement of Vic Thompson, Mr. Beech, and other established leaders, they began.

In 1977, at the National Walking Horse Trainers' Horse Show held in Louisville at the Kentucky State Fair Exposition Hall, I was invited to give a one-hour working clinic one free afternoon. Linda Fischer, one of my most treasured riders and helpers, went with me to ride her equitation horse.

The response was overwhelming. I do not believe that a single person left his seat during the one hour that turned into two. On the way into the arena, I was overtaken by Vic Thompson, who said, "Give 'em hell, Helen—let's get these kids to shine their boots and ride those horses. Just tell it like it is."

I believe that I enjoyed that clinic more than any I have ever given. About a dozen participants rode and accepted positive criticism on riding form, tack, proper horse performance, collection, controlled use of the body and the artificial aids, etc. At the end, one father came up to me in a state of extreme excitement. I will never forget his words: "Mrs. Crabtree, God bless you. My little boy fell off his horse at the last show and I just knew he couldn't reach his stirrups. Now, today I hear you say those stirrups were too long. I'm not going to quit the business, I'm going out and buy two more horses for my boy."

I tell this only to prove a point; children and parents are not dumb. They want the best and they know that proper attention to the development of young riders is possible for all trainers to give if they will just decide to study their own lessons and impart their knowledge to the youngsters.

As a footnote to the clinic, I was told that every participant who rode again in that show improved his placings.

The very facts that the Walking horse's true gaits are so easy to ride and the horses are so generally even-tempered make it possible for almost anyone to "ride" a Walking horse. Now riding and riding well are night and day, so the very qualities that make for the popularity of the Walking horse have contributed to the lack of progress in riding style and attainment that represents so much more work in the saddle breeds that require posting. The "Git 'n Go" school of Walking horsemanship was about to swallow up the very hand that fed it and was unknowingly its own worst detriment to progress and perfection. As I have said so often, young riders influence the trainers and the showmen certainly impress the youth. When a child and a trainer are standing together with their blue ribbons and a passer-by says to the child, "You rode beautifully," and then turns to the trainer and says, "Congratulations," the message is loud and clear—the paying customers not only want to see a winning ride but they yearn for beauty as well. And in riding, as in any other sport, beauty and perfection are one.

As the pictures of the Walking Medal Final winners so dramatically illustrate, two factors stand out. Laura Brandon is there—in 1977 with a good rider and a simple trophy. Compare the 1980 picture. Every trophy represents an establishment or a group of people who know how important Walking Horse Equitation is to the entire industry. And as the song title states, "We've only just begun."

With great determination and imagination the Walking Horse Trainers Auxiliary has evolved the idea of cash incentives to encourage the trainers to include good equitation instruction in their training barns. Begun in 1981, and spearheaded by the hard-working Laura Brandon, $1500 will be offered annually, to be paid out at the National Walking Horse Celebration in Shelbyville, Tennessee: $750 will be given to the trainer whose rider wins the Equitation Medal Final, providing that rider has competed in at least ten qualifying medal classes that year; an additional $750 will be paid to the trainer who puts the most equitation riders into the show rings that year. Conceivably the same trainer could collect both awards.

The originating idea is to make up the money from donations and from an annual auction and "roast," the first honoree being the universally recognized Vic Thompson.

Since the Walking Horse Medal Final is a challenge cup, it is evident that Final winners may continue to compete, which makes this division differ from the other three seats recognized by the AHSA. We must admire the tenacity of those people whose only thought is the betterment of the sport when they conceive a unique idea. With such unselfish drive and interest, it must work and many future trainers will have these dedicated few to thank for their prosperity.

As stated before, anything that is good looks easy, but the opposite does not necessarily hold true. This is the siren call of Walking Equitation—if you can sit in the middle of a horse, know "whoa" from "go," and have a well-trained horse that canters well on faint cue, then this rider can fool himself and the general public. This is why the trainers and teachers must teach good basic training and horse psychology. The quality of the gaits has to be of supreme importance and a rider cannot get perfection without knowledge. If a rider who is blessed with an unusual physical attractiveness is mounted on a superior horse in equitation, it could be possible for a "fake" rider to win because the gaits are so easy to sit to. This is the trap that the trainers and the riders, too, must avoid at all costs. The "how to" is not the important factor. The "why" is. You must realize the monster you are creating when you fail to teach the rider why the horse reacts the way he does, because if you do not teach completely, then when the untutored winner hits the open classes, he is lost.

One aspect of Walking-horse riding has been the emphasis on hand motion. How often we have seen horses almost literally "pumped" off of the ground in a hesitation that is not only physically erosive to the horse but grotesque to ride and to watch. This particularly applies to the canter and frequently results in a very unorthodox gait. A canter is a three-beat gait, initiated in one hind foot, followed by the next diagonal pair, and completed by the remaining front foot, which is the "leading foot." Excessive lifting can result in the "leap and lurch" type of canter which really is not a canter at all—being a highly restrained four-beat gait.

A good equitation judge cannot and will not reward a rider who produces an illegal gait. Here is where the wonderful influence of strong equitation can really help to change the complete picture of the walking breed by returning to the beautiful-to-watch, elegantly flowing canter that the Walking horse used to do. Saddle Seat Equitation on the Saddlebred was in this same dilemma thirty-five years ago when the riders just rode the tack and not the horse, when children drilled through their seventeenth year keeping their heads up and· their heels down. Then . . . after equitation, they "progressed" to a trainer who could begin to teach them how to show a horse!

But the task of closing that gap will not take years with the Walking horse. It can be done today because perfect balance can be attained in less than thirty days, and then we can get to the immediate delight of learning to understand our horse, physically and mentally.

The "big lick" that is the hallmark of the Walking breed is an intelligent blending of collection with the distinctive conformation of the breed. The exceptional make-up and mobility of the horse's "motor," mainly the stifle and gaskin, permit this horse to lower his hind quarters and reach forward with the long rear overstride. In order to keep the front motion high and hesitant enough for the longer, slower hind strides to keep synchronized, the rider must aid the horse's front end in this waiting process. The head must be high for the rear to drop down. The motion must be high to take up the time off the ground, otherwise the rear will rise, the forehand will drop and we will have a bobby-going horse that will be perilously close to racking or trotting. Now, with just this cursory examination of the flat walk and the running walk, the rider should be able to understand what an instructor means when he says, "Get into him, take hold of him." He is simply asking for collection and balance, not a circus performance. God and selective breeding did much of the rider's work, so the process of collection should be relatively easy and unobtrusive. The hunched, overtly pumping rider—whether he intends to or not—is giving the impression that his horse is not really much and only by the hardest effort is the rider able to make him any kind of a competitor. What a disservice it is to a wonderful breed to make this lovely animal look like a clown. Just study the pictures of our good young riders in this section and see how they can get results with a firm but sympathetic hand on the reins, a strong seat down in the saddle with the strength running right down through the heels, where calf pressure can encourage that horse to drop down and reach with his hind feet.

Open knees, slack legs, swinging feet with hit-or-miss spurring are not only common faults, they are just plain ugly. There is no excuse for sloppy riding. The old-fashioned seat was winning years ago when trainers and promoters were trying to show the world how easy-riding the Walking horse was. That is a well-established fact and no longer needs the fancied exaggeration of earlier days.

Now, a word about spurs. If the rider sits firmly in the saddle with strong calf contact and stirrup pressure, the horse will respect these aids and respond with the hind quarters with no need for spurs. The tendency to use overlong stirrups complicates the use of spurs as many riders' feet are well below the horses' bellies. This causes tiptoeing in the stirrups and upward swinging of the heels. Actually, spurs are a poor crutch and very difficult to use. I see trainers spurring away at some poor horse's stifles and then they spend fortunes on blacksmiths to try to remedy the horse that wings his stifles at each stride. The horse is just trying to avoid the spurs.

Collecting the horse must be a combination of force (seat) and restraint (hands). The horse that lugs is no equitation horse unless he is lugging because the rider never relaxes on the reins. The unattractive "bottoms up" stance at the reverse would not be necessary if we had not deadened the horse's jaw in the first place. So use your head to have good hands. Since you have only the one bit in the horse's mouth, the rider must be smart and know his horse so he can hold his form without cutting off the feeling in the chin. Never freeze on the reins and do take advantage of change of gaits to "pitch the bit" in the horse's mouth to refresh it.

Since the mechanics of figure work transfer from breed to breed because the correct approach is psychological, the chapter on workouts in the earlier section should suffice.

For riding without stirrups, the picture of Lee Minish in the 1977 Finals Presentation is an excellent example of good position. Since posting is never required here, the main elements of a deep seat, firm knees, and strong lowered heels fulfill the test very well.

At the canter figure eight, if a forward toe to the desired lead is being employed, one must be an excellent student if one's horse is to get the timing correct. Horses who are taught the toe aid generally respond at touch and your touch must occur just as the horse begins the forward movement of the desired leading shoulder. With the signal originating in the rear, the indication to move the hind leg is given to the horse but there is more freedom of timing for the horse to actually align all four feet correctly. With the toe aid the horse will lift the indicated foot when signaled, often regardless of the placement of the other three feet, and the chances of getting a disunited canter are great. If you are sure you understand timing and your horse's response, then use the toe aid. If it gives you trouble, then teach the horse to use the outside calf cue. Whichever you do, always be sure to employ the inside leg aid to bend the horse's body around the circle. Jan Pennington of Talmo, Georgia, has graciously taken the photographs for me that pictorialize much of these basic principles. The steps of addressing reins are particularly good and need no further explanation. She has been very moderate in her illustration of the too long stirrup, as this fault is so very often much more exaggerated, with the tip of the toe barely reaching the stirrup bar and the heel consequently high. If I were to select one fault that is the most flagrant in riding and showing the Walking horse, it would be the tendency to ride stirrups much too long. If for no other reason than aesthetics, the moderate-length stirrup simply looks better. Feet hanging below the silhouette of the horse's belly are very distracting to the entire picture and serve no useful purpose at all. The new saddle illustrated in the front of the book will allow any rider to use his legs to the rear without having to resort to the extra-long leather. That this has been a problem in the past has been proven by the many times in each show that the class waited while a fallen stirrup was put back on the saddle. The new type, with the stirrup mountings that can be moved to the rear, will let the legs stay back with the seat. No longer will the rider be forced to sit in the rumble seat with his feet on the dashboard!

Several years ago I was at Oklahoma City and Vic Thompson invited me to ride a smart little Walking mare one morning. In fact, she was the current World's Champion lady's mare. Like a real friend, I said, "I'd love to but do you think I could hold her?" Well!!! If looks could kill I would be six feet under, but he only said, "Helen, if she doesn't have as good a mouth as any horse you ever rode, I'll give her to you." Needless to say, Vic was safe with that remark because I never had a more enjoyable ride. I was invited to show at the Celebration, but it would have been a no-win situation. If I had won, I would have been rightfully resented by every lady exhibitor and if I had lost I would have been the world's prize dummy . . . so I declined. But I have always wished that I could have shown at the Celebration.

41

Tennessee Walking Horse
Equitation Rules

TENNESSEE WALKING HORSE EQUITATION.

SEC. 1. SEAT AND HANDS. (AS PRINTED IN THE 1980–81 AHSA RULE BOOK)

(a) General. It should be stressed that the required Equitation Walking Seat is a natural, coordinated and comfortable riding position and should in no way be rigid or exaggerated.

A rider should convey the impression of effective and easy control, with the general appearance of being able to ride for a considerable length of time with pleasure. To show a horse well he should show himself to the best advantage. Ring generalship shall be taken into consideration by the judges. The appearance, presentation and alertness of the rider and his mount make the over-all picture of utmost importance.

(b) Mounting and Dismounting. To mount, take up reins in left hand and place hand on withers. Grasp stirrup leather with right hand and insert left foot in stirrup and mount. To dismount, rider may either step down or slide down.

(c) Hands. The hands should be held in an easy position, waist or elbow high, over pommel, with palms downward, slightly turned toward body, wrists rounded slightly. The hands should be in unison with the horse's mouth, showing adaptability as well as control. How and where the horse carries his head determines the height the hands are held above the horse's withers. Hands and wrists should be flexible and not held extremely separated. (From the rider's view the hands should be in a V shape, close enough for thumbs to touch.) The fingers should be closed over reins, firm but not rigid. Pressure between thumb and index fingers to secure ends. Closed (or crossed) reins shall be used, with both hands on the reins, and the bight of the rein should be on the off side.

(d) Basic Position. To obtain proper position rider should sit comfortably in the middle of the saddle and find his center of gravity by sitting with a slight bend at the knees, without use of the stirrups. While in this position, have stirrup leathers adjusted to fit so that irons will be under ball of foot with even pressure on entire width of sole and center of iron. The foot position will be natural and comfortable if the knee and thigh are rolled inward and the heel is slightly lower than the toes. From the front or rear view, the lower leg will be held naturally away from the horse, depending on the anatomy of the rider and the size of the horse. Knee should rest against saddle.

(e) Position in Motion. The position in motion should be natural, co-ordinated and graceful, attained only with practice. From the side view a straight line can be drawn perpendicular to the ground through the rider's head, neck, shoulder, hip and ankle. The rider's toe should never be any more forward than his knee, thereby keeping his center of balance directly above his feet and ankles. Upper arms should fall naturally from the shoulder toward the hip bones, and should be flexible, never clutched to the body, extended forward, or spread away from the body. Hands should be in a comfortable waist-level position, depending on how and where the horse carries his head. The use of the hands should be smooth and gradual, without jerking or pumping at any of the gaits, or jerks on the reins when parked.

SEC. 2. APPOINTMENTS.

(a) Personal. Entries are judged on ability, but with neat and properly fitted riding habits; all exhibitors enhance their appearance in the show ring. The following requirements are based on simple, good taste, which is always in style and correct at all times.

The riding habit with two or three-button type coat in dark blue, dark brown, dark grey or black with matching accessories is always correct, day or evening. The semi-formal or tuxedo-type, one-button coat with continental tie is suitable to be worn at night only. For the more informal morning and afternoon classes, the simple, well-tailored habit of medium weight material, suitable for daytime wear, is preferred. In the summer a matching straw hat is acceptable.

Riding suits should be neatly pressed and jodhpur boots polished and in good condition. The riding suit should fit the rider, and a moderate fullness is better than too snug a fit. Coats should be finger-tip length when one is standing, and jodhpurs should be no more than one inch above the boot heel when mounted on the horse. Jodhpur straps should always be used. There is no equitation class in a horse show where conspicuous riding coats of bright color, plaid, stripe, brocade or sequins are acceptable. Satin, sequins, scrollwork, rhinestones and other added decorations belong only in a costume class or the circus.

The rider's hair must be neat and well groomed. Girls with long hair should have it styled so the back number can be seen easily.

Earrings and bracelets, as well as large rings, do not belong in the show ring; neither do flying hair ribbons, corsages and large flowers. Nothing should distract from the genuine beauty of a well trained horse and skilled rider.

Judges shall eliminate those contestants who do not conform.

(b) Tack.

Bridles: Should be of the type commonly used by Walking Horses, with single pair of reins. Brow bands decorated with rhinestones, etc. do not belong in equitation classes. Clean, well-kept bridles and shining silver bits are far more attractive. Martingales or similar tie-downs are prohibited.

Saddles: Should be of the flat, English-type, and of the correct size for the rider. Forward seat or western saddles are prohibited.

Boots: Clean, white boots of proper weight and design should be well fastened before horse enters ring. Boots are not removed during class as horses are not being judged. Boots may or may not be used.

Braid: Neatly attached at forelock and mane. Color should blend well with rider's habit and brow band.

▪ Action Devices: May be used provided they are in accordance with Part I, Sec. 2. All tack should be neat and clean, in good condition, and fit correctly on the horse.

SEC. 3. CLASS ROUTINE.

Enter ring at the flat-walk, turning to right and proceeding in counter clockwise direction. The class shall proceed at least once around the ring at each gait, and on command reverse and repeat. Riders may reverse mounts either forward or away from the rail. The gesture of stopping, leaning forward in the saddle and feeling of the curb chain is permissible if necessary, but certainly not desirable, and should be avoided. Entries shall line up on command and any or all riders may be required to execute any tests listed.

SEC. 4. TESTS FROM WHICH JUDGES MUST CHOOSE.

Tests may be performed either individually or as a group, and should be asked for after the entire class is lined up after performance both directions of the ring.

1. Pick up Reins; A quick check on muscular control and sensitivity of hands.
2. Backing; Must be required, as a check on hands, arms, thighs, knees and lower legs, feet, and voice commands.
3. Dismount and Mount; To be done quietly and as gracefully as possible.
4. Group Performance Around Ring; To check on maneuverability, ring generalship, etiquette and sportsmanship.
5. Individual Performance on Rail; Any or all gaits and tests may be required, including change of canter leads. See rider in motion from both front and rear at all three walking horse gaits.
6. Ride Without Stirrups; Any or all gaits may be requested.
7. Change Canter Leads Down Center Of Ring; Change leads, stopping at each change.
8. Figure Eight At Canter On Correct Lead; Full stop required on each change of lead. Pattern to begin at center of two circles so as to show one lead change.

SEC. 5. JUDGES.

Judges for Walking Horse Equitation classes are to be selected from the current Roster of Recognized Judges in Walking Horses or Saddle Seat Equitation.

Barbara Irvine has earned herself a unique place in Morgan annals through her excellent work with equitation riders. Hers was the honor of putting her student, Ann Hutcheson, in the winner's circle for the first AMHA Equitation Championship Finals in 1973. Stacy Ann Catlow, pictured here, is a present-day representative of this hard-working lady who contributes to every facet of the Morgan breed at her stable in Midland Park, N.J. *Instructor photo by Haviland, Student photo by Moseder*

326

Judy Nason is doing great work in Morgan Equitation at her stable in Dover, N.H. Darlene Kay was her first AMHA Final winner but she will have more.

Pictured here is Desiré Kay, a 1975 walk-trot winner for Judy. *Instructor photo by Bob Moseder, Student photo by Hilary Dollier*

In Dexter, Mich., Judy and Joe Dunville operate a very successful Morgan stable. Judy is an excellent equitation instructor working with both juveniles and adults. A fine example of her work is Pam Gunhiecl, AMHA Medal winner and one of many strong riders from this stable. *Instructor photo by Harold Koch, Rider photo by Moseder*

Susan Walker, who with her husband, Garn, operates a very successful Morgan training stable in Livermore, Calif., has had a positive impact on that breed in the West. Her equitation students have been outstanding, and through Susan reflect the early influence of Roy Register, who was her professional mentor in earlier years.

Elizabeth Goth is one of Susan's most successful students, shown here on Devan Lexington. *Instructor photo by Fallaw, Rider photo by Howard Schatzberg*

Penny Price is the equitation instructor for the famous Carrousel Stables of Bellevue, Ohio. A top trainer and rider, Penny proved that she could impart her knowledge when Linda Brown of Brighton, Mich., shown here, won the AMHA Gold Medal in 1975. *Instructor photo by Moseder, Student photo by Johnny Johnston*

42

Walking Equitation Do's and Don'ts

I can never adequately thank Jan Pennington for her cheerful and tireless efforts in preparing this section on Walking Horse Equitation. The breed must be proud of this fine worker.

ADDRESSING REINS

STEP ONE

STEP TWO

STEP THREE

STEP FOUR (Crossing Reins)
Photos by Jan Pennington

SOME COMMON FAULTS

HANDS TOO CLOSE

HANDS TOO FAR APART

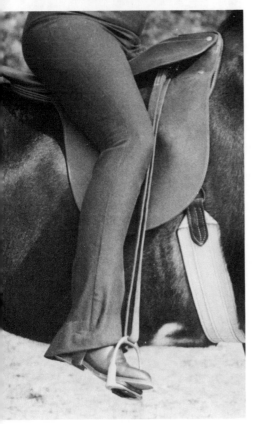

STIRRUPS TOO SHORT

STIRRUPS TOO LONG
Photos by Jan Pennington

Excellent leg position. Showing strong leg and thigh contact with the rider's foot pressure evenly distributed on the stirrup bar. *Photo by Pennington*

Perfect posture for Walking Horse Equitation—or any breed of horse. Balance is the keystone of all seats for all riding. *Photo by Pennington*

This splendid picture of Kim Williams in a victory pass represents Tennessee Walking Equitation at its best. Perfect balance of both rider and horse reflects the result of hours of studious riding and many more hours of just plain watching and learning. No class is too insignificant to educate the inspired learner. Very often one can learn more from watching and analyzing poor performances than can be gleaned from perfection.

I especially like the solid seat, the obvious body influence of rider on horse, and the attention to detail that makes such perfection possible. This rider is having fun and her horse's performance reflects the joy of accomplishment. Kim is self-taught, an inspiration to those who do not have access to professional help. It is the long way around, but it can be done.
Photo by Jamie Donaldson

43

Tennessee Walking Horse Trainers' Auxiliary Medal Final Winners

RIDER		INSTRUCTOR
Lee Minish, Commerce, Ga.	1977	Jan Pennington
Virginia Ann Taylor, McComb, Miss.	1978	Ron Eads
Kim Williams, Bishopville, S.C.	1979	Self-taught
Kim Williams, Bishopville, S.C.	1980	Self-taught

Lee Minish of Commerce, Ga., taught by Jan Pennington of Talmo, Ga., had the honor of being named winner of the first Tennessee Walking Horse Equitation Medal in 1977. Held at the National Walking Horse Celebration each year since, the Medal and the growing interest and respect it generates are vital parts of this huge show.

Laura Brandon is presenting the trophy in this class she worked so hard to institute. *Photo by Segroves, Shelbyville Times-Gazette*

Nineteen seventy-eight was the second year for the Medal, and the intense crowd at the famed Walking Horse Celebration saw Virginia Ann Taylor of McComb win it. Ron Eads, Waco, Tex., was her proud instructor. The solid seat and undeniable style shown here in action must have made a great impression on the judge. *Photo by Jim Dixon*

Kim Williams, Bishopville, S.C., went the distance to win the Medal in
1979. This self-taught rider did not rest on her laurels but worked even
harder and returned in 1980 to take the Medal for a second time. Such
self-discipline and willingness to work for improvement are to be com-
mended. The impressive trophies are evidence of the rapid growth of interest in Walking Horse Equitation in just four years. *Photo by Segroves,
Shelbyville Times-Gazette*

Jan Pennington of Talmo, Ga., is the outstanding instructor of Walking Horse Equitation. Her riders have a correctness of seat and a distinctive "Pennington" style. She is an instructor who is willing to give her time and energies to the promotion of equitation, as she understands so well where the future of any breed lies—in young riders. Charlene Brown, WHOA High Point Winner in 1978, is a fine example of her teaching. *Instructor photo by Pennington, Rider photo by Donaldson*

Ron Eads, now from El Dorado, Ark., trained the 1978 Medal winner, Virginia Ann Taylor. Her picture in this section shows that, with such teaching, Ron Eads will have many more correct riders in the ring. *Photo by Jim Brewster*

Here are two people who match their ideas with effort. Mr. and Mrs. Wallace Brandon, by their own examples of perfection, have created a fine image for all aspiring riders to emulate. Their stable is in Franklin, Tenn. By their unselfish efforts they are making things open up in the Walking Horse Equitation. They will succeed because they are right. *Photos by Sargent*

44

Development of Arabian
Saddle Seat Equitation

It has been only in the last decade that Saddle Seat Equitation on Arabian horses has gained the recognition it deserves. Prior to 1968, many shows had equitation classes for different age groups, but there were no medal classes or national titles and only the largest shows had a championship.

It was in 1968 that a number of prominent Arabian horsemen, including Tom Townsend, a fine equitation rider himself in previous years, Mona Betts, Carol Chapman, and others were instrumental in establishing the first Arabian Saddle Seat Equitation class at the Nationals in Albuquerque. Though not considered a "National class," which meant there was no qualification necessary and a different trophy than the traditional National trophy was awarded, the response was good, with twenty-eight to thirty riders participating. Cheri Barber, taught by her mother Imogene, both of Oklahoma City, was the first winner.

The same procedure was used the following year in Oklahoma City, where Lu Anthony, a successful equitation rider of saddle horses for many years under the guidance of Harold Adams, borrowed an Arabian and delighted a home-town crowd as she defeated a large class of riders following a grueling, never-to-be-forgotten workout without stirrups.

Noting the large turnout for these classes in their first two appearances at Nationals and the growing interest in this division, the International Arabian Horse Association decided to sanction a Saddle Seat Medal type of championship for the first time in 1970. Shows around the country were quick to add this class to their premium lists, but only 14 riders arrived to compete for the National Championship title. The two class winners from 1968 and 1969 were allowed to compete again, but a few years later their victories were recognized as National Championships as well. Cathy Crier of Dallas, started by

Joanne Crockett of Van Alstyne, Texas, took home the first National trophy awarded in this division, a 24-inch Arabian horse in bronze.

From the beginning, Arabian Saddle Seat Equitation was dominated by riders and instructors from the Southwest. Region 9, which includes Oklahoma, Texas, Arkansas, and Louisiana, boasts more champions and reserves than all other regions combined in the first twelve years. Gwen Nix of Carealot Farm in Houston began turning out champion after champion and, in fact, has never failed to have a Top Ten rider each year since the beginning in 1968. In Arabian Equitation events, the Top Ten riders in the nation are selected without being ranked after three phases of workouts, and from those ten a champion and reserve are selected. Gwen's students, Lois Finch, Louisa Craft, and Leslie Greg, were National Champions in 1971, 1973, and 1974. Her riders, Jane Latimer, Trudy Braden, and Kathy Craft, were reserve in 1968, 1971, and 1972, and in 1979 she made a clean sweep by winning both the championship with Bob Affleck and reserve with Derek Cook (both boys are from near Salt Lake City, Utah) and went on to win with Derek in 1980.

Joanne Crockett, who operates a training stable with her husband, Bruce, north of Dallas, trained Lisa Williams of Dallas, who was reserve in 1972 and in 1973. In 1977 she put another rider in the winner's circle when Rebecca Lampton of Oklahoma City was crowned National Champion. This was the year that the Finals began to look more as they do today, with tough competition from areas outside the Southwest. Entries had jumped from 47 the previous year to 71, and for the second time a Saddle-horse judge was asked to officiate, along with two judges from the Arabian divisions.

By 1978, the Arabian Saddle Seat Equitation division had overcome the problems which could be expected in early years in the judging system and class procedures and was finally established as one of the most important and most exciting classes at the Nationals. In 1979 we saw the largest increase in entries, with 120 riders from coast to coast competing at Louisville in three phases of workouts for the title. It was won for the first time by a boy, Jay Clark, a popular exhibitor from Piedmont, Oklahoma, who was trained by Peggy Richardson of Oklahoma City.

Tawne Markley of Scottsdale, whose instructor was the well-known Saddle-horse trainer and judge, Bunny Jeffery of Reno, Nevada, won the National title in 1976. Only two riders who neither lived in nor were taught by someone in Region 9 were National Champions in those first twelve years: Mary Jane New of Clayton, Ohio (1972), and Lori Schroeder of Des Moines, Iowa (1975).

Today Saddle Seat Equitation has become an important part of every Arabian show in America, and the excitement generated by this class at Nationals is a credit to that handful of individuals who started it all just thirteen years ago. Outstanding riders are being developed in all parts of the country by a "new breed" of instructor who recognizes the beauty and purpose of this form of competition, who appreciates and perpetuates its tradition, and who realizes the opportunity which exists for him in a new and exciting division of Saddle Seat Equitation—Arabian-style.

Because equitation is so new in the Arabian world, there are often discrepancies among judges, and judges with little or no background in equitation are faced with judging these large, highly competitive classes. It would be well for anyone planning to judge equitation to do some preparation before leaving home. He should become familiar with the workouts found in the AHSA Rule Book and use only variations for these. He should be aware of rules governing the class. He should have the announcer read the workout and repeat questions and answers so that everyone in the class hears the same directions. He should make sure that the written directions and accompanying diagrams are consistent with each other and listen carefully to the announcer as it is read. He should consider logistics when making up a workout, taking into consideration the size of the ring, position of the gate and judge's stand, etc., before designating a certain number of steps or other directions. He should make sure all riders understand the pattern before the first one begins to work.

In an Arabian Saddle Seat class, a judge may ask a rider to pull down from a canter to a trot without losing momentum; to make a "simple" change of leads, which means walking between leads; to canter a circle on the wrong lead (this should be discouraged) or to do a figure eight showing two changes of leads, which requires three circles. These are not usually asked for at Saddlebred shows.

Often a judge will have all riders do a workout, even in a preliminary class, and ask them to work in numerical order. Some judges fail to consider the evaluation of the rider's rail work, in which case they are faced with judging the class only on the basis of the workout. Many times a poor or weak rider on a "dead broke" horse will then defeat the better, more aggressive riders who might make a slight error and be left out of the money. The same thing happens with young, short-legged riders whose legs lie against the saddle and don't move and who are riding a "dead broke" horse. They are frequently tied over an obviously more experienced rider when the workout is not difficult enough to differentiate between them. Inexperienced equitation judges will tie ho-hum workouts every time.

These judging weaknesses do not belong to the Arabian judges only. But these tendencies may be more pronounced because the format of the Finals puts so much emphasis on workouts and the pre-publishing of patterns before the show that there will continue to be a tendency to tie the negative. In this situation, the possibility is very real that a "do nothing" rider will be tied over a rider who dares to ride his horse up to his best performance. We say it so many times, but it is frustratingly true, that an absence of mistakes is made the main criterian for judging. We must encourage our riders to RIDE THE HORSE, NOT JUST THE PATTERN. And we must encourage our judges to educate themselves to the point where they can recognize a superior rider by his positive actions.

In many cases, riders and instructors have found that an Anglo-Arab (Half-Thoroughbred) or an Arabian-Saddlebred cross has many characteristics which make a rider look good. Whether a purebred or a Half-Arabian is used, however, there are a few basic and essential elements required in an equitation mount: a strong, sound trot; an elevated head carriage; a size that suits the rider; and, probably the most important, a cheerful, willing attitude.

45

IAHA *National* Saddle Seat
Equitation Finals

IAHA offers to Recognized Shows three National Qualifying Classes open only to Juniors who have not reached their 18th birthday, riding a purebred Arabian stallion, gelding or mare, or a registered Half-Arabian mare or gelding.

IAHA National Saddle Seat Equitation Qualifying Class Open to Juniors who have not yet reached their 18th birthday. A rider must win a class or classes necessary to earn the required number of points to qualify for the Finals Competition. Winner of each class will receive a silver medal. Two or more individual tests, 1–12, shall be required of at least ten contestants, if available. To fill a class, five competitors with proper appointments must be entered, shown and judged.

In 1980, qualifications for the Arabian Saddle Seat National Finals were changed.

A rider must receive a total of six points to ride in the Finals. The winner of a qualifying class will receive a total of six points if his class has six or more riders. If only five riders compete, then five points will be awarded and the winner can compete again until one more point has been earned in a qualifying class. Stock Seat riders need only five points.

The judges are asked for suggestions on workouts before they arrive at Nationals. The Equitation Committee then selects the patterns that will be used.

Since 1977 three phases needed to be used because of the large number and quality of entries, but the procedure has been different each year. In 1978, twenty-one riders rode for Top Ten and the champion and reserve were selected at the same time (the riders who had the highest score). In 1979 the Top Ten were selected in the second phase and only that ten rode in the Finals for champion and reserve.

Prior to 1968 there were equitation classes at most shows, but only the major shows had championships. In 1968 an equitation class was offered at Nationals with no qualification necessary. This year and the next, the trophies presented to the winners were not like National trophies and first through tenth places were awarded. There were 28 to 30 entries.

Records of equitation as a National Championship began in 1970, with a medal required for entry. Former winners were allowed to enter and were later given the opportunity to purchase the National trophy which was given from 1970 on. Only eight places were given because of the number of entries.

In the first few years, three of the National's judges who had any experience in equitation were asked to judge it. For two years (1976 and 1977), one Saddle-horse judge was brought in to work with two Arabian judges. In 1978 and 1979, three Saddle-horse judges were used, then for 1980 they reverted back to one Saddle-horse judge (Annie Cowgill) with two Arabian judges, Cecile Hetzel and Lenora Wilson.

INTERNATIONAL ARABIAN HORSE ASSOCIATION
NATIONAL EQUITATION CHAMPIONS

RIDER		INSTRUCTOR
Cheri Barber, Oklahoma City, Okla.	1968	Mrs. Imogene Barber
Lu Anthony, Oklahoma City, Okla.	1969	Harold Adams
Cathy Crier, Dallas, Tex.	1970	Self-taught
Lois Finch, Houston, Tex.	1971	Gwen Nix
Mary Jane New, Clayton, Ohio	1972	Rev. Abraham New
Louisa Craft, Houston, Tex.	1973	Gwen Nix
Leslie Gray, Houston, Tex.	1974	Gwen Nix
Lori Schroeder, Des Moines, Iowa	1975	Carol Stohlman
Tawne Markley, Scottsdale, Ariz.	1976	Bunny Jeffery
Rebecca Lampton, Oklahoma City, Okla.	1977	Annie Cowgill
Jay Clark, Piedmont, Okla.	1978	Peggy Richardson
Bob Affleck, Salt Lake City, Utah	1979	Gwen Nix
Derek Cook, Sandy, Utah	1980	Gwen Nix
Reserve, Bridget Weatherford, Richmond, Tex.	1980	No Instructor

Balance of Top Ten – 1980

Todd Dearth, Corrales, N.M.
Andy Gray, Houston, Tex.
Kellie Ann Harding, Downey, Calif.
Karin Johnson, Edmond, Okla.
Lisa Hampton, Oklahoma City, Okla.
Kammie Milligan, Cypress, Tex.
Jerry Peay, Provo, Utah
Whitney Ross, Grand Blanc, Mich.

Pictured here is Cheri Barber, Oklahoma City, Okla., who won the first Arabian championship offered—not a Top Ten class, but an added class. The show was in Albuquerque, N.M., being the U.S. and Canadian Arabian and Half-Arabian Championship Show. The year was 1968 and marked a very important trend—the sponsoring of the ever-increasing equitation division in the Arabian shows. Cheri's mount was a purebred Arabian. *Photo courtesy I. Barber*

Tawne Markley, 1976 IAHA National Equitation Champion. *Photo by Schatzberg*

Rebecca Lampton, 1977 IAHA National Equitation Champion. *Photo by Sparagowski*

Jay Clark, 1978 IAHA National Equitation Champion. *Photo by Richardson*

Bob Affleck, 1979 IAHA National Equitation Champion. *Photo by Spara-gowski*

Derek Cook, 1980 IAHA National Equitation Champion. *Photo by Art of Glory*

46

Some Faults of
Arabian Saddle Seat
Equitation Riders

There is essentially no difference between Saddle Seat Equitation on an American Saddlebred, where it began, and on an Arabian horse. There are, however, differences in the horses themselves, so, in order to have the same finished product, one must compensate for these factors when showing an Arabian.

Arabians generally have shorter backs than Saddlebreds, and saddles are often placed too far forward. This causes one of two problems: if the horse is high-headed, the rider will lean back at the waist; if the head is low, the rider's arms will extend forward over the neck. In either case, the rider's back tends to look stiff, the post is choppy, and smooth transitions are difficult. Momentum will often cause the rider to fall forward when coming down to a walk, and there is no way the horse's back end can be kept beneath the rider when the rider's weight is being supported primarily by the horse's shoulders. Model, Lynn Roberts. *Photos by Peggy Richardson*

The Arabian's smaller size and way of going cause problems for the equitation rider. Frequently a horse has a "soft" trot or racky way of moving, or is allowed to carry his head too low and leave his hocks extending behind him. The remedy for the first problem is obvious; find a horse that is large enough to suit the rider, preferably with a long neck that comes up straight from the shoulder. A soft or racky trot can often be "cured" with shoeing by lowering the heels, using a flat shoe, and wearing the foot as long and shoe as heavy as allowed. However, because of shoeing restrictions, which limit the amount of correction that can be accomplished, a horse with this way of moving would be better overlooked as an equitation horse.

A bit of training, mouthing, and the use of leg aids can raise the horse's head, keep him from diving into the bridle, and keep his hocks under him. When this is not accomplished the rider is off balance and the overall picture is that of going downhill. Since Arabians do not have as much hock action as Saddlebreds, they do not help a rider

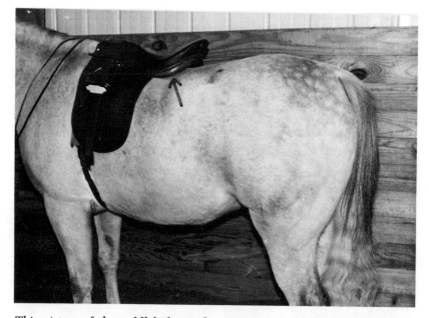

This picture of the saddle's forward position is a perfect example of what happens so frequently, all because the normal narrow heart girth and quickly sprung ribs of the Arabian horse do not permit the saddle to be moved back. There is shoulder-pommel interference that limits or hinders free front motion in the horse. Obviously we are tacking the animal in such a way as to give the appearance of a long back, which is not true. The arrow indicates an area of extreme pressure which cannot fail to influence the mobility of the hind quarters. *Photo by author*

leave the saddle as smoothly when posting. Riders must be careful not to pull themselves up with the reins, post too high, or get ahead of the horse when posting. It should appear to be effortless, though the rider is, in fact, doing most of the work.

In fact, if one were to summarize the problems most frequently found among Arabian Saddle Seat riders, it would be one of extremes.

The Half-Arabian shows longer heart girth which will permit a saddle to remain back in comfort to both horse and rider. There is no problem here as the alert posture of both horse and rider proves. Proper placement of the saddle is truly a basic necessity. The tailoring of the riding suit could be better but the proportions are good. Model, David Owen. *Photo by author*

In this pose, David has assumed a posture fault quite common in Arabian Equitation. In an attempt to sit back to enhance his horse's appearance and inadvisedly to "sit up," he has turned into a living statue. His weight has zeroed in on the cantle of the saddle, causing obvious discomfort to his horse's back and hind quarters. The rider's torso is behind his center of gravity. Only labored posting and restricted mobility of the rein action can result. Probably the basis of all of these faults can be traced to the extreme forward placement of the saddle. Model, David Owen. *Photo by author*

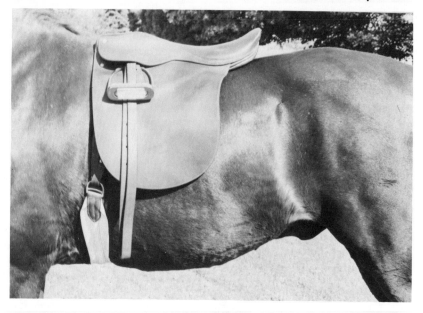

This illustration is like the well-worn joke: "First I have some good news, then I have some bad." The good news is that this saddle has been properly placed to keep from interfering with the comfort and movement of the horse's withers and the moving shoulders. The bad news is the extreme forward mounting of the stirrup leather. There is no way that head, hips, and heels can line up to attain unhindered balance for the rider. *Photo by author*

Perhaps it is because the Arabian's body is smaller or perhaps only because of riders' bad habits, but one frequently sees legs extremely flared. Model, Carmelle Moller. *Photo by author*

In this picture we see what happens when the rider sits where the stirrups and the seat of a poor-fitting saddle dictate. In a vain effort to appear in the middle of the horse, the rider has leaned back at the waist, destroying her balance and having her head thrust forward in an attempt to regain her balance. The saddle must fit the proportions of the rider, especially the thigh. Model, Carmelle Moller. *Photo by author*

Now the rider has moved into excellent balance. Head, hips, and heels line up to effect an alert, appealing, and workable position. Will she be able to ride the trot and look like this? No! The stirrups that are drawn back at the standstill will swing forward as soon as the rider rises to the post —a very common cause of swinging legs. The majority of rider/saddle incompatibility cases is caused by the stirrup hangers being mounted too far forward. Model, Carmelle Moller. *Photo by author*

When a horse carries his head too low or roots into the bridle, leaving his hocks, the rider is either tilted forward, giving the appearance of trotting downhill, or leans back with legs forward to brace himself. Even when good posture is maintained the overall picture is unattractive. Model, Lynn Roberts. *Photo by Peggy Richardson*

Here hands are too low, which is frequently seen on Arabians. The elbows tend to go out and use of the wrists and forearms is impaired. Model, Lynn Roberts. *Photo by Peggy Richardson*

Thick saddle pads are often seen on Arabians but they make it virtually impossible for a rider to put his legs in the proper position. They should be used only when unsoundness is a real threat to that particular horse. Model, Dee Ann Vaughn. *Photo by Peggy Richardson*

Posting entirely on one foot and "propping" with the other is so unsightly that we are surprised to see it so often. If both knees are kept supple and calf pressure is stressed, this fault will be cured. Model, Dee Ann Vaughn. *Photo by Peggy Richardson*

If you hang on to the curb in the lineup your horse will pull you right up on his neck, no matter how you resist. Get on your snaffle —your problems will disappear. Model, Lynn Roberts. *Photo by Peggy Richardson*

With stirrups and reins too long, the rider has sacrificed hand and body control. The horse is literally out of control and definitely not collected. Model, Dee Ann Vaughn. *Photo by Peggy Richardson*

When the rider forces the heels down too far, the hands tend to go down, and the head too. Model, Dee Ann Vaughn. *Photo by Peggy Richardson*

This rider, in working to get her horse's head up in the lineup, has completely forgotten the proper position of strong seat and legs.

The torso is fine, the horse alert and comfortable. But our rider has overcorrected her loose leg position. Now the legs are splayed, with the weight running to the little toe.

Now we have it all put together. The rider's position is balanced and firm. The horse is collected and alert. The rider could sit back more toward the cantle, but that is a matter of teacher's preference depending on the horse. Model, Lynn Roberts. *Photos by Peggy Richardson*

A rider should use his legs to push the horse's hocks up underneath him so he can post straight up out of the saddle. The wrists are stiff in this illustration, and even though curb bit use is setting the horse's head for collection, the action is better achieved with more supple and arched wrists. Model, Lynn Roberts. *Photo by Peggy Richardson*

The walk is so frequently over-looked by teacher and pupil. It is not a rest period. It is the root of all gaits and must be aggressive, alert, and ground-covering as shown here. As in all four of these fine illustrations, the rider's wrists appear to be rigid. You must be aware of not only what you are doing but how it may "appear" to the judge.

A splendid example of collection at the trot.

Good balance at the rise of the post. Softer wrists may have taken up the shock as the horse shied and raised his nose.

Excellent balance of horse and rider at the canter. Stirrups mounted more to the rear would permit the rider to move back to the curve of the cantle. Rider, Lynn Roberts. *Photos by Peggy Richardson and Ben Gay*

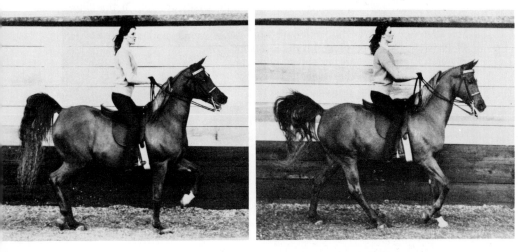

Finally we arrive at the well-balanced rider. Carmelle looks smart and alert, as does her horse. The ribs are up out of the rider's belt and her body weight flows evenly throughout the saddle contact down to the firm foot in the stirrup. This saddle is within an inch of perfection as the stirrup leathers should be set back. Next year the saddle and rider will be perfect for each other. *Photo by author*

The author would like to give special thanks to Carmelle Moller, David Owen, and their instructor, Delores Lowe of Lowe's Riverside Farm, Flushing, Mich., for their patience in setting up these technical studies. Equally grateful thanks go to Lynn Roberts and Dee Ann Vaughn, students of Peggy Richardson of Oklahoma City, Okla. Without Peggy's hours of research for the earliest days of Arabian Equitation and her superb camera work and the technical ability to set up the proper riding situations, this section would have been impossible. My further thanks to Ben Gay, photographer, who worked so hard with Peggy Richardson to get these analytical pictures. From left to right: Dee Ann Vaughn, Peggy Richardson (standing), and Lynn Roberts. *Photo by Ben Gay*

47

Arabian Equitation Instructors

If every breed had a Peggy Richardson it would indeed be blessed. Peggy teaches equitation in Oklahoma City, Okla. Her students are tops and so is she. An expert trainer and show rider, Peggy got her start showing and owning American Saddlebreds. She has been a personal friend of the author for many years. I have nothing but praise for her knowledgeable help in researching this section. The Arabian world owes Peggy Richardson a vote of thanks for her unselfish work on behalf of Arabian Equitation. *Photo by Sparagowski*

Of the twelve winners of the Arabian Equitation Nationals, five have been students of Gwen Nix of Carealot Farm, Tomball, Tex. Many reserve champions and many more Top Ten finalists put Gwen Nix in a class by herself. She must be considered the most influential teacher at the beginning of the '80s and a challenging model for the many young instructors just beginning. Here are two of her excellent students, Jennifer Nix and Julie Calhoun. *Instructor photo by Nix, Students photo by Bruce Bennet*

Bunny Jeffery, native of Louisville, Ky., now residing and teaching in Reno, Nev., has been affiliated with Saddle Seat Equitation for thirty-five years. Bunny is a past student of the author, a member of Saddle Seat Equitation Committee of the AHSA, and has judged the major shows in the country, including the national event Finals, AHSA Medal and UPHA Finals, and the International Arabian Saddle Seat Finals. She is in constant demand for equitation clinics and continues to be a great asset on the west coast in the development of young riders. Pictured here is a product of her outstanding work, 1976 International Arabian Saddle Seat Champion, Tawne Markley of Palm Springs, Calif. *Instructor photo by Anderson, Rider photo by Schatzberg*

Mrs. John Cowgill has been a guiding force in equitation since 1934 when she instituted a horsemanship course at Stephens College in Columbia, Mo. Besides conducting a Summer School of Horsemanship for twenty-five years at Jo-Ann Stables, she has been an active member of the AHSA, serving on various committees and as a director. Presently Mrs. Cowgill is assisting her daughter, Margaret C. Hankins, with a busy program of horsemanship, training, and breeding at Jo-Ann Stable, Inc., Springfield, Mo. They have been working with Arabians and their young and old owners for the past sixteen years. Pictured is her fine student, Rebecca Lampton, a big winner in 1976 and 1977. *Instructor photo by Mignard, Rider photo by Johnny Johnston*

Joanne Crockett, Crockett Training Center of Van Alstyne, Tex., consistently turns out top Arabian Equitation riders. A gifted horsewoman, Joanne Crockett is most recently successful with the Lampton girls of Oklahoma City. Pictured here is Lisa Lampton, Top Ten in the Nationals in 1980. *Instructor photo by Richard Lampton, Rider photo by Sue Wooldridge*

Dee (Delores) Lowe and her son, Jim, operate a lovely stable called Lowe's Riverside Farm and Training Center in Flushing, Mich. The author had the pleasure of working with three of Mrs. Lowe's students and they were extremely well versed. Since 1979, her equitation program has burgeoned and continues to grow in size and importance every year. Dee and Jim were most helpful in setting up some photos used in this text. Pictured is Jim Lowe in Egypt preparing to bring several head of horses to the United States. *Instructor photo by Rousseau, Group picture by Lowe*

48

Basic Psychology of Training

The psychology of training the horse has appeared throughout this entire book. Without the realization that we must understand what motivates a horse and how rider control depends upon this understanding, we would be able neither to train horses nor to teach riders.

In the first edition of SADDLE SEAT EQUITATION the extent to which I went with horse psychology was somewhat restricted by the limited experience of the riders who would be helped by that particular book. It is obvious that the new subjects dealt with in this expanded work merit a deeper study of the underlying motivations of horses and how much the rider can comprehend and better his riding with the understanding.

In early discussions with my editor I was trying to determine how to go about writing this book—what to retain, what to enlarge. Finally, in desperation, I told her that either I had written a darn good book or I had not learned anything in the ten intervening years. It was then that she suggested that all of the original book could be retained and then enlarged in text and ideas with anything that might further the education of the reader. So this I have done, and I have left for the last the subject dearest to my heart. The following illustrates this conviction as well as anything I could write.

Last year I had a group of very young riders who were avid to learn anything they could about riding a horse. We were in the arena, at the lineup, and it suddenly occurred to me that right at that very moment we had an opportunity that rarely occurs in any learning situation. There was I, a professional by the age of twelve, with fifty years of training and teaching behind me, and there sat four young riders whose thirst to learn could never be quenched. I told them about our situation and what a great opportunity there was for our group to combine my experience and their young, fresh, and intelligent approach to an expanded understanding of the basic psychology of the domesticated horse—particularly the modern show horse.

Those children loved the challenge and what I have to write here is a compendium of our ideas.

Much has been written about animal behavior, particularly in view of the recent interest in the endangered species. Scientists have gone to the far mountains to live with the apes and countless hours have been spent listening to the "language" of the porpoise, but very little has been examined about the modern show horse.

The wide spectrum of animal behavior has been explored for centuries but we have not been brought up to date on or delved into the deepest sources of show-horse behavior. *Equus* magazine, a most worth-while publication about horses, has touched this subject and will continue to do so, but its editors have not yet translated motivation into show-ring situations, and that is what concerns the learning rider (and that includes every one of us who trains).

The first thing we have to understand about our horse is that he would rather not be ridden or shown. Given his "druthers," the horse would prefer to stay in his safe stall. If you doubt this, observe the next horse that loses his rider. He does not go to the rail and continue his work. With a big kick and breaking into a run, he makes a direct dash to his stall. If this happens in the alien territory of the show ring, he will either find the out-gate or, being a herd animal, he will join the lined-up horses.

We all applaud the freed horse who snorts, throws his tail up over his back, and goes a spine-tingling "pasture trot." Certainly exuberance can claim some of the inspiration, but I think that "acting big" is just as much a defense mechanism as it is a show of spirit. It is a clever trainer who can completely train a horse and yet keep him fresh enough and responsive to show-ring stimuli to retain some of this "acting big."

The primeval instincts of self-preservation and procreation of the species underlie everything that the animal does. In prehistoric times when a horse was a small, totally defenseless creature, his survival depended upon escape to safety. Almost every misdemeanor that a show horse commits or even the making of a compliant but indifferent performance can be traced to this most basic fact. The word "domesticated" encompasses centuries of the horse's exposure to man and his training and utilization of the horse. That much we have had done for us. What will never be erased is the horse's return to original fear when we put him in a frightening situation. If every rider who has had to contend with a "stubborn" or willful horse would simply return to the cave and then work back to the problem, the solution would generally emerge. It has to go without saying that an understanding of conformation and how it affects performance must go hand in hand with psychology. But even here the horse's resistance to commands that he is physically incapable of doing merely revert to the primeval instinct—fear.

Now if we understand right back to prehistory why a horse has made a mistake, then we are better equipped to deal with it. Instead of automatic punishment, try eliminating the situation that put the horse back several million years. Gradual, sensible, mutually enjoyable riding is the sort of training that is predicated on understanding the natural timidity of our horse.

There will be moments of forcing in all training. The great opera star, Pavarotti, did not arrive at La Scala without running his scales, but what any rider must avoid is setting up contradictory situations in which we mean one thing and imply another. That can be frightening to humans, so pity the green horse.

For a good horseman the understanding and use of fear can be one of his most powerful allies when he trains. If a show prospect has been left alone until he is a two-year-old and then exposed to human control, he will begin with a healthy natural fear of the trainer.

Back-yard pets are the bane of a trainer's existence. This is very difficult to explain to proud owners who have bred their child's mare because they want to raise their own show prospects and they cannot resist the temptation to try to make pets of the foals. How wrong owners are to do this. What they do not understand is the power of fear in teaching an animal to do something he really does not want to do. (Remember the cave.) Colts who have been fooled with until they lose this natural fear are in for some rough treatment to put the fear back. Because good training has to be based on reward when the horse reacts properly—not punishment when he fails to respond—we start with calming the frightened colt and rewarding him when he makes the first learning step. Psychologists will tell you that touching is a basic human need. I think this applies to animals too.

Those colts that have been hugged and petted for stepping on your feet, laughed at indulgently when they pinned their ears back because you failed to produce another sugar cube—those colts will not respond to rewarding kindness during training. What they will require instead is very rough treatment to make them respectful of authority so that the trainer can, hopefully, return to square one where the young horse has the normal fear and responds to the praise that comes with learning. I believe that the psychology of training colts is very close to the methods of handling the two-year-old child. And it remains a constant factor throughout the horse's lifetime.

We have a different challenge when we deal with show horses. Their very name explains that we are asking for contradictions. We want a horse that is totally subservient to the rider's command while at the same time he is supposed to appear wild and free. When you examine your demands, you must realize the enormity of the task. You need all of the help you can get, and understanding the origin of fear and how it is a help, not a hindrance, to the thinking trainer is the first step.

Take an entire lesson period and spend the time analyzing the horse's reactions to the rider commands. Forget form, diagonals, etc. Just concentrate on the mental aspects of riding. That riding is 90% brains and 10% muscle has been repeated so often that it has joined all of the other clichés in this book. But let's hear it for clichés! If they were not worth while they would not have survived!

To return to the 90%; thinking, understanding, and experimenting are the trade instruments of a good rider. We all know that learning for a horse comes with repetition. Add something pleasant and you have a rewarding conditioned response. Add something bad and your conditioned response will nullify any progress you have hoped to make. Certainly the essence of training has been oversimplified here. It would take an entire volume to get into the exceptions that make up serious behavior problems. That is the reason that we have horse trainers. You would never dream of removing your own appendix, but anyone can deal with a simple stomachache.

I will always remember that day of discussion and bless the opportunity to share opinions and theories with young people who had so much to contribute. If there is one thing that has kept me enthused and stimulated for each succeeding lesson over these many years of teaching, it has been that I, too, am the learner.